# BATTLES OF THE CIVIL WAR

CURT JOHNSON & MARK McLAUGHLIN

# BATTLES OF THE CIVIL WAR

This edition published by
Barnes & Noble Inc.,
by arrangement with
Carlton Books Ltd.

1995 Barnes & Noble Books

Reprinted 1999

Copyright © 1977 Roxby Press

ISBN 1-56619-755-4

Printed in China

# CONTENTS

# THE WAR IN THE WESTERN THEATER

Includes operations in the Carolinas and Georgia.

**1861**
APRIL 12–13 Bombardment and surrender of Fort Sumter, Charleston, SC.
AUGUST 10 Battle of Wilson's Creek, MO.
**1862**
FEBRUARY 6–16 Grant captures Forts Henry and Donelson, TN.
MARCH 7–8 Battle of Pea Ridge, AR.
APRIL 6–7 Battle of Shiloh, TN.
APRIL 25 Farragut captures New Orleans, LA.
OCTOBER 8 Battle of Perryville, KY.
DECEMBER 31–JANUARY 2 1863 Battle of Stones River (Murfreesboro), TN.
**1863**
MARCH–JULY Grant's final campaign against Vicksburg, MS.
MAY–JULY Siege of Port Hudson, LA.
JULY 4 Capitulation of Vicksburg.
JULY 9 Surrender of Port Hudson.
SEPTEMBER 19–20 Battle of Chickamauga, GA.
NOVEMBER 23–25 Battle of Chattanooga, TN.
**1864**
MARCH–MAY Red River Campaign.
MAY–SEPTEMBER Atlanta Campaign.
JULY 20–28 Battles around Atlanta, GA.
AUGUST 5 Naval battle of Mobile Bay, AL.
SEPTEMBER 2 Fall of Atlanta.
SEPTEMBER–JANUARY 1865 Hood's Tennessee Campaign.
NOVEMBER–DECEMBER Sherman's March to the Sea (Savannah Campaign).
NOVEMBER 30 Battle of Franklin, TN.
DECEMBER 15–16 Battle of Nashville, TN.
DECEMBER 21 Confederates evacuate Savannah.
**1865**
MARCH 19 Battle of Bentonville, NC.
APRIL 26 Johnston surrenders to Sherman in North Carolina.

# THE WAR IN THE EASTERN THEATER

Unless indicated, battles, campaigns, and sieges occurred in Virginia.

**1861**
JULY 21 First Battle of Bull Run (Manassas).
**1862**
MARCH 9 Duel between ironclad gunboats *Monitor* and *Virginia* (*Merrimac*) in Hampton Roads.
MARCH–AUGUST Peninsular Campaign.
MAY 31 Battle of Seven Pines (Fair Oaks) in the Peninsular Campaign.
MAY–JUNE "Stonewall" Jackson's campaign in the Shenandoah Valley.
JUNE 25–JULY 1 Battles fought in the Peninsula include Gaines's Mill (June 27–28) and Malvern Hill (July 1).
AUGUST 29–30 Second Battle of Bull Run (Second Manassas).
SEPTEMBER 17 Battle of Antietam (Sharpsburg, MD).
DECEMBER 13 Battle of Fredericksburg.
**1863**
MAY 1–4 Battle of Chancellorsville.
JULY 1–3 Battle of Gettysburg, PA.
**1864**
MAY–APRIL 1865 Grant's Richmond Campaign.
MAY 5–7 Battle of the Wilderness.
MAY 8–19 Battles at Spotsylvania.
JUNE 3 Battle of Cold Harbor.
JUNE 15–APRIL 1865 Siege of Petersburg.
**1865**
APRIL 2 Confederate evacuation of Richmond and Petersburg.
APRIL 9 Lee surrenders to Grant at Appomattox Court House.

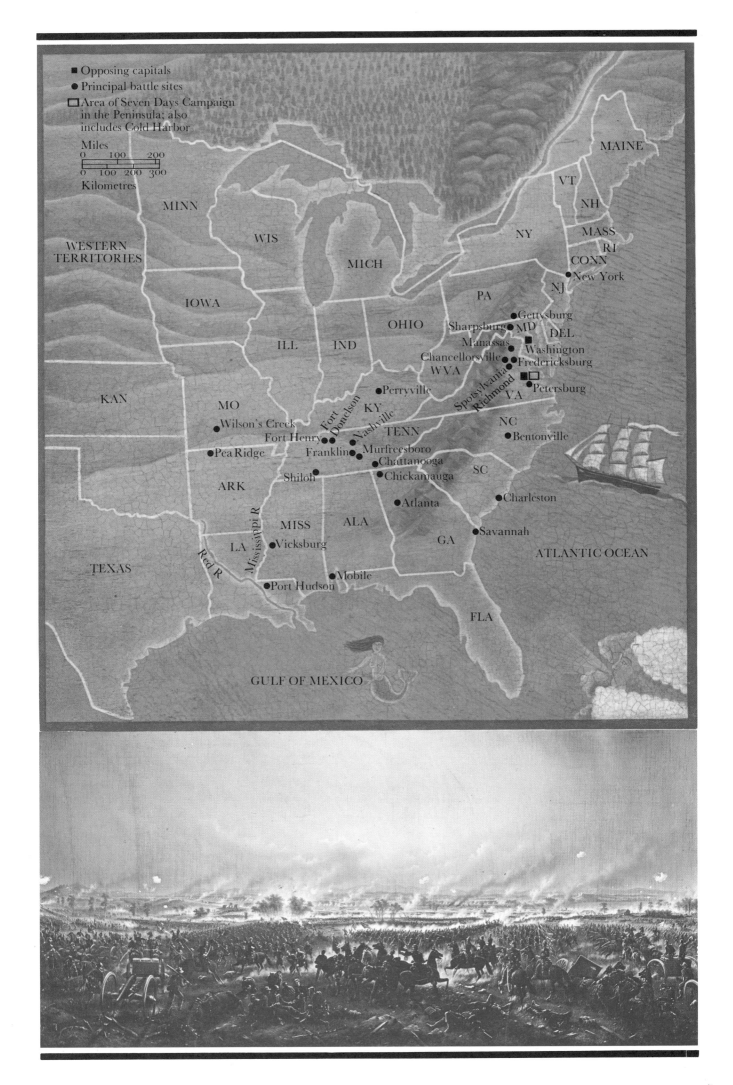

- ■ Opposing capitals
- ● Principal battle sites
- ☐ Area of Seven Days Campaign in the Peninsula; also includes Cold Harbor

Miles

0     100     200

0    100   200   300

Kilometres

MAINE

WESTERN TERRITORIES

MINN

WIS

MICH

VT

NH

NY

MASS

RI

CONN

● New York

NJ

PA

IOWA

OHIO

● Gettysburg

Sharpsburg ●  MD  ● DEL

Manassas ●  ● Washington

Chancellorsville ●  ● Fredericksburg

ILL

IND

WVA

Spotsylvania ●  ● Petersburg

Richmond ☐

VA

KAN

● Perryville

MO

Fort Donelson

KY

Nashville ●

TENN

NC

● Bentonville

● Wilson's Creek

Fort Henry ●

● Pea Ridge

Franklin ● ● Murfreesboro

● Chattanooga

SC

● Charleston

ARK

● Shiloh

● Chickamauga

● Atlanta

● Savannah

Red R

Mississippi R

MISS

ALA

GA

ATLANTIC OCEAN

LA

● Vicksburg

● Mobile

● Port Hudson

FLA

GULF OF MEXICO

"On our arrival in Boston we were marched through the streets—the first march of any consequence we had taken with our knapsacks and equipments. Our dress consisted of a belt about the body, which held a cartridge-box and bayonet, a cross-belt, also a haversack and tin drinking-cup, a canteen, and, last but not least, the knapsack strapped to the back . . . constantly giving the wearer the feeling that he was being pulled over backward. My canteen banged against my bayonet, both tin cup and bayonet badly interfered with the butt of my musket, while my cartridge-box and haversack were constantly flopping up and down—the whole jangling like loose harness and chains on a runaway horse. As we marched into Boston Common, I involuntarily cast my eye about for a bench."

From "Going to the Front", the recollections of Private
Warren Lee Goss, as recorded in Johnson & Buel, *Battles &
Leaders of the Civil War* (1887).

# PART I

# THE WAR AND ITS CONDUCT

Curt Johnson

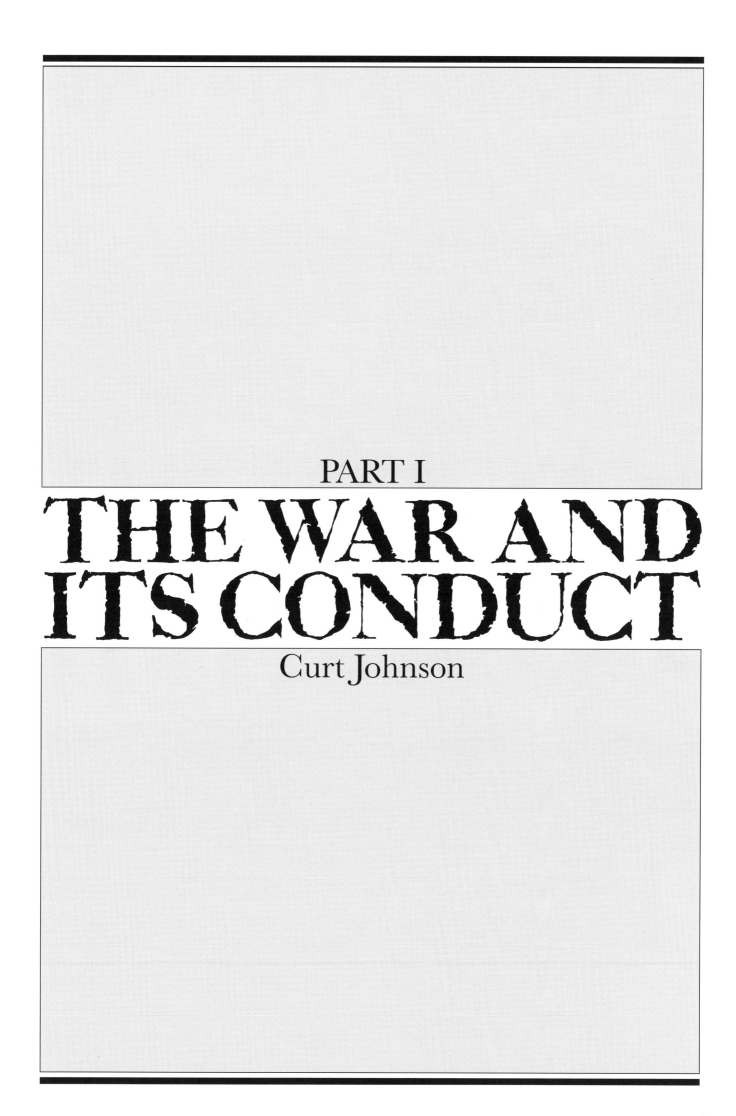

# CAUSES OF THE WAR

Above left
Several generations of slaves, all born on the same plantation near Beaufort, South Carolina. The photograph was taken in 1862.

Left
Poster for a slave auction of 1829.

Above
To arms! Volunteers of the Sumter Light Guards (Company K, 4th Georgia Regiment) in April 1861. Their flag has seven stars, one for each of the seceding states that formed the original Southern Confederacy.

Below
Damage from the war's first day: the heavily shelled Gorge front of Fort Sumter on April 13, 1861, the day after Beauregard's opening bombardment. The photograph is a composite of four plates taken from the same spot on the wharf opposite; some distortion is evident.

The Civil War and its fractious step-child, Reconstruction, represent perhaps the most important collective experience of the American people, a national trauma with roots reaching back beyond the foundation of the Republic and branches extending toward an uncertain future. The war's centenary passed years ago, but the process of binding up the nation's wounds, about which Lincoln spoke so eloquently in his Second Inaugural Address, continues to this day.

Historians have long debated the causes of the war, but they have never been able to arrive at a consensus and, of course, never will. Their debates, however, have helped to clarify the complicated sequence of events preceding the war. Few cite slavery as a direct cause of the war, though all agree that but for its existence armed conflict might never have occurred. As the historian Bernard DeVoto wrote, "Slavery was at the very heart of our disequilibrium. It was the core of the social, the economic, the political, and the constitutional conflicts . . ." Southerners referred to slavery as a "peculiar institution," but it might more appropriately have been described as a "persistent institution." At one time almost universal, slavery by the 19th century continued to exist in few places outside the Americas. In the United States, gradual abolition had been the trend for some time, and by 1846 all the Northern states had outlawed the institution. The South might have followed the North's lead except for the enormous impact of the

Industrial Revolution on the region's economy.

There had never been much industry in the agrarian South, and nearly all its money and credit were tied up in plantation land, the slaves who worked the land (and represented an estimated $2.5 billion investment in 1860), and cotton futures. The whole system was wasteful, inefficient, and sluggish, and might anyway have collapsed had not two developments revitalized it: first, Eli Whitney's invention in 1793 of the cotton gin made possible the rapid processing of raw cotton; second, the growth of the British textile industry created a seemingly insatiable market for the crop. Cotton became the nation's leading export, and the "Cotton Kingdom" expanded to meet the demand. The old, depleted Piedmont lands were abandoned, and new plantations were created on tracts owned by poor dirt farmers in the Midsouth. Although Congress had prohibited the overseas slave trade in 1808, the mania for land on which to grow cotton was such that speculators would anticipate the acquisition of territory by the Government and smuggle slaves into certain areas in search of a quick profit. In states like Maryland and Virginia, where neither the plantations nor the slave system itself were any longer economically feasible, a new industry, "rearing slaves," came about.

The boom in the demand for cotton and the expansion of the growing lands into the Gulf states affected the mind of the South as much as it did the economy. The apparently limitless economic possibilities of "King Cotton" inspired confidence in the region's potential for separate development and a resolve that the system must not be torn down. The South had effective control of the Government until 1860, but Southerners were jealous of their hegemony and sensitive to Northern efforts, real or imagined, to undermine it. Political compromises in 1820, 1833, and 1850 allayed sectional antagonism, maintained the delicate balance of power in the Senate, and allowed for the limited expansion of slavery, but the underlying problem remained: the North, allied with the non-slaveholding Midwest, was fast outstripping the South in every index of economic and demographic growth and bidding to upset the political equilibrium in the national government. Moreover, on many important issues affecting the nation as a whole–the protective tariff and internal improvements, for example–the North was using its growing political power to "outmuscle" the South. And the South was not slow to show its resentment of this turn of events.

Because the political and economic power of the planter oligarchy was founded on slavery, Southerners banded together to protect the institution and fell prey to a curious siege mentality. Parochialism, state rights, and sectional patriotism became the watchwords of the "slaveocrats," and talk of secession was commonplace, especially in the 1850s when the South pressed for the extension of slavery into the territories west of Iowa and Missouri. Abolitionist agitation and slave revolts, like Nat Turner's bloody insurrection in Virginia (1831), served only to intensify Dixie's xenophobia, while the formation in 1854 of the Republican Party provided a strong anti-slavery lobby and gave added notice of the North's determination to force changes.

The struggle intensified when, in 1854, Congress passed the Kansas-Nebraska Act, legislating that the question of whether the territory should permit slavery or be free would be decided by "popular sovereignty," i.e., by vote of the settlers. What followed was unrestrained and often gruesome violence as pro-slavery "Border Ruffians" from Missouri and bands of anti-slavery fanatics like that of the free-soiler John Brown engaged in open warfare that claimed more than 200 lives.

The episode of "bleeding Kansas" was nothing more nor less than a large-scale dress rehearsal for civil war. Sectional ill-will continued unabated and the violence spread, even into the halls of Congress, where Charles Sumner, the anti-slavery senator from Massachusetts, was beaten insensible by the South Carolina representative, Preston Brooks, after Sumner had made a speech entitled "The Crime Against Kansas." In 1859, John Brown and 18 followers seized the federal arsenal at Harpers Ferry, Virginia, and called upon the slaves to rise up, arm themselves, and fight for their freedom. Not one slave responded to Brown's call, and the coup was speedily suppressed by Federal troops (led by Colonel Robert E. Lee). Even so, the South was alarmed by the specter of a slave insurrection potentially as destructive as the horrific Haitian uprising of 1800. Brown was hanged for his act, but Northerners hailed him as a martyr who, in Emerson's words, would "make the gallows glorious like the cross."

In this atmosphere of fiery partisanship, extremists came to the fore and vied with moderate politicians for leadership. In the South these fanatics were called "fire-eaters"; among them were Alabama's William Lowndes Yancey, South Carolina's Robert Barnwell Rhett, and Virginia's Edmund Ruffin. Armed conflict between the sections was hastened when the equilibrium in the Senate was upset by the admission of two free states, Minnesota (1858) and Oregon (1859), without any counterbalancing increase in representation for the slaveholding interests. Then, in the presidential election of 1860, the Democratic Party, split by the intransigence of the "fire-eaters," lost badly to the Republicans, who ran Abraham Lincoln of Illinois. Lincoln's victory was viewed with horror in the South, where he was regarded as "a baboon," a wild man from nowhere, and the worst type of "Black Republican." It was the last straw. Southern fears of coercion and abolition multiplied, and Dixie's leaders, like Mississippi's Senator Albert Gallatin Brown, urged succession. "Disunion is a fearful thing," said Brown, "but emancipation is worse. Better leave the Union in the open face of day, than be lighted from it at midnight by the incendiary's torch."

The climax of decades of verbal skirmishing, rising fears, and increasing violence occurred during "secession winter"–the four-month interval between Lincoln's election and his inauguration (November 6, 1860–March 4, 1861). First South Carolina and then six other Deep South states seceded from the Union and formed the Southern Confederacy. The new Confederacy raised an army and seized Federal property within her borders, including forts, arsenals, and customs houses. War broke out on April 12, 1861, when Major Robert Anderson, the Federal commander of the Charleston, South Carolina, forts, resisted the demands of Confederate authorities that he surrender Fort Sumter, his post in Charleston harbor. Rebel shore batteries commanded by General P. G. T. Beauregard bombarded Fort Sumter for 40 hours and compelled Anderson's surrender. This attack unified the South and led directly to the secession of four more Southern states: Virginia, Tennessee, Arkansas, and North Carolina. North and South now drew up their war plans.

# PLANNING FOR VICTORY

Above
President Lincoln, visiting the Antietam front in October 1862, discusses the progress of the war with General McClellan and staff officers. At that stage the Northern generals had dismally failed to assert their superiority in numbers and equipment.

Left
The quelling of the South: inhabitants of the besieged city of Vicksburg cower before an unexploded shell. Painting by Howard Pyle.

The strategic objectives of the two sides may be simply described: the North, seeking to restore the Union, had to take the offensive and crush the rebellion by destroying the Confederate armies in the field; the South had to defend its territory, to persevere until the North wearied of war and recognized Southern independence, or until European powers such as Britain and France were compelled, for economic reasons, to intervene on her behalf.

Initially, little thought was given to strategy. Both sides expected a short, relatively bloodless war and fielded armies of enthusiastic citizen-soldiers, led largely by politician-generals. The advice of professional soldiers went unheeded, and the raw armies met at Bull Run (July 21, 1861) in the war's first great battle. First Bull Run was a disaster for the North, but it dispelled the romantic "short-war" illusion and forced the Lincoln government to prepare seriously for a long, hard conflict. The South, on the other hand, reaped few rewards from victory. Most Southerners rejoiced in the battle's outcome and concluded erroneously that they had little to fear from Northern arms. As a result, the South never fully mobilized for war, and the Rebel armies were continually hampered by unnecessary shortages of men, foodstuffs, and matériel.

Winfield Scott, the aged, gouty General-in-Chief of the Union Army before McClellan, laid the foundation for the North's winning strategy with his famous Anaconda Plan. A thorough professional, Scott predicted before Bull Run that "300,000 men under an able general might carry the business through in two or three years." His plan proposed the economic strangulation of the South by means of a naval blockade, while land armies gained control of the Mississippi Basin and captured the Rebel capital at Richmond. The Anaconda Plan was ridiculed at first, but the concept was sound, and Lincoln adopted it in all its major features.

During the first two years of the war, however, the Northern armies met little success. The problem, basically, had to do with poor leadership and lack of direction from the General-in-Chief. Both McClellan, who succeeded Scott as General-in-Chief in November 1861, and Halleck, who was supreme commander from July 1862 until March 1864, when Grant took over, lacked strategic sense and were unable to coordinate the moves of all the Union armies. Time and again, as in the Peninsula, at Shiloh, Second Bull Run, and Chickamauga, the Confederates combined against isolated, dangerously exposed Northern armies and defeated them.

The few clear-cut Northern victories of this period–Gettysburg, Vicksburg, and Tullahoma–were less decisive than they might have been because generally the Rebels were allowed time to rest and recoup their losses, often by drawing troops from quiet sectors of fronts where no pressure was being exerted. Thus, Lee, after Gettysburg, reinforced Bragg with nearly one-third of his army, and Bragg subsequently crushed Rosecrans at Chickamauga. Neither Grant nor Meade, who commanded the two other Union armies, had been ordered to combine their operations with Rosecrans to prevent reinforcements from being sent to Bragg.

When Grant went east to assume the general command in March 1864, he brought with him a plan for common action by all the Union armies. Recognizing the superiority of the North's resources of men and matériel, and, conversely, the extreme poverty of the South in these categories, and fully aware that for

Above
By 1864 the North, under General Grant's leadership, was at last getting on top. Here Union soldiers enforce Grant's plan to destroy the Confederate heartland, tearing up railroad tracks around Atlanta, the South's stricken industrial center.

Right
Thinning ranks at a Confederate roll-call late in the war.

political reasons the victory must be clear and beyond dispute, he directed Sherman to operate against the Confederate heartland and Johnston's Army of Tennessee, while he, with Meade's Army of the Potomac, engaged Lee in an all-out battle of attrition in the Virginia theater. For the first time in the war, every effort was made to engage the Confederate armies all along the line. Constant contact with the enemy, a hallmark of modern warfare, became the order of the day, the ultimate objective being to hammer the Rebel armies into submission.

In operation, Grant's strategy was costly but effective. Lee could not be lured into the open and preferred to fight from behind skillfully prepared entrenchments that seemed to move with his army. In one month's fighting, Grant's losses exceeded the total strength of his adversary's army, but he kept pushing on and finally cornered Lee at Petersburg, where the armies settled down to a nine-month siege. Sherman, meantime, captured Atlanta and marched virtually unopposed across Georgia, bisecting the heartland and wrecking what remained of the South's war-making capacity. The end came in April 1865, when Lee abandoned his untenable Petersburg lines and sortied westward. Grant's pursuit surrounded Lee's remnants at Appomattox Court House, and on April 9 the proud "Gray Fox" was forced to surrender. Within the month, the war was ended.

Of Confederate strategy, little need be said. President Davis ran the Southern war effort from Richmond in a strange, severely autocratic manner; the advice of field commanders, even that of the revered Lee, was neither sought nor welcomed, but the cold hand of Richmond meddled in every area of the military effort, extending even into niggardly details of army command and administration. "I have been greatly surprised today," wrote General Joseph E. Johnston in 1862, "to receive an order from the War Office detailing a private for a working party here. I hazard nothing in saying that in time of war, a Secretary of War never before made such a detail."

Davis's interference in petty military matters might be overlooked as a peculiarity of character but for the fact that he rarely provided operational directions for his armies and instituted no strategic policy beyond that of passive defense. From the first, Confederate forces were parceled out among military departments and geographical divisions, each of which, according to a War Office clerk, was "a separate nation for military purposes without divisions, cooperation, or concert." In Davis's scheme of cordon defense, each army, whatever its size or strategic relationship with neighboring forces, was responsible for its own territory. Cooperation with other Confederate armies or concentration against a Union threat was virtually impossible because all interdepartmental correspondence was routed through Richmond. Thus Vicksburg was lost because Davis refused to allow troops from the Trans-Mississippi Department to cross the Mississippi and operate against Grant's besieging army from the rear.

Davis's defensive strategy handicapped the field armies of the Confederacy in another way. Troops needed desperately at the fighting front were scattered hither and yon in garrisons or detached from parent organizations at politically opportune moments. State governors also withheld troops from the front on the pretext that they were needed for local defense. The whole system was so chaotic and inefficient that of the 480,000 men on Confederate muster rolls in January 1864, barely a quarter were actually in service with the two remaining field armies.

# THE FIGHTING MEN

A Union volunteer of 1861,
frozen in splendor by the studio camera.
Romantic attitudes to the war faded as the realities
of the harsh struggle became more widely felt.

A patriotic assemblage of Confederate generals and flags,
grouped around that most worshiped of men, Robert E. Lee.

"War," said Oliver Wendell Holmes, Jr., shortly after he enlisted in the 20th Massachusetts in 1861, "is an organized bore." At the beginning, however, there were few Americans, North or South, who would have agreed with the young Bostonian, later a distinguished Supreme Court justice. The first battles of the war were fought by "Sunday soldiers'–militia 'rarin' for a fight," men whose whole image of war was colored by zealous patriotism and blind romanticism.

It was more or less the way Americans had always gone to war. The Regular Army was small (numbering some 15,000 men in 1861) and dispersed in garrisons along the frontier, and so was not a major factor in the government's plan to put down the rebellion. As it had been in the past, the main reliance initially was on the state militia organizations which could be mobilized by the President for short-term service in national emergencies. The militiamen had never been very good or very reliable soldiers, but they were, in 1861, the only ready reserve of trained manpower.

Both sides anticipated a relatively short and bloodless war, and the first calls for troops reflected this belief. On April 15, 1861, Lincoln called for 75,000 militia to serve for 90 days "to cause the laws to be duly executed," while Davis, for his part, enlisted 100,000 men for one year. These early measures proved to be largely shortsighted and inadequate: the 90-day men present at First Bull Run fought well enough, but many others had left the army abruptly

on the eve of the battle, claiming quite correctly but most inopportunely that their term of enlistment had expired. General James B. Fry thought that these shirkers should be shot but found that "unfortunately they were voters, and therefore sacred."

The failure of this brief experiment with the militia companies and the sudden realization after Bull Run that the war would be a protracted struggle requiring immense resources of men and matériel caused the Lincoln government to reevaluate its manpower policies. It was plain that the enthusiasm and bravado of the militia could not begin to make up for their shortcomings as soldiers and their relative invulnerability to army discipline; they were not, as McDowell remarked, an army. At this juncture, the Administration began to recruit volunteers–a more permanent force of essentially national troops (although the regiments retained the name of the state in which they were raised).

With the minor exceptions of the hastily mobilized militia units and the comparatively small numbers of draftees and substitutes raised by conscription (164,331 Northerners and an indeterminate but smaller number of Southerners), nearly all the troops that served in the Civil War were volunteers, enlisted for terms of service ranging from three months to three years. In total, the North raised nearly 2.8 million men (soldiers, sailors, and marines), while an estimated 1.1 million saw service under the Confederate flag. Casualties were, proportionately and numerically, the worst in American history: the dead alone numbered some 360,000 for the Union and an estimated 260,000 for the South. Three-fifths of the Northern dead and two-thirds of the Confederates

*Prisoners from the Front*, by Winslow Homer.
For these Confederates a period of, at best, grim inactivity awaited;
disease was rampant in the prison camps, and life there was little safer than on campaign;
some 49,000 men died in the prison camps of both sides,
not so much from design as from the inability of the Administrations to cope with the problems
that the camps posed.

died as a result of disease–the soldiers' greatest hazard until this century.

With the passage of time, the volunteers became steady veteran troops–by some accounts the best the world has seen. General Thomas J. Wood, who commanded a division at Chickamauga (1863), preferred volunteers over regulars. Commenting on the difference between the two, he said: "They [the volunteers] will 'stick' you; you can fight them as long as you please . . . The regulars are too sharp. They know when they are whipped but the volunteers don't; they will fight as long as they can pull a trigger." Another Union general, John M. Schofield, felt that the genius of the volunteer lay in his battlefield pragmatism. "The veteran American soldier," said Schofield, "fights very much as he has been accustomed to work his farm or run his sawmill: he wants to see a fair prospect that it is going to pay." Even Lee, the most formal and dutiful man of his generation, felt that his splendid veteran soldiers were, in 1864, more battle-wise than their superiors, many of whom were new to command, having replaced the terrible casualties sustained by the officer corps at Gettysburg. And the Confederate General Daniel Harvey Hill paid the volunteer soldiers of both sides the highest compliment when, in his comments on the Battle of Malvern Hill (1862), he wrote: "The Confederate infantry and Federal artillery, side by side on the same field, need fear no foe on earth."

Both sides used similar systems of organization for the three battlefield arms–infantry, cavalry, and artillery.

**Infantry** The Regiment was the building block of the infantry and represented the smallest battlefield unit of maneuver. More commonly, the brigade was the tactical unit and the division or corps the grand tactical unit. Confederate regiments were, on the whole, bigger than their Union counterparts because Northern regiments were allowed to waste away while fresh manpower was channelled into "new and superfluous regiments," which in turn meant that "new and superfluous colonels" could be created. This inane system was in large measure responsible for the uneven quality of Federal units; in any campaign, whole brigades and divisions were raw or untested. It was, however, politically expedient, since in the volunteer regiments the state governors controlled the appointment of field officers. The system did have its defenders. Schofield, for one, felt that the small, finely honed veteran battalions of the war's last years were much superior as tactical units, flexible, responsive, and easily handled. Confederate units generally had a majority of veteran troops leavened by replacements. Even late in the war, when recruits were simply unavailable, units shattered in battle were amalgamated with other units, all the while retaining their old identity. Thus, Edward Johnson's division, most of which was captured at Spotsylvania (1864), was reformed as a brigade. This expedient meant that until late in the war at least, Rebel units were up to strength, while in the Union Army any number of "phantom" units served beside those which were at full strength.

Another organizational difference between the armies lay in the mode of brigading regiments: where possible, the Confederates combined regiments from the same state together, while in the Union Army regiments were most often brigaded haphazardly,

Confederate prisoners at Point Lookout, Maryland. Two activities are shown: on the left, "Catching Rats,"
on the right, "Cooking Rats." In the captions to the original picture each man has his say, as follows:
Man No. 1: "Boys thats my rat if you kill him, he been eating my bread for the last three days."
No. 2: "Dont let that rat get away, put your foot on him."
No. 3: "Let him alone I'll get him."
No. 4 "Hello Sam! what are you going to do with them rats, are you going to eat them?"
No. 5: "Certainly I am they are as good as squirl [sic], and they make a fellows rations hold out
–go and get your bread and come and take dinner with me."

without regard to state or origin. The Southern practice undoubtedly helped the morale and improved the *élan* of the men; most brigades rapidly developed an "identity" or reputation much like that of certain ancient regiments of European armies. Examples of this include Hood's Texas brigade of Lee's army and the Kentucky "Orphan Brigade" of the Western army. Union troops were rarely brigaded in this manner, but when they were, they generally performed superlatively. The most remarkable case was that of the famous Vermont brigade of the Army of the Potomac, a fine unit that retained its singular identity throughout the war and, in the savage fighting of the Wilderness Campaign (1864), lost 1,645 of its 2,800-man complement–the greatest loss sustained by any brigade over a brief period in the course of the war.

The pattern of infantry organization was as follows:

### U.S. REGULARS
A regiment consisted of 2–4 battalions. Each battalion had 8 companies of 62–100 men each.

### U.S. & CONFEDERATE VOLUNTEERS
A regiment consisted of 10 companies of 64–82 men each. The strength (officers and men) of a Union regiment varied from 869–1,049; late in the war, "small battalions" averaged 500 men. Confederate brigades and divisions were generally larger than Union brigades and divisions.

**Cavalry** The North began the war with five regular cavalry regiments and later added a sixth. These regiments were never grouped and therefore had very little impact in the subsequent fighting. The bulk of the horse regiment, North and South, were volunteers. Southern troopers had to supply their own

horses (the government provided mounts for the Union horsemen), which seriously handicapped the efficiency of the Rebel regiments because the men tended to conserve their animals in much the same manner as the French cavalry of the 18th century. The lack of a Remount Corps sapped the effective strength of Confederate regiments: many troopers who should have been in the line of battle were dismounted–searching for a horse. The Richmond government would pay compensation for a horse lost in battle, but would not compensate the trooper for a horse lost to disease. On average, a cavalryman used up five mounts a year. In one month of 1863, the 10–14,000-man Cavalry Corps of the Army of the Potomac required 7,336 remounts. Under these conditions the battlefield strength of the cavalry regiments of both sides fluctuated widely.

The cavalries were organized as follows:

### U.S. REGULARS & VOLUNTEERS
A regiment consisted of 4–6 squadrons. Each squadron had two companies of about 100 men each. Ideally, the regimental strength was no lower than 818 men, but by 1863 Union regiments averaged 333 men, and by 1864, 250.

### CONFEDERATE VOLUNTEERS
The Rebel cavalry had no regular organization, but in general a regiment comprised 10 companies of 10 troops, the latter each having 60–125 men. Average regimental strength fell from 500 troopers per regiment in 1861-62 to 300–350 in 1863. By the end of the war, most Rebel cavalry regiments mustered about 100 men.

The proportion of horse to foot in the armies seems to have remained relatively constant throughout the war, generally 1:6, In current practice in

Europe this was considered a proper proportion for wooded and broken country. The tactical unit was the regiment or brigade, but as the war progressed, the cavalry of both sides frequently maneuvered and fought in larger-sized bodies.

**Artillery** During 1861-62, both sides dispersed their artillery matériel throughout their armies, attaching individual batteries to infantry brigades for close fire support. This practice made the massing of guns for concentrated effect difficult. On occasion, however, as at Shiloh (Ruggles's massed battery) and Malvern Hill, resourceful local commanders did manage to mass guns and use the cannon as Napoleon had recommended, "like pistols aimed at the heart of the enemy." Subsequently, the artillery was reorganized into larger unit–battalions and brigades. These were attached to infantry divisions and corps or, as artillery divisions, formed the army's reserve of artillery.

The proportion of guns to men in the armies ranged from 1–4 guns per 1,000 men; 3 guns per 1,000 seems to have been the average. In the last campaigns, the artillery was reduced considerably. Sherman had 1 gun per 1,000 men on the March to the Sea, and Grant, just before Spotsylvania, reduced the Army of the Potomac's artillery park by 100 pieces. In the first instance, Sherman desired mobility in a countryside of poor clay roads; in the second, Grant found himself facing Lee in tangled, heavily wooded country where artillery was useless except in defense.

The artilleries were organized as follows:

## U.S. REGULARS & VOLUNTEERS

A light (field) battery contained 6 guns. These were all of the same type, usually 12-pounder Napoleon smooth-bores or 3-inch Parrott rifled guns. A horse artillery battery contained 8 or, more usually, 6 guns. They were all of the same caliber, usually 3-inch Rodmans or Ordnance rifles. An artillery brigade consisted of 2 or more battalions, while a battalion contained 2 to 5 batteries.

## CONFEDERATE VOLUNTEERS

A field or horse artillery battery contained 2–8 guns, usually 4. The gun types were mixed, but 12-pounder Napoleons were prevalent. Brigade and battalion strengths were as for the Union Army.

Napoleon, himself something of a tactical innovator, once observed that a people ought to change its tactical system every 10 years in order to stay ahead of its enemies. But soldiers generally are a conservative race, usually better prepared to fight the last war than the next. This phenomenon is especially apparent in ages when advances in weapons technology occur at a rapid rate and are unaccompanied by changes in tactical doctrine. Such was the case in the decades preceding the Civil War: the armies that fought the war inherited a tactical system unchanged since the Napoleonic Wars, but faced weapons that made those tactics suicidal. Only gradually did the soldiers come to see their mistake and alter their tactics to accommodate the new weapons.

As mentioned elsewhere, the chief agents of tactical change were the rifle musket, the pistol, and the magazine rifle. These new weapons, coupled with certain chemical and physical discoveries which made possible advances like the percussion cap, improved powder, and the elongated Minié bullet, conferred a tremendous advantage on the defensive. The "danger zone" of concentrated, aimed small arms fire increased from the Napoleonic standard of less than 100 years to 500 yards or more. The artillery, formerly a decisive offensive weapon, was forced to stand off at greater ranges because its primary and antipersonnel round, canister, was most effective at up to 350 yards only (the maximum effective range was 700 yards). The tactics of Napoleon's time, with massed columns of infantry charging home after an intensive short-range artillery preparation, were no longer practical; the artillery could not get close enough to the enemy's line to "soften it up," and the defending infantry and artillery were left free to savage the attackers with pointblank rifle fire and canister. This was the reason for the many bloody repulses of the war, such as those that occurred at Fredericksburg, Pickett's charge at Gettysburg, and Cold Harbor.

**Infantry Tactics** Historically, American infantry had fought in shallow (two-man deep) linear formations, a tactical arrangement that maximized firepower but could be broken by a determined bayonet charge if the enemy weathered the storm of musketry and closed. After the American Revolution, the British adopted this formation, which became the "thin red line," and broke the offensive impetus of Napoleon's massed battalion columns. Strangely, however, in the wake of the Napoleonic Wars, most nations abandoned the line in favor of the shock-power of the dense column. Academically, at least, this was the case in the U.S. too; the military schools taught the value of the line as a defensive formation, but emphasized the column for offensive maneuver.

Nevertheless, Civil War troops rarely maneuvered in the dense columns employed by European powers. Loose columns, really a succession of lines–"waves" in modern terminology –were more frequently used, being better suited to the character and temperament of American volunteers. This gave the column less mass, but made it much more flexible and, incidentally, cut casualties on the approach. Even so, the blizzard of musketry and canister encountered in the last several hundred yards of any offensive usually wrecked the head of the column and often stopped the succeeding "waves." The utmost valor and discipline were needed to push on to the objective; green troops usually gave way and "skedaddled," while veterans sought cover or stood manfully and exchanged volleys with the enemy at the closest range until one side or the other bolted. This was what happened in the Wheatfield on the second day of Gettysburg, part of the fire-fight being carried on at the murderous range of 40 yards, neither side giving ground until the issue was decided by events on both flanks.

Where European-style dense columns were employed for attack, as at Kenesaw Mountain (1864), casualties were frightful. The officers who ordered these ill-fated offensives were brave, often in General John Gibbon's phrase, refusing to "play ornament to the rear rank," but they were also misguided and foolish, refusing to recognize the new realities of modern warfare. Similar tragedies would be enacted on other battlefields, much removed in time and space: Worth, St. Privat, the Marne, Flanders, and the Somme.

Ultimately, both rankers and officers adjusted their approach. The year 1863 was, in Sherman's words, the first "professional" year of the war, and the veteran soldiers of both sides, having "seen the elephant" (soldiers' slang for combat), elected to change their tactics. Concealment and cover were utilized to a greater extent than ever before, and the "deserted battlefield" of our own time became a possibility. The front was no longer a host of men facing each other in lines arrayed over half a dozen miles of countryside; instead, elaborate, wide-ranging trench systems, always roughly parallel and encompassing a shell-torn "no-man's land," marked the ever-changing boundaries of the arena of combat. Armies moved (there was as yet little diminution of mobility) and their trenches moved with them. "No regiment," recalled General Oliver Otis Howard, "was long in front of [Joe] Johnston's army without having virtually as good a breast-work as an engineer could plan." And Virginia and northwestern Georgia, the scenes of the titanic spring campaigns of 1864, were scarred by hundreds of miles of trenches, continuous works not unlike the great trench systems of World War I; Petersburg and Atlanta were, in many respects, miniature Verduns.

Such defensive arrangements quite naturally increased the strength of the defense, which, as we have noted, was already supreme. Concentrations of artillery, interlocking zones of fire, and defensive aids such as wire obstacles and abatis, made offensives not just prohibitive but suicidal. New tactics were experimented with–open order and attacks in "rushes" (see diagrams)–but the generals were slow to abandon the older formations. At the "Hell Hole" in Georgia, Hooker lost ten times as many men as the defenders, and at Cold Harbor 7,000 men fell in a single assault that lasted 20 minutes. Progressive officers like the brilliant Union Colonel Emory Upton lamented these reverses. Of Cold Harbor, Upton commented: "I am disgusted with the generalship displayed. Our men have, in many instances, been foolishly and wantonly sacrificed . . . Thousands of lives might have been spared by the exercise of a little skill."

The trenches also increased the area over which a battle might be fought, since extensive lines could be held by limited numbers of troops. Lee, with barely 40,000 men, held 35 miles of entrenchments at Petersburg against an army nearly three times as large. At Atlanta, Hood held the lines encompassing the city with militia and a handful of regulars while he sortied against Sherman with the bulk of his army. A complete stalemate, such as occurred on the Western Front during World War I before the breakthroughs of 1918, was prevented only because the Confederacy, physically and materially exhausted by late 1864, was extended beyond endurance in the last campaigns. The trenches certainly prolonged the war and added

hundreds of thousands of names to the casualty lists, but they could not avert the end.

**Cavalry Tactics** At the beginning of the war, cavalry on the old model, employing the saber-swinging shock tactics of the past, was as "obsolete as the crusaders" (to quote G. F. R. Henderson). The American cavalry tradition, however, had always emphasized firepower over shock (the mounted rifleman being the most prevalent type), so the horsed arm adjusted readily to the changes wrought by the revolution in small arms. All the cavalry of the war were mounted infantry of a new type–men who could fight skillfully both mounted and dismounted, who were as adept with the saber as they were with the pistol, carbine, and magazine rifle, but who much preferred the modern weapons.

The tactical field itself, with its snares and traps for the mounted man, belonged to the infantry, and Civil War cavalry rarely become closely engaged in proximity to the infantry line of battle (Nashville, with its inviting open flank, was a notable exception). Rather, the cavalry was best employed as an "army in motion," divorced from the plodding infantry, gathering information, raiding communications and bases of supply, and creating diversions. Late in the war, the North created separate cavalry armies which combined firepower and mobility in a new way and contributed mightily to the ultimate defeat of the South, which could not check their depredations. This development served as a model for the German *Blitzkrieg* of World War II and represented the apogee of development for the horsed cavalry.

**Artillery Tactics** Artillery, the "Queen of Battles," had for a long time been the major determining factor in battles, but had been eclipsed and bypassed in the technological revolution that followed the Napoleonic Wars. Nonetheless, artillery played a major role as a defensive weapon during the war. The hitting power of massed guns using spherical case (shrapnel), shell, and shot at long range, and canister and grapeshot at close range, was demonstrated on several occasions. Malvern Hill, a Union victory, was won virtually by the guns alone, and at Murfreesboro and Gettysburg, the employment of massed batteries by the skilled Union artillerists was what decided the outcome of those battles.

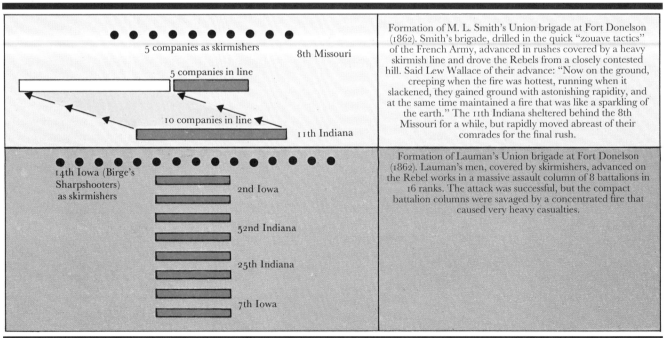

5 companies as skirmishers

8th Missouri

5 companies in line

10 companies in line

11th Indiana

Formation of M. L. Smith's Union brigade at Fort Donelson (1862). Smith's brigade, drilled in the quick "zouave tactics" of the French Army, advanced in rushes covered by a heavy skirmish line and drove the Rebels from a closely contested hill. Said Lew Wallace of their advance: "Now on the ground, creeping when the fire was hottest, running when it slackened, they gained ground with astonishing rapidity, and at the same time maintained a fire that was like a sparkling of the earth." The 11th Indiana sheltered behind the 8th Missouri for a while, but rapidly moved abreast of their comrades for the final rush.

14th Iowa (Birge's Sharpshooters) as skirmishers

2nd Iowa

52nd Indiana

25th Indiana

7th Iowa

Formation of Lauman's Union brigade at Fort Donelson (1862). Lauman's men, covered by skirmishers, advanced on the Rebel works in a massive assault column of 8 battalions in 16 ranks. The attack was successful, but the compact battalion columns were savaged by a concentrated fire that caused very heavy casualties.

General Burnside's troops (foreground) at First Bull Run. The nature of the battlefield changed radically after 1861: in place of these lines of unprotected troops blazing away at each other, the armies adopted sophisticated entrenchments that anticipated the Western Front of World War I.

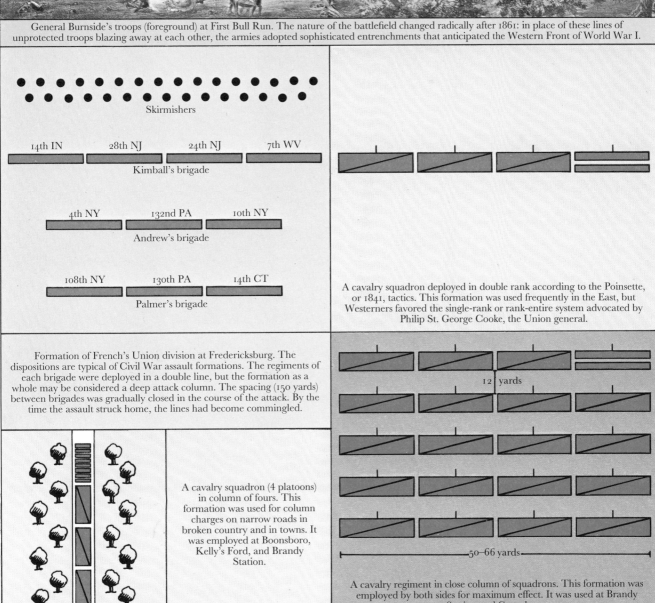

Skirmishers

14th IN    28th NJ    24th NJ    7th WV
Kimball's brigade

4th NY    132nd PA    10th NY
Andrew's brigade

108th NY    130th PA    14th CT
Palmer's brigade

A cavalry squadron deployed in double rank according to the Poinsette, or 1841, tactics. This formation was used frequently in the East, but Westerners favored the single-rank or rank-entire system advocated by Philip St. George Cooke, the Union general.

Formation of French's Union division at Fredericksburg. The dispositions are typical of Civil War assault formations. The regiments of each brigade were deployed in a double line, but the formation as a whole may be considered a deep attack column. The spacing (150 yards) between brigades was gradually closed in the course of the attack. By the time the assault struck home, the lines had become commingled.

12 yards

50–66 yards

A cavalry squadron (4 platoons) in column of fours. This formation was used for column charges on narrow roads in broken country and in towns. It was employed at Boonsboro, Kelly's Ford, and Brandy Station.

A cavalry regiment in close column of squadrons. This formation was employed by both sides for maximum effect. It was used at Brandy Station and Gettysburg.

Why cavalry rarely charged a gun line. The diagram shows how cavalry, deployed 1,000 yards from a battery, would cross the intervening ground in 7 minutes at its normal sequential pace of walk, trot, gallop, and final charge. In that time, each gun of the battery (presuming smooth-bores-rifles would be slower to load) would fire at least 11 rounds of solid shot and 5 of canister. Even aggressive horsemen such as General Forrest warned against such suicidal odds.

| 200 yards | 400 yards | 400 yards |
|---|---|---|
| 2 canister | 2 solid shot and 3 canister | 9 solid shot or spherical case (shrapnel) |

# THE WAR AT SEA

Above
The opening stage in the amphibious assault on Fort Fisher, in January 1865. The Union monitors are pounding the Confederate fort at close range; troops were then sent ashore, and they secured the fort's surrender.

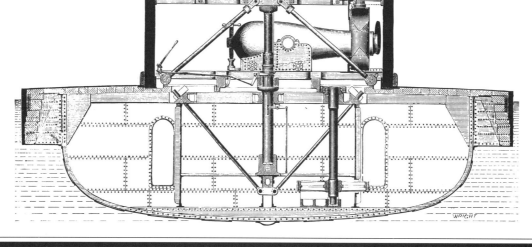

Left
Anatomy of a monitor: a transverse section through the turret and pilot-house of the Union *Montauk*; her design is typical of the seagoing vessels of the monitor type.

On April 19, 1861, just five days after Fort Sumter's surrender, President Lincoln proclaimed a blockade of Southern ports. At the time this strategy seemed absurdly optimistic, and, in one respect at least, positively harmful to the Union cause. The United States Navy, with 90 ships, most of them obsolete (only three were available for immediate duty on blockade) and 8,800 officers and men, was plainly incapable of closing over 3,500 miles of Southern coastline, and Lincoln, in adopting this policy, inadvertently conferred belligerent status on the Confederacy, since under international law only belligerents could be blockaded. Foreign powers, which would not treat or trade with rebels, welcomed Confederate emissaries and opened their ports to Southern commerce.

Because of the weakness of the Union Navy, the blockade began inauspiciously; in fact, it was no blockade at all. International law stipulated that "blockades, in order to be binding, must be effec-tive—that is to say, maintained by a force sufficient really to prevent access to the coast of the enemy." Until late 1863, the blockade was anything but effective, and blockade-runners—long, nimble steamships painted gray to avoid detection—slipped in and out of Southern harbors at will.

Powerful neutrals such as Britain and France objected to this "paper blockade" and might have made common cause with the South in destroying it, but every time the question was raised in the parliaments of Europe, Union sympathizers produced statistics proving that the blockade was effective. These statistics were not falsified; the Confederate government, wholly beguiled by the "King Cotton" delusion, actually embargoed cotton shipments during 1861-62, hoping to ruin Europe's economy and force foreign intervention in the war. By the time this grievous policy error was corrected, the Union Navy had grown large enough to enforce the blockade, and the South's economy, desperately short of foreign exchange, was a shambles.

As the war progressed, the blockade became

The Confederate ironclad ram *Stonewall*, built in France
and reputedly the most powerful ship in commission with either navy during the Civil War.
She arrived too late to participate in the fighting.

highly efficient: in 1861, only 1 in 10 blockade-runners was captured; by 1864, chances of capture had risen to 1 in 3. To achieve this, the blockaders used a variety of techniques, many of them revolutionary. Southern ports were close-blockaded and assaulted by combined army-and-navy task-forces. Out at sea, a cruising blockade was set up in international waters, along sea lanes and off neutral ports such as Matamoros in Mexico. The Confederate Secretary of State Judah P. Benjamin called the cruising blockade illegal and "a predatory cruise against the commerce of Europe . . . under pretense of a blockade of our ports."

In addition to the blockade, the Union Navy performed vital service on the "inland sea," the maze of rivers and lesser waterways draining the Southland. Whole fleets were constructed on the inland waters to assist the Army in its job of penetrating Jefferson Davis's cordon defense and bisecting the Confederacy along the line of the Mississippi. Typical were the Eads gunboats–seven casemated ironclads built in record time by engineer James B. Eads on the Mississippi near St. Louis, Missouri.

If the Union Navy began the war unprepared for the immense task confronting it, the Rebels' situation was immeasurably worse. Stephen Mallory, the Confederate Secretary of the Navy, is said to have described the Confederate Navy in 1861 as consisting entirely of an unfurnished room in Montgomery, Alabama, where naval policy was made. The South began the war without ships, machinery, or money, but fortunately obtained the services of many trained, able officers. One-sixth of the U.S. Navy's officer corps went South, among them the great navigator, Matthew Fontaine Maury, and the Commandant of the Washington Navy Yard, Franklin Buchanan.

Confederate naval strategy was characterized by two elements: commerce destroyers and ironclad river and harbor-defense vessels. The commerce destroyers, modeled on the privateers of the Revolution (when 16 British warships and 2,980 merchantmen were taken or destroyed by privateers alone) and the War of 1812 (1,344 British merchant-men captured), were meant to scourge the seas, destroying the Union merchant marine and drawing Union

Above
The Union sloop *Richmond* engaged with the massive Confederate ram *Tennessee* in Mobile Bay.
Painting by 2nd Assistant Engineer Robert Weir, who served on board the *Richmond* during the battle.

Below
The building of the Confederate ram *Albemarle* at Edward's Ferry, North Carolina.
Her protection was to consist of a shield of two layers of 2-inch-thick iron plate.

warships away from the blockade. Many of these vessels, like the British-built *Alabama* and John Maffitt's *Florida*, were spectacularly successful, but they did not seriously impede the Union war effort; the merchant marine, however, was dealt a blow from which it did not recover until World War I.

Confederate ironclads were mostly built in makeshift yards and designed strictly for defensive purposes. None of these indigenous ironclads was very seaworthy, so their chief purpose was to attack and destroy the vulnerable wooden blockading fleet in the harbors and rivers of the South. Altogether, 37 armored or iron-hulled vessels (including the turtle-

like *Manassas*, America's first ironclad) was built or converted for the Rebel Navy. Many of these warships never saw action, and 21 were destroyed to prevent their capture; seven were surrendered.

Southern agents tried to buy ironclads abroad, but Union diplomats prevented delivery of all but one of these foreign-built ships. The exception, the *Stonewall*, was built by France, sold to Denmark, and then transferred to the Confederates. Shadowed by Union warships which respectfully kept their distance, the powerful *Stonewall* arrived off the North American coast too late to take part in the war, was surrendered, and ultimately sold to Japan. The Confederate iron-

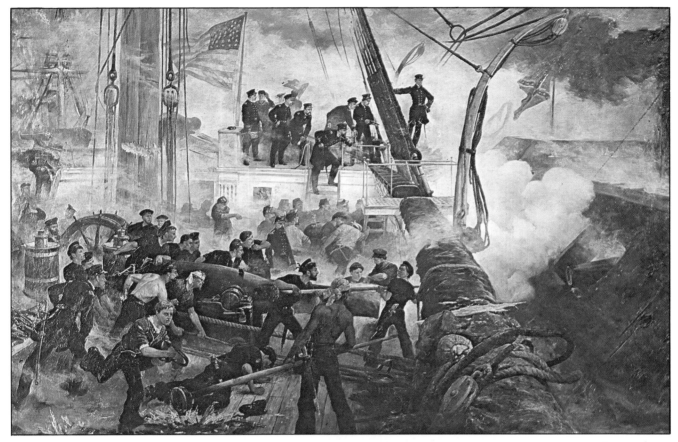

clads which did engage blockaders were clumsy but awesome weapons, mostly casemated like the *Virginia*, which served as the prototype for the rest; contemporaries considered them the most powerful warships afloat. The Union Navy countered with monitor-type vessels, based on a design by the inventive Swede John Ericsson. Ericsson's monitors won every duel with Rebel warships and clearly established their supremacy in ship-to-ship battles.

Without the blockade and the services of the river flotilla, the Confederacy might have resisted forever, defying Union arms from secure, well-supplied trench-lines and mountain redoubts. Thus, in the last analysis, the Union Navy's role was decisive. Lincoln recognized this fact when, late in the war, he paid tribute to the soldiers and seamen of the Union: "It is hard to say that anything has been more bravely, and well done, than at Antietam, Murfreesboro, Gettysburg, and on many a field of lesser note. Nor must Uncle Sam's web-feet be forgotten. At all the watery margins they have been present. Not only on the deep sea, the broad bay, and the rapid river, but also up the narrow muddy bayou, and wherever the ground was a little damp. Thanks to all. For the great republic—for the principle it lives by, and keeps alive—for man's vast future—thanks to all."

# THE IMPACT OF SCIENCE

A train of the U.S. Military Railroad on a troop-guarded bridge of the Orange & Alexandria Railroad.

The U.S. Military Railroad's chief executive, Herman Haupt (standing right),
supervises construction work on a stretch of track in Virginia;
the locomotive in the picture is named after him.

The Civil War has been called "the last of the old wars and the first of the new." While in many respects it resembled the conflicts of earlier times, it also foreshadowed modern "total war," especially in its final phase. The genesis of this remarkable transition lay in the tremendous changes sweeping the West in the wake of the Industrial Revolution, which began in Britain in about 1730 and transformed Western society by revolutionizing the technology at man's disposal. Archaic methods of production, in use for centuries, were supplanted by complex machines driven by steam or electric power, and great factories replaced the small-scale business enterprises of the past. Capital was accumulated in the industrial nations as a result of massive increases in trade and investment, and science, now allied with capital, flourished. In the U.S., the number of workers engaged in scientific endeavors doubled every decade.

These radical changes affected every aspect of life, including the nature of war, with the result that many items of military equipment that we regard as commonplace today first appeared during the Civil War. As a rule, technological change most affects tactics, since the weapons available at a particular time largely determine the nature of the battle in which they are used. But during the Civil War, strategy too was transformed being subjected to its first great metamorphosis since the invention of the wheel. The chief agents of this change were the railroad and the telegraph.

The railroads had begun to spread their ribbons of iron across the nation in the 1830s, experiencing their greatest period of prewar growth in the 1850s, when the total mileage increased from 9,000 to more than 30,000. In effect, the building of the railroads also helped to hasten the war in that it contributed to the South's isolation: Northern lines snaked across the Appalachian Mountain barrier to link the industrial Northeast with the agricultural Midwest, firmly bonding the two sections economically and politically. Southern railroads, on the other hand, made no such intersectional links: they were used for cotton-hauling and ran mainly from the interior plantation belt to the coastal cities. And when the war came, the North was found to have the better system from a strategic viewpoint.

During the war, both sides used the railroads

Signal communications were used extensively.
This is a Union signal tower at Petersburg in 1864.

A field telegraph battery wagon,
photographed in 1864.

extensively from the beginning; indeed, the armies were almost entirely dependent on rail and river transportation, and most of the great campaigns were fought along the lines of the railroads. The Confederates first demonstrated the striking strategic possibilities of rail transport at First Bull Run (1861), when they reinforced one army, already embroiled in battle, with another brought to the scene of the action by rail. The arrival of the second force, impossible without the railroad, was decisive and delivered victory to the South in the war's first great battle.

The use of the railroad in the Civil War was not a "first"–the Allies in the Crimea (1855) and the French in Italy (1859) had made limited use of the new transport–but the American experience dwarfed these efforts and revolutionized strategic geography. The most militarily progressive European powers took note, and by 1914 the railroad had become the most important logistical instrument, essential for military transportation and supply.

The telegraph, invented by Samuel F.B. Morse in 1844, had a similarly profound effect on the conduct of the war. For the first time in history, military policymakers, generals in the field, and numerous lesser lights were able to communicate spontaneously and almost instantaneously. By 1864 General Grant, from his post in the field with the Army of the Potomac, could control the activities of a multitude of units operating on widely separated fronts as if he were present with each. The telegraph did not immediately displace more antiquated modes of communication such as the dispatch rider, but by the end of the war nearly all strategic and a large proportion of tactical communications (especially in the Union armies) were being handled telegraphically. Both governments adopted the existing civilian telegraph network for military use, but the North did so more efficiently, and for two reasons: first, the Confederate President, Jefferson Davis, was loath to interfere with private companies, preferring loose supervision to govern-

ment control; second, Edwin Stanton, Lincoln's powerful Secretary of War and himself a former executive of the Atlantic and Ohio Telegraph Company, secured the active cooperation of Northern firms and created the Federal Military Telegraph System, which operated under his direct supervision. This organization at first worked in tandem with the U.S. Signal Corps (established since June 1860), then in late 1863 all telegraphic communications, both strategic and tactical, became the responsibility of the civilian operators of Stanton's Military Telegraph System. The Signal Corps continued to operate, but was limited to visual signaling in tactical situations.

In the realm of tactical weaponry, there were no less striking advances. New weapons, chiefly the rifle musket, the revolver, and the repeater or magazine rifle, helped to bring about the greatest change in the shape of the battlefield confrontation since the socket bayonet was coupled with the flintlock musket at the end of the 17th century. The infantry, although slow to master the tactical implications of the new hardware, were no longer forced to maneuver and fight in archaic masses; and as ranges and rates of fire increased, so battlefield formations became looser and more attenuated. The cavalry adapted quickly to the changed conditions: they became a kind of highly mobile infantry, using their horses for movement but dismounting to fight. The artillery, which had been the main tool of the Napoleonic conflicts, benefited least from the advances in technology: gunners found they could not maintain a position in the open within rifle range of the enemy except at great cost; but they remained useful when on the defensive, where the awesome firepower of massed cannon was still important.

The rifle musket, which became the chief infantry firearm in the 1850s, replacing the venerable smooth-bore musket, represented the first improvement in shoulder arms in 150 years. Earlier muskets, like the British "Brown Bess," were smooth-bores,

Union troops being transported by rail on the Nashville & Chattanooga Railroad; in the background is an encampment of the Pioneer Brigade. The devastations of war closely followed the lines of the railroads.

The well-armed trooper.
This Rebel horseman carries a Sharps carbine, twin Colt revolvers, and a saber.

accurate to about 40 yards and effective to 100 yards or slightly more. They were entirely dependent on the clumsy flintlock mechanism that ignited the propellant charge of powder, and they were generally inefficient, prone to misfires (flashes in the pan), and were useful only to massed units. The new weapon utilized two inventions that improved its range, accuracy and efficiency. The unreliable flintlock was replaced by the percussion lock, which ignited the propellant charge when the musket's hammer struck a percussion cap of copper coated on the inside with fulminate of mercury. In addition, the rate of loading and firing was increased from 1–2 to 3–4 rounds a minute thanks to the Minié bullet. This was the invention of a French Army captain, Claude Minié, who, to avoid the problems of laboriously forcing an over-sized lead ball down the rifled bore to "take" the rifling, by 1847 had developed a bullet-shaped projectile with a hollow base that expanded on firing to fit the rifling. Rapid, accurate fire to ranges of 500 yards or more became possible, and this established the infantry as the dominant force on the battlefield.

The mass-produced American Springfield (several models, .58 caliber) and its English cousin, the Enfield (.577 caliber), were the most prominent small arms of the war. Beside the Enfield, much coveted by the soldiers of both sides, a variety of mostly obsolescent foreign rifles was imported or run through the blockade to supply the needs of the two armies. As the war progressed, both sides became more uniformly armed. By mid-1864 the Union Army was almost wholly armed with Springfields, and the Confederates, unable to manufacture or import enough weapons, made good their wants with battlefield captures. Big hauls of weapons were made in the East in 1862, when Lee's men defeated the armies led by Banks, McClellan, Pope, and Burnside, and captured the Harpers Ferry Arsenal during the Maryland Campaign. Nevertheless, after Hooker's defeat at Chancellorsville, the Rebels gleaned fewer muskets from battlefields, since rarely again were they left in possession of a field. Even so, Colonel C. S. Venable, Lee's ADC, stated that after Chancellorsville all the men of II Corps were armed with Springfields, and some authorities assert that by the end of the war the Confederates were armed as well as or better than their opponents.

In addition to the rifle musket, which had previously seen service in the Crimea and in Italy, two entirely new types of firearms appeared during the Civil War–the breech-loader and the magazine rifle. Breech-loading arms had been around since the advent of gunpowder weapons, but there had never been very many of them, large or small, because it had proved difficult to create a gas-tight seal at the breech. Even when this problem was solved (largely by the introduction of metallic cartridges, first used in the Civil War) and safe, effective breech-loaders became available, stodgy ordnance officers opposed the new weapon as wasteful.

The first really good single-shot breech-loading system was patented in 1848 by Christian Sharps. Lever-operated, the Sharps (.52 caliber) could be fired at a rate of 10 rounds a minute. About 100,000 were used during the war, mostly carbines purchased by the Union government for the cavalry, but also some rifles, which were used to arm special units like Berdan's green-jacketed 1st U.S. Sharpshooters. The effectiveness of Berdan's men with the new weapon helped to convince the authorities of the superiority of the breech-loader over the muzzle-loader.

A still greater advance in weaponry was the repeater, a gun that could be fired many times in succession before the magazine had to be replaced or replenished. The most famous repeaters of the war were the Spencer (.52 caliber) seven-shooter, of which approximately 230,000 saw service, and the Henry, a .44 caliber rifle with a 16-shot magazine (the precursor of the Winchester level-action magazine rifles so familiar to viewers of Western movies); only about 10,000 Henrys were used in the war. The Spencer was without a doubt the outstanding shoulder arm in service. Capable of being fired 15–20 times a minute, it was an efficient, mechanically reliable weapon. The soldiers liked it for its simplicity and for the ease and rapidity with which it could be loaded and fired. The magazine, a replaceable tube containing seven metallic cartridges, passed through the butt of the stock and fed the chamber, which was opened and closed by a lever-operated breech-block. Firing could be accomplished in four motions. Most Spencers were carbines, produced for the Union cavalry, which by 1864 was uniformly armed with them and the Sharps. In the face of these weapons, the *élan* of the Rebel infantry and the skill of the gray-clad horsemen went for naught. The Union troopers, on the other hand, gained new confidence and began to assert themselves. A cavalry general, James H. Wilson, remarked: "My division was the first division in the Army of the Potomac that had first-class repeating arms. Green regiments, that you couldn't have driven into a fight with the old arms, became invincible the very moment that good arms were placed in their hands

Men of Berdan's 1st U.S. Sharpshooters in action at Malvern Hill (1862).
The Sharps breech-loader brought many advantages and was greatly preferred to the standard rifle musket. It had a rapid rate of fire and could be reloaded from a prone or kneeling position; because he did not have to stand and fumble with a ramrod in order to reload, the soldier was less exposed and better able to use cover.

. . . there are only two arms that cavalry should use in modern warfare–the repeating magazine gun, either rifle or carbine, and the revolver."

The magazine rifle quite literally changed the tempo of the war. In the Virginia Campaign of 1864-65, on Sherman's March to the Sea, with Sheridan in the Valley and Thomas in Tennessee, and on the final, massive cavalry sweeps that "ate out the vitals of the South," the repeaters led the way. With more than 50,000 repeater-armed horsemen at the front in 1865, many of them in separate "cavalry armies," the North had a fighting force that combined firepower and movement in an unparalleled manner and prefigured the *Blitzkrieg* of World War II.

The artillery, although relegated almost wholly to a defensive role, underwent certain technological changes that helped to compensate for its diminished status. Rifled pieces, used for the first time in large numbers (by 1863, about half the Union artillery, consisted of rifled guns), contributed toward re-establishing the artillery's role in offensive operations, and on occasion, as at Nashville (the end of 1864), the concentrated long-range fire of rifled guns was devastatingly effective. However, other factors worked against the new cannon being used to maximum effect, most notably the broken and wooded terrain over which much of the war was fought–which limited the opportunities for long-range fire–and the ineffectiveness of the primitive rifled shell, which had thick walls and a comparatively small bursting charge.

By preference and force of circumstance, the Confederates employed mostly smooth-bores in their field artillery, but in one respect at least–the use of breech-loading cannon–they were well to the fore. The best of the breech-loaders were British imports and included the sleek Whitworth 12-pounder, capable of throwing its solid hexagonal shot up to six miles, and the Armstrong 12-pounder, a gun already proven in the Third China War of 1860, but unhappily prone to premature explosions in the breech. The few Whitworths in Rebel service were outstanding weapons, but lacked the punch of comparable smooth-bores. Still, Confederate artillerists prized them, and it was a Whitworth two-gun section that fired the sighting shots for the artillery bombardment preceding Pickett's charge at Gettysburg (1863). With remarkable accuracy the shots landed among the Union ranks on Cemetery Ridge.

The machine gun, a major weapon of modern warfare, made its debut on Civil War battlefields. Dr. Richard Gatling's six-barreled revolving cannon was patented in 1862, but production problems and mechanical defects prevented its employment until late in the war when General Butler, who was fascinated by "freak" weapons, reportedly used a few at Petersburg (1864-65). The early Gatling fired at a rate of 250 rounds a minute, but Army Ordnance remained unimpressed, and adoption of the gun was deferred until 1868. Other machine guns may have seen action, among them the Agar "Coffee Mill" gun and the Confederate 1-pounder Williams gun. A Northern war correspondent spotted 10 of "the Devil's coffee mills," probably Agar guns, at Chattanooga (1863), and reported his impressions after one was fired in demonstration: "It was tick, tick, tick, sixty to the minute, as fast as you could think." The gun, he thought, "might do tremendous execution in skirmishing, were it not as liable to get out of order as a lady's watch."

The war witnessed the widespread use of "infernal machines," especially marine "torpedoes" (mines) which the Confederates planted to defend their rivers, harbors, and inlets. A constant threat to the Union Navy, these devices claimed 27 ships during the war. Both sides used spar torpedoes, bombs attached to long poles, with great success. These were driven to the target vessel by a torpedo boat or submarine, then rammed home at or below the waterline, opening a great hole in the side of the victim. The first successful sinking of a large surface ship by a submarine occurred in this manner during the night of February 17, 1864, when the Confederate submersible *Hunley*, a modified cylindrical steam boiler propelled by a hand-cranked screw propeller, sunk the USS *Housatonic* off Charleston. The unlucky *Hunley*, which had already sunk three times in trials, drowning 20 men, was dragged to the bottom with the *Housatonic*, carrying her gallant volunteer crew of nine with her.

In the skies, as well as on land or below the waves, the inventors and daredevils were at work. A handful of balloonists, led by Professor Thaddeus Lowe, Chief Aeronaut, Balloon Corps, Union Army, pioneered aerial observation and, in one instance, telegraphically directed artillery fire onto Rebel positions. Lowe's little air force eventually grew to a strength of seven balloons, but was inexplicably disbanded after Chancellorsville. The Confederates, too, fielded a few balloons but gave up after their best-remembered "gas bag"–the "Silk Dress Balloon," so named because it was made from strips of dresses donated by patriotic Southern women–was captured in 1862. General James Longstreet, in a rare moment of romanticism, bemoaned its loss as "the meanest trick of the war."

Where there were balloons, there were bound to be antiballoon measures. Chief among these were camouflage and antiballoon artillery fire. The Confederates used camouflage to deceive Union aerial observers, who from their airborne stations could count tents and guns and arrive at accurate estimates of their enemy's strength. Beauregard suggested camouflaged sheds and "Quaker guns" of blackened wood to represent entrenched cannon. More often, however, masked batteries waited for balloons to draw near and then let loose a salvo of shellfire–the world's first antiaircraft fire. Tom Rosser's battery of the Washington Artillery of New Orleans is said to have shot down one of McClellan's observation balloons in this manner, but "shot down" may have meant "forced down," since there is no record of a Union balloon being so destroyed, nor of a Union aeronaut being lost to Rebel gunfire.

In so brief a survey, it is impossible to chronicle all the new devices and weapons that to greater or lesser extent were employed in the Civil War. Others such as wire entanglements, flame throwers and gas shells (called "stink bombs") also made tentative appearances on the battlefield. It will nonetheless be clear from these pages that during the war substantial breaks with the past were achieved, ending several centuries of inertia in military science and technology, and forging many new patterns for the military tools and techniques of the future.

Battery D of the 5th U.S. Artillery in action at Fredericksburg (1863).
The artillery had lost much of its offensive power to the infantry,
but the massed firepower of cannon was still indispensable to the defense.

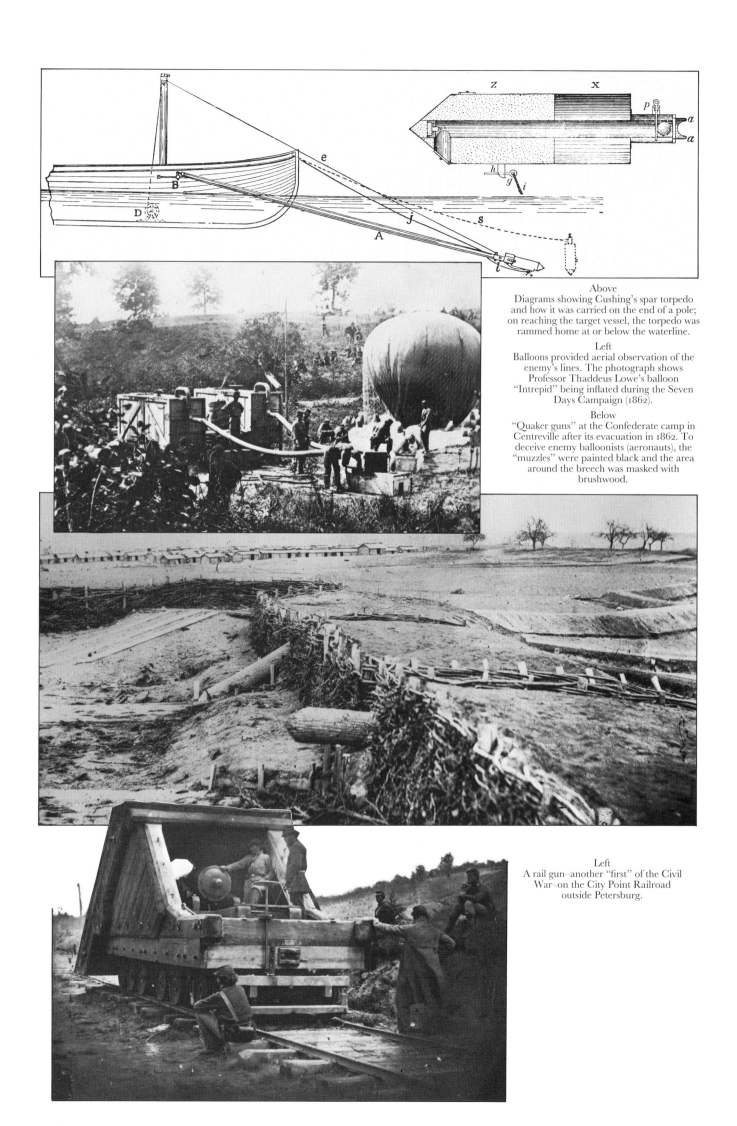

Above
Diagrams showing Cushing's spar torpedo and how it was carried on the end of a pole; on reaching the target vessel, the torpedo was rammed home at or below the waterline.

Left
Balloons provided aerial observation of the enemy's lines. The photograph shows Professor Thaddeus Lowe's balloon "Intrepid" being inflated during the Seven Days Campaign (1862).

Below
"Quaker guns" at the Confederate camp in Centreville after its evacuation in 1862. To deceive enemy balloonists (aeronauts), the "muzzles" were painted black and the area around the breech was masked with brushwood.

Left
A rail gun–another "first" of the Civil War–on the City Point Railroad outside Petersburg.

"The view of this field of battle was horrible. Dead Dead Dead everywhere in every imaginable position and most of them stripped nearly naked. And among them hundreds of our poor wounded who had been on the field without food or water or any attention two days and some of them three during which scorching sun and heavy rain. And then the amputations at which we assisted and the sufferings of the night following that on which we arrived on the field . . . I could not sleep but must up and go to them groping in the darkness and stumbling over dead bodies–almost choked by the stench from dead horses, thickly scattered over the field. Nothing but the excitement kept me up."

Part of a description of the battlefield of the Second Battle of Bull Run
written by J. Spencer Kennard, a civilian, in a letter to his
father. Reproduced by permission of Dr. Ralph J. Kennard.

# PART II
# THE BATTLES

Curt Johnson
and
Mark McLaughlin

# FIRST BULL RUN

July 21, 1861

Private Francis E. Brownell, 11th New York Fire Zouaves. Before the battle Brownell's commander, Elmer Ellsworth, was killed by a citizen of Alexandria for tearing down a confederate flag from the roof of a tavern. Brownell shot and killed the man.

"The great fact is upon us," remarked the *New York Express* of April 15, 1861. "Civil War has commenced. The news of the Union withdrawal from Fort Sumter acted like a catalyst, decisively ending Lincoln's policy of "no policy" and so terminating the vacillation and attempts at conciliation that had characterized the Government's actions since the secession of South Carolina in December 1860.

The newly inaugurated President reacted swiftly. On April 15 he published a proclamation calling on the states to furnish 75,000 volunteers to suppress the incipient rebellion. Throughout the North, the people responded to this call with wild enthusiasm. Crowds took to the streets in every city, town, and hamlet. Militiamen mustered, patriotic rallies were held, speeches made and bonfires lit. Popular excitement was so widespread and intense that the episode is now widely referred to as "The Uprising of the People." It was, in the words of Senator John Sherman of Ohio, "a thrilling and almost supernatural thing."

War fever swept the South, too. Newspapers called for the occupation of Washington and the extirpation of "Black Republican" government. The people, elated by the easy victory in Charleston harbor, hailed General P. G. T. Beauregard as their first national hero and clamored for him to lead an invasion of the North. More significant, however, was the secession of four border states, Virginia, Arkansas, North Carolina, and Tennessee, in response to Lincoln's proclamation and the sudden militarization of the conflict. Three other slave-holding states, Maryland, Kentucky, and Missouri, were perilously close to adopting a similar course.

For a short time following the Fort Sumter episode and the President's call for troops, Washington had lain virtually defenseless–a lone rock breasting the tide of secessionist sentiment that threatened to engulf it, a city paralyzed by fear, unaware as yet of the great awakening of the North. The secession of Virginia (April 17) and the uncertain status of Maryland had combined to place Washington in a virtual state of siege. Virginia troops, acting with surprising rapidity, seized the Harpers Ferry Arsenal and the Norfolk Navy Yard (both of which had been partly demolished by retreating Union forces) and cut the Baltimore & Ohio Railroad, Washington's only rail communication with the West. In Maryland, meantime, a mob of secessionist rowdies (the so-called plug-uglies) rioted in Baltimore and bloodied the 6th Massachusetts Regiment, which was in the vanguard of a host of Northern volunteers rushing to the defense of the capital. Rail, telegraph, and mail communications with the North were severed, and for a while the advocates of disunion seemed to hold the upper hand in the state.

Washington's dark days continued until April 25 when, quite unexpectedly, two fine regiments of militia, the New York 7th and the 8th Massachusetts, detrained at the depot and paraded down Pennsylvania Avenue to the wild cheers of the citizens. Much of the credit for lifting the siege belonged to Ben Butler, a politician-turned-general from Massachusetts. Butler did not get many things right during the war, but this was his finest moment. It was he who had outwitted the Baltimore mob and opened a roundabout route to Washington via Annapolis and a feeder line of the Baltimore & Ohio Railroad. It took Butler just about a month more to clear the northern approaches

to the capital; after the 25th the flow of troops became a torrent, and Maryland, cowed into submission, voted to remain in the Union. Washington was transformed into a garrison town, groaning under the weight of the largest army the Republic had ever known. Soldiers were billeted everywhere, including the Capitol and many public buildings. "Bayonets," claimed one wag, "have replaced buncombe."

In Virginia, another army was building up. The defense of the state, so vital to the infant Confederacy, was in the capable hands of Major-General Robert E. Lee, who until April 18 had been a colonel in the U.S. Army. On that date he had been offered command of the Union Army. Torn by conflicting loyalties, he had resigned his commission rather than take up arms against his native state.

Lee's plans were strictly defensive: since the Confederacy existed, so its leaders maintained, it had only to continue to exist in order to gain eventual recognition as a nation. The defense of the capital at Richmond was of paramount importance to the Confederacy's leaders. Richmond was, and continued to be, the major strategic objective of the Union armies in the East–not because it had any overriding military significance, but because the political consequences of its fall would have a catastrophic effect on the South's credibility abroad.

At the very heart of Lee's defensive arrangements were two armies operating near the Potomac River in Northern Virginia and the Lower Shenandoah Valley: Brigadier-General Beauregard's force of 20,000 men based at Manassas Junction and General Joseph E. Johnston's 12,000-man Valley Army at Harpers Ferry. Beauregard, protecting the most direct overland route to Richmond via the Warrenton Turnpike and the Orange & Alexandria Railroad, faced Brigadier-General Irvin McDowell's burgeoning army of 30,000 men, which was poised for an offensive on the Virginia heights opposite Washington (the Union army occupied the heights on May 24). Johnston, too, was outnumbered, having to contend with some 18,000 Federals commanded by an aged general of Pennsylvania militia, Robert Patterson.

Beauregard's position, called the "Alexandria Line," encompassed much of northern Virginia, but was based ultimately on Bull Run, a meandering tributary of the Potomac situated 26 miles southwest of Washington. Bull Run was not really defensible, but it was at least an obstacle to the expected Union advance and covered the approaches to Manassas, an important rail junction some four miles south of the creek. At Manassas, the Manassas Gap Railroad from the Valley met the Orange & Alexandria Railroad from Gordonsville.

If the Yankees managed to defeat the Confederates at Manassas, Lee's whole defensive army in the Valley would become unhinged, since Johnston's army in the Valley would then be flanked and forced to quit its position on the Upper Potomac. The two Confederate forces were thus strategically interdependent, but they did at least enjoy the advantage of interior lines–an advantage improved immensely by the rail link of the Manassas Gap line. Though locally outnumbered by their opponents, Beauregard and Johnston could use the railroad to combine quickly and defeat one Union army before the other could march to its aid.

In Washington, meantime, McDowell was perfecting his plan of invasion. The young brigadier proceeded reluctantly, knowing full well that his raw, untrained troops were not fit for combat. Both he and

Winfield Scott, the 75-year-old General-in-Chief, had objected to an early offensive, but the President insisted on a move in July, before the enlistment terms of the three-month militia expired. Mindful of the political consequences of inaction, he had parried the protests of his generals by stating, "You are green, it is true, but they are green, also; you are all green alike."

McDowell's plan, essentially, was to overwhelm Beauregard at Manassas while Patterson pinned Johnston's force in the Valley. Patterson's role, of course, was crucial. McDowell enjoyed a three-to-two numerical superiority over the Confederates at Manassas, but if Johnston slipped away from Patterson and joined Beauregard, the Confederates would then outnumber McDowell. To prove this, Scott wired Patterson to hold Johnston in check while McDowell delivered the decisive stroke. Unfortunately, Scott had lost the facility of writing simple, direct orders. His telegrams to Patterson were fuzzy

"The nation is at war and must have men." Henry Harrison Young, who was later to command Sheridan's Secret Service, harangues the men of a Rhode Island village in the spring of 1861. Illustration by Howard Pyle from *Young*, by William Gilmore Beymer.

and imprecise. Patterson, like Scott a septuagenarian, had himself lost the ability to act decisively. In the critical week preceding the battle at Manassas, Patterson, thoroughly confused, allowed his army to drift away from Johnston's main body, thereby creating the strategic basis for a Union disaster.

McDowell's offensive was launched on July 16. The 20-mile march to Centreville, where the army would concentrate for the attack on Beauregard, consumed two and a half days, an embarrassingly slow rate of progress. The main course of this tortoise-like advance seems to have been McDowell's fear of surprise by Confederate "masked batteries" (a prominent bugbear of the Union High Command that spring). March discipline was erratic, furthermore, and straggling was endemic; eventually the greater part of the army was simply shepherded to Centre-

ville. Once there, a minor disaster occurred. General Daniel Tyler's advance guard moved down to Blackburn's Ford on Bull Run to "feel" the Confederate defenses and became involved in a skirmish that turned into something of a rout. This affair at Blackburn's Ford (called by the Confederates the battle of Bull Run) had serious consequences for McDowell's army. The demoralization of Tyler's men soon affected other units, and spirits on the Union side plummeted.

The skirmish confirmed McDowell's worst expectations. He now felt certain that his green troops would be near-useless in a frontal assault, and determined to outflank the Confederate line and fight Beauregard's troops in the open behind their earthworks. On the 19th and 20th, he scouted the Bull Run crossings, finally settling on a move by his right flank across Sudley Springs Ford,

Beauregard had not been idle either. Informed of McDowell's march from Washington almost the moment it had begun, he had immediately wired Richmond for reinforcements. Johnston, then at Winchester, wasted no time in responding to his colleague's call for help, and his vanguard, Brigadier-General Thomas Jackson's Virginia brigade, de-trained at Manassas on the afternoon of the 19th.

Jackson's brigade, 2,600 men strong, had left their camp at Winchester at about noon on the 18th, marched 17 miles to Paris, where they rested, then continued six miles to Piedmont. Arriving at 8 A.M., they boarded the freight cars of the Manassas Gap Railroad for the 34-mile trip to Manassas Junction. The first trains started at 10 A.M. and arrived in Manassas at 1 P.M. The entire march, covering some 57 miles, represented a triumph of logistics. It was the first time the railroad had been used for strategic transportation in war.

During the next few days, indeed even during the battle itself, the troops of the Valley Army continued to arrive, swelling Beauregard's numbers beyond 30,000. Other commands, too, were *en route* or arriving, including T. H. Holmes's strong brigade from Aquia Creek and the Hampton Legion from Richmond. General Johnston himself arrived at Manassas on the 20th and conferred with Beauregard that afternoon. Because he was the ranking officer, Johnston assumed command, but being unfamiliar with the countryside, he approved Beauregard's scheme to attack the Union left by means of the country roads converging on Centreville. Before he retired, he directed Beauregard to make the necessary dispositions for the offensive and to strengthen the left flank near the Stone Bridge, which was held by a single isolated brigade.

McDowell was just as interested in the Confederate left. He had no scouts, so his own staff was charged with reconnoitering the Confederate line. For two precious days, the 19th and 20th, the Union army idled in its camp, while blue-coated staffers scouted the upper fords of Bull Run. But their work was amateurish, and in the end McDowell was forced to plan his turning movement in almost complete ignorance of the terrain and the crossings above Stone Bridge. Finally, on the evening of the 20th, satisfied that he had done the best he could with what information he had, the Union commander summoned his field officers for a council of war.

McDowell's plan was sound but in effect too complicated to be carried out properly by the raw soldiers and untutored officers of the Union army. The major attack, set for 7 A.M. the next day, was a wide turning movement by way of Sudley Springs Ford, a major crossing more than two miles upstream from Stone Bridge, where the extreme Confederate left was thought (correctly) to lie. Two divisions, the Second (6,000 men under Brigadier-General David Hunter) and the Third (7,200 men under Brigadier-General Samuel Heintzelman), were assigned to make this circuit and envelop the enemy's left and rear. To divert the attention of the Confederates from the main attack, two secondary attacks, really feints, were to be made. Tyler's First Division was to demonstrate at the Stone Bridge, and Colonel Israel B. Richardson's brigade was to make a "false attack" toward Blackburn's Ford. The Fourth Division, consisting wholly of unbrigaded militia regiments, was to be held in reserve at Centreville.

As an example of grand tactics, the Union plan was excellent; but it broke down in its execution. The Union column, with Tyler's division in the lead, left

Springs. It was already well past dawn, and the possibility of surprise had diminished,

At 6.30 A.M., the big Parrott thundered, and the battle began. The Confederates at Stone Bridge, "Shanks" Evans's 1,100-man demi-brigade, watched Tyler's demonstration mutely; their own artillery pieces were outmoded smooth-bore howitzers, unable to match the range of the big Union rifle. Even so, Evans awaited the inevitable attack with equanimity. He was certain his two regiments could stave off any assault over the narrow bridge. Two hours passed. The Federals showed no disposition to attack. Their fire was desultory. Then, at 8.45, Captain E. Porter Alexander, the engineer officer in charge of Beauregard's signals unit, wigwagged a message to Evans: "Look out for your left! You are turned!"

From his post on Signal Hill, eight miles away, Alexander had seen what Evans could not see–sunlight dancing off the musket barrels and bayonets of the Union flanking column at Sudley. His report to

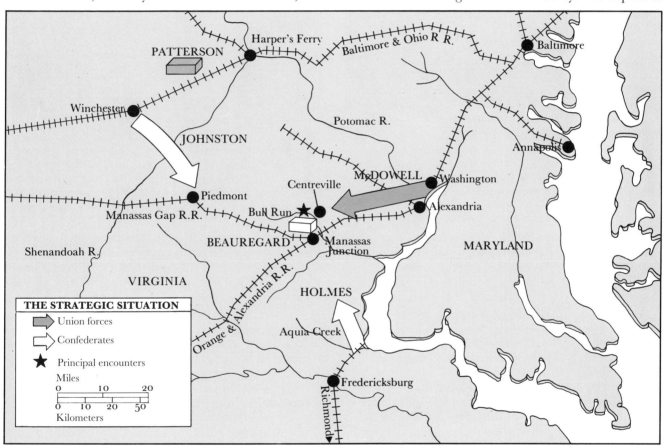

Centreville by the Warrenton Turnpike at 3 A.M. Hunter and Heintzelman followed Tyler. The distance to Stone Bridge was about four miles–an easy march along a straight road. At about the halfway point, the column would pass Cub Run, a minor stream; Tyler would continue toward Stone Bridge, but Hunter and Heintzelman were to veer right along a little-used track which was believed to lead to the fords at Sudley Springs. The problem here was that no one knew just how long this route was, nor indeed just where it led.

Tyler's progress was painfully slow. Someone had imprudently placed the mammoth 30-pounder Parrott rifle of Carlisle's battery at the head of the march column, and the great gun, weighing over 6,000 pounds, moved so slowly that it delayed the entire operation. Finally, at about 5.30 A.M., Tyler's men took up positions near the Stone Bridge. Further back, the divisions of the main attack diverged from the turnpike and began their march toward Sudley

Evans was another military "first"–the first battlefield use of the familiar wigwag field-telegraph system. Alexander's message confirmed what Evans had half-suspected. Abandoning the insignificant skirmish with Tyler, he swung his command across Young's Branch and marched northwest to Matthews's Hill, where he formed a new line at right angles to his old position. Carefully, he disposed his small corps to meet the new Federal threat; the infantry, six companies of the 4th South Carolina (four having been left to watch Tyler) and Major "Rob" Wheat's tough zouave battalion, were posted in a thicket near a copse of pines; two howitzers anchored the flanks.

Evans's men did not have long to wait. At 10 A.M., Colonel Ambrose Burnside's Rhode Island brigade, the van of the still-developing Union line of battle, emerged over the rolling fields separating them from the Confederates. The Rebels had the advantage of cover and a secure defensive position, and their fire hit the Rhode Islanders hard, stopping them

# THE COMMANDERS

Major-General Irvin McDowell, USV

General P. G. T. Beauregard, CSA

Irvin McDowell (1818-85), the reluctant commander of the Union army at Bull Run, was a burly man with a prodigious appetite and a bluff, rough-and-ready manner. Although he had few friends in the army, McDowell was well liked by the politicians of the Lincoln Administration. His military background was impeccable, and few Regular Army officers possessed more knowledge of military theory. It was, perhaps, for these reasons that he was promoted from major to brigadier-general and appointed to lead the army that was to make the North's first large-scale invasion of the Confederacy.

McDowell did not lack confidence, but at no time did he seem secure in his position; rather he appeared almost overwhelmed by the enormity of the task facing him. He had first of all to improvise an army from the motley bands of citizen-volunteers in Washington. No one could be certain that these men would fight, and McDowell had few illusions. "This is not an army," he confided to his friend John Bigelow. "It will take a long time to make an army." He also had to formulate a plan of campaign that stood a reasonable chance of success. This he did, working long hours alone with inadequate maps.

The campaign and battle that ensured demonstrated McDowell's strengths and weaknesses as a soldier. He was strong on organization and planning–staff work was his forte. But he became curiously indecisive in the face of the enemy, wasting time when he might have attacked with advantage. During the battle itself, he seems to have lost contact with the bulk of his army; instead of directing the overall attack, he was seen time and again at the head of single regiments. Consequently Bull Run was, as Sherman expressed it, "one of the best-planned battles of the war but one of the worst-fought."

After the battle McDowell was replaced by McClellan. A corps commander at Second Bull Run, he was relieved of command afterward and did not hold a field command for the rest of the war.

Pierre Gustave Toutant Beauregard (1818-93) was born in Louisiana, the son of a wealthy Creole planter. His youthful background was entirely Gallic, and he inherited an excitable temperament. Although his primary education was patchy, he was a good student and very early showed an interest in military history, especially the campaigns of Napoleon Bonaparte. His parents enrolled him in a French military academy in New York City, and in due course he entered West Point. There, ironically, he was instructed by Robert Anderson, the future defender of Fort Sumter, and was a classmate of Irvin McDowell, his opponent at Bull Run.

His military education completed, Beauregard served as an army engineer in various postings and built up an excellent record as a staff officer in the Mexican War. He was briefly Superintendent at West Point in 1861, but was removed because of his secessionist sympathies. Returning to Louisiana, he was chagrined to find that the authorities had appointed Braxton Bragg commander of the state's armed forces. In a fit of resentment, he enlisted as a private in the Orleans Guards. But the Confederacy could not overlook his obvious talents, and he was subsequently named the first brigadier in the South's Provisional Army. After his triumph at Charleston Harbor, he served as second-in-command at First Bull Run and Shiloh. His greatest contribution, however, was his stubborn defense of Charleston in 1863.

As a soldier Beauregard was imaginative but not always realistic. His plans were often far-fetched. Jefferson Davis deplored the last trait, which he described as "drivelling on possibilities." "Old Bory" was not a great field commander, but in 1861 he was the South's man of the hour.

Beauregard served throughout the Civil War: in its final phase he commanded the defenses of Richmond and Petersburg. In 1863 he gave further proof of his interest in the theory of warfare when he published *Principles and Maxims of the Art of War*.

in their tracks. More Union brigades shouldered into line, extending their combined front to the right and left far beyond the limits of Evans's position. The Confederates were forced to disperse and fight in small groups to guard their flanks. "It was impossible at this time to concentrate them at any point," recalled a soldier, "each was fighting in his own style–'bush-wacking,' as it is called." Major Wheat fell, shot through both lungs. Given up for dead, he protested, "I don't feel like dying yet." In the event he lived, only to predict his own death in action at Gaines's Mill less than a year later.

Despite his efforts, Evans could not long resist the Union tide. Anxiously, he cast about for help. Behind him, on the Henry House plateau, two Confederate brigades had recently arrived, those of General Bernard E. Bee and Colonel Francis Stebbings Bartow, both of Johnston's army. These men had been ordered to march to the left earlier in the day when Tyler's firing had caused Beauregard some concern for his weak flank. Now Evans urged them to join him.

At first Bee demurred. He held a better position on the commanding Henry Hill, and he did not wish to sacrifice his men needlessly in the maelstrom near Matthews's House. He hoped Evans would have sense enough to disengage and fall back on his (Bee's) lines. Evans, however, could not be budged from his position. Reluctantly, Bee led his men to Evans's line, which they extended to the right.

Bee's troops were fresh, but there were not enough of them. The battle had become a meeting engagement, and McDowell was pushing troops to the front in greater numbers. In addition to Burnside's brigade, Colonel Andrew Porter's and Colonel William B. Franklin's were not engaged. Additionally, two of Tyler's brigades, those of Colonel William Tecumseh Sherman and Colonel Erasmus D. Keyes, had discovered an obscure ford above Stone Bridge and were crossing Bull Run to add their weight to the fight. The decisive element, however, was the Union artillery. Three full batteries–those of Ricketts, Griffin, and the 2nd Rhode Island–were tearing the Confederate line to pieces at close range.

It was more than men could stand. The Rebel line, hammered unmercifully by artillery and pressured from front and flank, broke up. The men ran down into the valley of Young's Branch, past the Stone House and across the turnpike to Henry Hill. As they ran, they were harried by shellfire. The crisis of the battle was approaching. The Confederates had to hold the Henry plateau or risk defeat on the plains of Manassas beyond.

Beauregard and Johnston were not unaware of the fight on the Confederate left, but throughout much of the morning they were preoccupied with the execution of the main Rebel attack, which, as we have noted, was to be carried out by the right-wing troops. The attempt, however, stalled in mid-course. Beauregard's orders for the offensive were poorly written and confusing, and at least one set failed to be delivered. By mid-morning Johnston had become exasperated with the delays; he was also worried by the rising volume of fire on the left. Already the brigades of Bee, Bartow and Jackson, and Colonel Wade Hampton's Legion had been despatched to Evans's aid; but still the issue seemed in doubt. Finally at 11.15, Johnston waved his hand to the north and exclaimed, "The battle is over there. I am going!" Beauregard, still half-convinced his plan might yet be implemented, was disappointed but forced to concede that the action was now elsewhere. The two men put spurs to their horses and rode for Henry Hill.

McDowell's men had convincingly won the morning phase of the battle. They had only to pursue the fleeing Confederates to gain a complete victory. With veteran troops it might have been done quickly, and with precision; with militia it was a different matter. Burnside's brigade, for example, disintegrated and broke for the rear almost the instant Evans's troops ran from its front. Other commands were disorganized, too (though none so badly as Burnside's). Another factor was that many experienced field officers were already *hors de combat*: Generals Hunter and Heintzelman were wounded and Colonel John S. Slocum of the 2nd Rhode Island had been killed. The junior officers were as confused as the men. Some units, notably the brigades of Sherman and Keyes, did follow the Confederates, but the rest took an hour to reorganize. During this period McDowell brought up the unengaged brigades of Colonel Orlando B. Wilcox and Colonel Oliver Otis Howard for the final push.

John D. Imboden, the commander of the Staunton (Virginia) battery of Bee's brigade, had taken up a position on the northwest slope of Henry Hill, where he had dueled with Rickett's and Griffin's batteries during the morning's action. Now Imboden found himself alone. "No Confederate soldier was visible from our position near the Henry House," he recalled. Not 500 yards away, at the Stone House near the junction of the turnpike and the Manassas-Sudley Road, Federal troops were massing for the attack on Henry Hill. His battery now being in imminent danger of capture, Imboden ordered the guns to be limbered and drawn out of danger. As the battery retreated across the plateau through the dips and swales near Henry House, the Union guns redoubled their fire. Several shells burst in and about the house, killing Mrs. Judith Henry, an aged widow, and wounding her Negro maidservant. They were the first civilian casualties of the war.

Although Imboden may have felt deserted by his comrades, in fact desperate fighting raged several hundred yards away on the northeast slope of the plateau. There, near the house of James Robinson and along the turnpike–at that point nearly hidden by a deep road cut–Wade Hampton's 650-man legion intervened to stop the Union pursuit.

Hampton was reputedly the wealthiest planter in the South. The son of a Revolutionary war hero, he was intelligent, brave, immensely strong, and an accomplished horseman and athlete. He had recruited and equipped his men at his own expense from among the most eminent families of South Carolina. Like the New York 7th, the legion was a blue-blooded outfit. Hampton's unit had been in existence little more than a month, but at Bull Run its patrician-soldiers fought like veterans. In two hours' combat, fighting virtually alone, the legion lost 121 men.

The efforts of Hampton's men along the turnpike and in the farm lane of Robinson House secured the right flank of a new Confederate line formed by Jackson's brigade at the edge of a long belt of young pines which stretched in an arc from Robinson House along the eastern crest of the plateau. Keyes's Union brigade, which ought to have smashed this vulnerable flank, recoiled in confusion from Hampton's front and retreated to a wooded valley near the confluence of Young's Branch and Bull Run. There, out of harm's way, Keyes's men huddled together, thoroughly demoralized. They took no further part.

# THE TURNING POINT

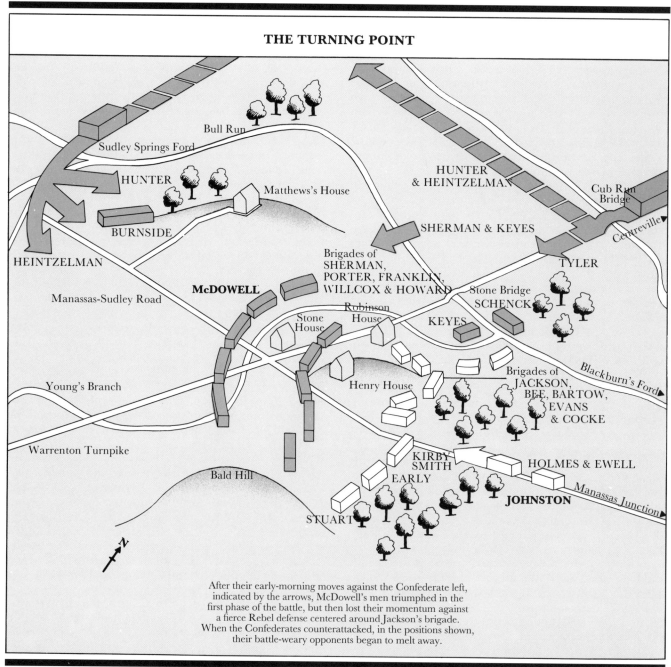

Bull Run

Sudley Springs Ford

HUNTER

Matthews's House

HUNTER
& HEINTZELMAN

Cub Run
Bridge

BURNSIDE

SHERMAN & KEYES

Centreville

HEINTZELMAN

Brigades of
SHERMAN,
PORTER, FRANKLIN,
WILLCOX & HOWARD

TYLER

**McDOWELL**

Stone Bridge
SCHENCK

Manassas-Sudley Road

Robinson
House

Stone
House

KEYES

Young's Branch

Henry House

Brigades of
JACKSON,
BEE, BARTOW,
EVANS
& COCKE

Blackburn's Ford

Warrenton Turnpike

Bald Hill

KIRBY
SMITH
EARLY

HOLMES & EWELL

STUART

**JOHNSTON**

Manassas Junction

N

After their early-morning moves against the Confederate left,
indicated by the arrows, McDowell's men triumphed in the
first phase of the battle, but then lost their momentum against
a fierce Rebel defense centered around Jackson's brigade.
When the Confederates counterattacked, in the positions shown,
their battle-weary opponents began to melt away.

Major "Rob" Wheat's Zouave battalion, the Louisiana Tigers.
This hard-fighting unit was recruited from the sweepings of the New Orleans waterfront.

## THE OPPOSING FORCES

### UNION ARMY
Brigadier-General Irvin McDowell

First Division (Brigadier-General Daniel Tyler):
First Brigade (Colonel Erasmus D. Keyes).
Second brigade (Brigadier-General Robert C. Schenck).
Third Brigade (Colonel William T. Sherman).
Fourth Brigade (Colonel Israel B. Richardson).
Second Division (Brigadier-General David Hunter):
First Brigade (Colonel Andrew Porter).
Second Brigade (Colonel Ambrose E. Burnside).
Third Division (Brigadier-General S. P. Heintzelman):
First Brigade (Colonel W. B. Franklin).
Second Brigade (Colonel Orlando B. Willcox).
Third Brigade (Colonel Oliver O. Howard).
Fourth (Reserve) Division (Brigadier-General Theodore Runyon): 9 unbrigaded regiments.
Fifth Division (Colonel Dixon S. Miles):
First Brigade (Colonel Louis Blenker).
Second Brigade (Colonel Thomas A. Davies).
Cavalry (Major I. N. Palmer): 7 companies of Regulars, attached to Porter's Brigade.
Artillery: 10 batteries, 9 of them Regular Army, and 2 guns attached to an infantry regiment–the 71st New York. Total guns: 49.

#### Estimated Totals

The total strength of McDowell's army has been accurately estimated at about 35,000 men and 49 guns. Of that number, however, only 18,572 rank and file were closely engaged in the battle.
Losses: 460 killed, 1,124 wounded, and 1,312 captured or missing. Total: 2,896.

### CONFEDERATE ARMY
General Joseph E. Johnston

#### ARMY OF THE POTOMAC
Brigadier-General P. G. T. Beauregard

First Brigade (Brigadier-General M. L. Bonham).
Second Brigade (Brigadier-General R. S. Ewell).
Third Brigade (Brigadier-General D. R. Jones).
Fourth Brigade (Brigadier-General James Longstreet).
Fifth Brigade (Colonel Philip St. George Cocke).
Sixth Brigade (Colonel Jubal A. Early).
Evans's Demi-brigade (Captain N. G. Evans).
Reserve Brigade (Brigadier-General T. H. Holmes).
Unattached infantry (2 regiments).
Cavalry (Various commands, about 3 regiments).
Artillery (Various commands, 29 guns).
Estimated strength: 24,000 men and 29 guns.

#### ARMY OF THE SHENANDOAH
General Joseph E. Johnson

First Brigade (Brigadier-General Thomas J. Jackson).
Second Brigade (Colonel F. S. Bartow).
Third Brigade (Brigadier-General B. E. Bee).
Fourth Brigade (Brigadier-General E. K. Smith).
Cavalry (1st Virginia, Colonel J. E. B. Stuart).
Artillery (5 batteries, 20 guns).
Estimated strength: 8,500 men and 20 guns.

#### Estimated Totals

Beauregard's Army of the Potomac had an estimated strength of 24,000 men, including Holmes's command of 2,500 men which arrived on the 20th from Aquia Creek. Johnston brought 8,500 men of the Valley Army's 11,000 effectives to Manassas. The total Confederate strength was therefore about 32,500 rank and file available for action on the 21st, and 49 guns. It has also been estimated that 18,053 men were actually engaged in the battle.
Losses: 387 killed, 1,582 wounded, and 13 captured or missing. Total: 1,982

---

The fiercest action of the day now began to build up around Jackson's line. Jackson himself was a complex man: brilliant, deeply religious, and something of an eccentric. His students at the Virginia Military Institute called him "Tom Fool" Jackson, but in battle he was calm and confident. He had arrived on the plateau earlier in the day after Bee and Bartow had joined the fight on Matthews's Hill. Coolly appraising the field, he had selected his brigade's position with care. The men were arranged in the concave line already described, sheltered from opposing artillery fire by the crest of the hill. In front of this line, which stretched from the Manassas-Sudley Road to Robinson House, the ground dipped and then rose again to Henry House, some 330 yards away.

This was Jackson's position when the debris of Bee's, Bartow's, and Evans's commands trailed back over the plateau following the morning's fight. Jackson's brigade and Hampton's legion were the only cohesive Confederate units in the vicinity. Bee, swept back with his men, rode over to Jackson and reported. "General, they are beating us back." Jackson, exhibiting the calm courage that inspired men about him to feats of unsurpassed valor, replied, "Sir, we will give them the bayonet!" Hearing this, Bee rode back to his

troops, stood in his stirrups, and gestured toward Jackson, saying: "Form! Form! There stands Jackson like a stone wall! Rally behind the Virginians!" The words had a magic quality. The troops of Bee, Bartow, and Evans did indeed rally and return to the fight. The nickname stuck; thereafter Jackson was "Stonewall", his brigade the "Stonewall Brigade," Moments later, Bee fell, mortally wounded.

Beauregard and Johnston were up now, rallying troops and leading them into line. Colonel Philip St. George Cocke's brigade came up and extended Jackson's front across the Manassas-Sudley Road. Colonel J. E. B. Stuart's 1st Virginia Cavalry lay nearby, concealed in scrubby pine thickets near Cocke's position. The Confederates, tired and thirsty but full of fight, awaited the final onslaught.

McDowell's attack commenced at 1 P.M. Four brigades, those of Sherman, Porter, Franklin, and Willcox, about 10,000 men altogether, supported by Howard's brigade, made straight for Henry Hill in an uncoordinated but spirited offensive. Struggling uphill in the scorching midday sun, these men drove the Confederates from Henry and Robinson Houses and swept right up to Jackson's line, where they were blasted back by volleys of musketry and rapid discharges of canister from several batteries. Thereafter, both sides fought with frantic energy to secure the plateau. Charge and countercharge boiled across the undulating ground between the lines–furious attacks launched piecemeal by regiments and companies long since separated from their parent units.

Sensing that he had gained the upper hand, McDowell played his trump card, ordering Rickett's and Griffin's batteries to the front and directing them to take up positions south of Henry House. It was McDowell's great mistake. The 11 guns, ranged in a 200-yard-long semicircle stretching from Henry House to the Manassas-Sudley Road, were quite incapable of harming the Confederates, who were concealed by the brow opposite them. Their fire, previously so effective, now made little impression.

The Union batteries had not been long in action when, at about 3 P.M., Colonel Charles Cummings's 33rd Virginia, Jackson's left-flank regiment, marched out of a little grove of trees in their front and advanced unmolested to within 70 yards of the gun line. Cummings's men wore their blue militia uniforms; at their head, the blue Virginia state flag hung limply from its staff. In the smoke and haze, they were mistaken for Union troops. Suddenly, 400 muskets were leveled, and a devastating volley swept the batteries, wrecking both and scything down 54 men and 104 horses.

As Cummings's exultant troops swarmed over the guns, Stuart's cavalry rode through the ranks of Union infantry ranged in support of the batteries. The attack was textbook-perfect. The Union forces, a battalion of Marines and the New York Fire Zouaves, broke. However, though stunning, Cummings's success was not decisive. The Union troops counterattacked, and once again the tempest raged to and fro across the plateau. Three times the guns changed hands before the Confederates won them at the last. Finally, at about 4 P.M., the Union army began to disintegrate. The men, as if with one mind, decided they had had enough. Having marched the better part of the night and fought all day on sun-baked fields and hills, they were thoroughly exhausted. As amateurs they had fought well, but victory had eluded them.

The majority had begun to straggle away before the next great Confederate counterattack stove

in the flank of Howard's brigade near Dogan House. This occurred when Johnston, who had earlier left the field to help direct newly arriving troops to the front, sent reinforcements up to the ridge to the west of the Manassas-Sudley Road. These men, the brigades of Colonel Jubal A. Early and Brigadier-General E. Kirby Smith, advanced along the ridge parallel to the road. They fell on the exposed flank of Howard's brigade, which was attempting to envelop the Confederate left on Henry Hill. Howard's unit fell apart. Simultaneously, the Confederates on Henry Hill advanced all along the line and swept the remaining Federals across the turnpike. Fear and panic struck the Union army; the retreat became a disorderly rout.

As the scared mob of fugitives streamed back across Bull Run, Del Kemper's Confederate battery unlimbered near the Stone Bridge and began shelling the Cub Run Bridge. One shell burst squarely in the center of the span, overturning a wagon and blocking traffic. A bottleneck soon developed, made worse as the hordes of stampeding soldiers and panic-stricken wagoners crossed the bridge and then became nightmarishly entangled with hysterical civilians who, hours before, had hired buggies and driven out from Washington expecting to witness a Union victory. Mercifully, there was no Confederate pursuit; the Rebels were too disorganized to do much more than collect prisoners.

The battle ended with this Union flight. McDowell's army was shattered but eventually reorganized at Washington, where, on the 26th, it received a new commander, General George B. McClellan. The exhausted Confederates, unable seriously to threaten Washington, limited their advance to Centreville, where they established a fortified camp, and awaited the next Union move. Thus now both sides were in virtually the same positions they had occupied before the battle.

Bull Run had several important consequences. Many Southerners, rashly assuming that the war had ended in victory for their cause, went home. Most Northerners, on the other hand, now recognized that the war could not be ended quickly. Congress promptly voted to raise an army of 500,000 long-term volunteers. The war, henceforth, would be fought in earnest; the day of the "Sunday soldier" had passed.

Men of the 33rd Virginia Regiment overwhelm Rickett's Union battery on Henry Hill.

Top
Sudley Springs Ford, where the Union
flanking column crossed Bull Run.

Left
Lieutenant-General Wade Hampton, CSA.
At the time of First Bull Run, he was a colonel
commanding a 650-man legion raised and equipped
at his own expense from among the most eminent
families of South Carolina.

Below
Robinson House, its walls heavily scarred with
bullets from the fight in which Hampton's legion
stemmed the Union pursuit.

# SHILOH

April 6–7, 1862

Prelude to Shiloh: General U.S. Grant supervises the reduction of Fort Donelson (center background). Soon to be nicknamed "Unconditional Surrender" when he refused to bargain with the capitulating Rebels, Grant in this campaign showed his great potential as a strategist and a fighter. In him, the Union Army was to find its winning leader.

In the beginning of February 1862, the troops of the Confederate General Albert Sidney Johnston manned an extended defense line in Kentucky and northern Tennessee. This line, the embodiment of Jefferson Davis's ill-conceived cordon-defense policy, was well over 300 miles in length, stretching from the Mississippi River in the west to Cumberland Gap on the Virginia border in the east; to defend it Johnston had no more than 45,000 men. These troops were scattered far and wide in detachments meant to contest the main invasion routes from the north and protect the vital agricultural heartland of the Confederacy to the south.

Johnston himself commanded the largest field force, an army of 22,000 men whose headquarters were at Bowling Green, Kentucky. The only other big concentrations were in garrisons: Major-General Leonidas Polk's command of 17,000 men at Columbus, Kentucky, and the 5,500 men assigned to the defense of Forts Henry and Donelson, important earthworks built just 12 miles apart on the narrow neck of land separating the Tennessee and Cumberland rivers below their confluence with the Ohio River. Thus the bulk of Johnston's force occupied a military frontier some 110 miles in extent. Johnston and Polk, on the right and left respectively, held salients projecting northward; between them, but well to the south, the two forts denied the Federals access to the interior along the great riverine highways of Middle Tennessee.

Opposed to Johnston were 125,000 Union troops in three armies: Major-General Don Carlos Buell's 75,000-man Army of the Ohio at Louisville, Kentucky; Brigadier-General Ulysses S. Grant's army of 20,000 men based at Cairo, Illinois; and Major-General John Pope's 30,000-man force operating in Missouri. Besides these armies the Union forces included the Western Flotilla, a powerful fleet of shallow-draft gunboats, many of them ironclads, designed and built specifically for use on Western waters. These gunboats, commanded by Flag-Officer A. H. Foote, were stationed at Cairo, where they could cooperate with Grant's army. The Confederates had nothing comparable to them.

The armies of Grant and Pope were directed by Major-General Henry W. Halleck, the Commanding General of the Missouri Department. Halleck was an ambitious man but a timid theoretician, a military pedant once described as "a large emptiness surrounded by an education." Both Grant and Pope menaced Polk's lines along the Mississippi, but Grant had latterly seized Paducah, Kentucky, on the Lower Ohio. Paducah became a sallyport, an advanced post from which Grant might at any time strike quickly at Forts Henry and Donelson. Buell, on the Union left-center, advanced cautiously along the line of the Louisville & Nashville Railroad toward the huge Confederate supply depot at Nashville. This offensive, in concert with the movements of Halleck's armies, was designed to use Union numerical superiority to maneuver the Confederates out of Kentucky and east Tennessee.

In the face of this overwhelming mass of men and matériel Johnston's strategic position was near-hopeless. Thus far, he had managed to maintain the semblance of a defensive line by bluff and guile, but earlier, on January 19, one of his advance detachments under Brigadier-General Felix K. Zollicoffer was routed in a battle at Logan's Cross Roads, and the Confederates were swept from eastern Kentucky

in the aftermath. Clearly, should the main Union armies make a concerted offensive, resistance would be futile and Johnston would be forced to retreat.

Ironically, Johnston's two greatest allies in this predicament were the Union commanders. Halleck was cautious and unwilling to take responsibility for any large-scale troop movement, while Buell, who might have crushed Johnston's army at Bowling Green whenever he wished, was a courageous soldier but a plodder. Then, too, Johnston's overblown reputation as a soldier helped to keep the Union armies at a distance. That left Grant, who was a more energetic opponent. Sometime that winter, Grant had conceived a plan to force Polk and Johnston out of their salients by capturing Forts Henry and Donelson and making a strategic penetration of the Confederate center. By following the rivers beyond the forts, he could split Johnston's army in two and imperil the heartland of the Confederacy.

Halleck, of course, opposed the plan, but allowed Grant and Foote to mount a limited expedition against Fort Henry, which fell to the gunboats on February 6. Grant next decided, on his own initiative, to move on Fort Donelson. His advance, however, was delayed by severe weather, and the army was unable to march until the 12th. In the interim, a few of Foote's gunboats steamed up the Tennessee as far as Muscle Shoals, Alabama, destroying the Memphis & Ohio Railroad bridge and some Confederate gunboats. On their return, they swung up the Ohio and turned into the Cumberland River to assist Grant in the reduction of Fort Donelson.

Halleck, meantime, was perturbed by Grant's bold scheme of campaign. To friends he moaned, "It is the crisis of the war in the West." He was nevertheless stimulated by the success at Fort Henry and busied himself forwarding reinforcements to Grant. If Grant failed, it would be Grant's defeat; if Grant succeeded, it would be Halleck's victory.

At this juncture Johnston made the greatest blunder of his military career. Perceiving the danger to his line of communications, he withdrew to Nashville from his exposed position at Bowling Green. Before retiring, however, he split his army, sending two divisions (about 12,000 men) to reinforce Donelson. Johnston's motive for doing this has remained a puzzle to this day. Military logic dictated either the evacuation of Donelson or a concentration of all available forces against Grant's vulnerable army. To make matters more complicated, the commanders of the Donelson reinforcement, Brigadier-General John B. Floyd and Brigadier-General Pillow, were among the worst incompetents to wear Rebel uniform. Grant knew both men, and his comments are instructive: "I had known General Pillow in Mexico and judged that with any force, no matter how small, I could march up to within gunshot of any entrenchments he was given to hold . . . I knew that Floyd was in command, but he was no soldier, and I judged that he would yield to Pillow's pretensions."

Grant's army invaded Donelson on the 13th, the day on which the last Confederate reinforcements arrived. Foote's gunboats attacked the next day, but were driven off after a hot fight with the batteries. On the 15th, the encircled Confederates made a desperate attempt to break out toward Nashville. Their attack caught the Union army by surprise and drove two of Grant's divisions away from the river road, this being the Rebels' chosen escape-route. At this juncture the Confederate commanders might have evacuated the fort and made good their escape as planned.

Instead, they began to argue among themselves and then ordered their troops back into the fort. Grant, who had been away conferring with Foote on his flagship, returned in time to rally his men and order a crushing counterattack which regained the lost ground and sealed the fate of the fort. The fighting, which proved to be the bloodiest of the war until McClellan's Richmond offensive, cost Grant's army 3,000 men; Confederate losses numbered 2,000.

That evening, Brigadier-General Simon Bolivar Buckner asked for surrender terms. (He had been left in command of the beleaguered garrison after Floyd and Pillow had stolen away on a steamboat, taking some 1,500 troops with them.) Grant's reply was harsh: "No terms except an unconditional and immediate surrender can be accepted." Buckner complained that the terms were "ungenerous and unchivalrous," but his position was hopeless and he was forced to accede. The next morning he surrendered the fort and its garrison of 15,000 men.

The surrender of Donelson was an unmitigated disaster for the Confederacy. Between them Floyd, Pillow, and a young cavalry colonel named Nathan Bedford Forrest had managed to save 3,000 men from the fiasco, but the losses were nevertheless crippling. Johnston, facing annihilation, abandoned Tennessee, drew in his detachments, and made a frantic appeal to Richmond for reinforcements. President Davis, still confident in Johnston's ability to retrieve the South's sagging fortunes, stripped the Gulf Coast and the Mississippi Valley of troops to shore up a new front south of the Tennessee River. This left many vital areas of the western Confederacy virtually undefended and in fact presented the Federal forces with one of their grandest opportunities to end the war.

Grant, now nicknamed "Unconditional Surrender" by a jubilant public, saw that "the way was open to the National forces all over the south-west." The quick follow-up he hoped for, however, was not to be. Halleck, with remarkable perversity, claimed the victory at Donelson for himself and then accused Grant of neglect of duty, inefficiency, and drunkenness. All these slanders were telegraphed to General McClellan at Washington who replied advising Grant's arrest "if the good of the service required it." On March 4 Grant was removed from command of his army. Brigadier-General C. F. Smith, who had commanded a division at Donelson, replaced him. In the aftermath of this cruel injustice, Halleck was appointed to the command of all Union forces in the West, including Buell's army which was then at Nashville.

Johnston, meantime, was concentrating his troops at Corinth, Mississippi, an important rail center at the junction of the Mobile & Ohio and Memphis & Charleston Railroads. Besides its value as an assembly point, Corinth provided a convenient base from which to defend the line of the Memphis & Ohio Railroad–the South's only adequate line of communications between the Mississippi and the Atlantic coast. At Corinth, Johnston's army ballooned in strength to about 60,000 men. Nevertheless, many of these men were sick and others had been detached to guard the railroads, so the effective total was nearer 40,000. The new army, organized into three corps and a reserve and dubbed the Army of Mississippi, was a hodge-podge of elements, some good, most bad. Beauregard, who had come from the East in February, was second-in-command. The corps commanders were a talented group: Polk and William J. Hardee had been with Johnston from the beginning,

but Braxton Bragg, a neurasthenic martinet who had brought 10,000 men from the Gulf, was new. John C. Breckinridge, elevated to the command of the reserve when Bragg removed George B. Crittenden for drunkenness, was a capable soldier and a former Vice-President of the United States.

Morale among the troops was high, but with the exception of Bragg's corps discipline was poor. Johnston appointed Bragg Chief of Staff to correct deficiencies in the army's administration and to improve discipline; even so Polk's corps, composed largely of Kentuckians and Tenesseeans whose loyalty was suspect, defied even his draconian measures. (Bragg, at his wit's end, referred to these men as "Polk's mob.") To complicate matters further, the army's supply system was grossly inefficient. The worst shortages were in food and munitions. Malnutrition and disease were common, and even mild illnesses claimed the lives of soldiers weakened by a poor diet. Most of the men were poorly armed, and the variety of weapons, including ancient flintlocks, shotguns, and fowling-pieces, made the army a veritable museum of small arms. Johnston corrected this deficiency somewhat when he requisitioned 18,600 British Enfield rifles–the cargoes of two blockade runners–for distribution to the troops. The cannon, too, were obsolete, being for the most part old smoothbores. Such was the state of the Army of Mississippi on the eve of Shiloh. Well might Bragg complain that the troops "were too poorly supplied, and too badly organized, instructed, and disciplined, to justify a hope of even carrying them to the point desired, much less a success against a well-organized foe."

Despite Bragg's misgivings, the Confederate army, however unprepared, was about to assume the offensive. The opportunity was provided by a chain of Union blunders. After boasting that he would "split secession in twain in one month" once he had the high command in the West, Halleck permitted Johnston's army–his true strategic objective–to slip from his grasp and reorganize unimpeded. Having chosen not to pursue, he opted for a policy of leisurely concentration. Buell was to march to the Tennessee River and join his command with Smith's; then Halleck would take the field and lead the combined armies against the Rebels at Corinth. Until Buell arrived, Smith was to select a suitable base on the river and conduct raids against the railroad.

It was during the course of one of these raids (March 16-17) that Brigadier-General William T. Sherman discovered Pittsburg Landing, a transfer point for goods shipped from the Tennessee River to Corinth. Just beyond the landing was a pleasant, verdant plateau hemmed in on two sides by creeks. Corinth was 22 miles to the southwest, connected to the landing by a country road. In Sherman's view, the area provided the best campsite in the region (despite being on the Confederates' side of the river), and he established his division there. Soon, the rest of the army followed.

Smith, meantime, had injured his leg and contracted a tetanus infection which was to prove fatal. When Halleck heard of this, he restored Grant to command. In due course, Grant arrived at Savannah, a river town eight miles below (north of) Pittsburgh Landing, and established his headquarters there. From this position it was clear that his army was concentrating on the "wrong" side of the Tennessee River within a day's march of the Confederate base at Corinth. If this bothered Grant, he gave no evidence of it. "Camp Shiloh," which took its name from

Shiloh Church, a tiny log meeting-house two and a half miles from the landing, was dry and convenient for the army's steamboats. The Confederates were thought to be demoralized and therefore no threat; besides, Buell was on his way. Grant's odd complacency was reflected in the haphazard arrangement of the army's campsites. Five of the six divisions were bivouacked in the narrow plateau-like triangle of land between the creeks which extended southwest from Pittsburgh Landing. The remaining division, commanded by Major-General Lew Wallace (the future author of *Ben Hur*), was posted five miles downstream at Crump's Landing.

No system was employed in arranging these camps. The rawest divisions, those of Sherman and Brigadier-General Benjamin M. Prentiss, occupied the most exposed positions. Sherman's camp at Shiloh Church constituted the right flank of the advanced line and covered the main approach to the landing via the Corinth Road. Prentiss's division,

convey an impression of weakness. Such was the situation of Grant's army before the Confederate attack. The men drilled or lolled about, enjoying the relaxed atmosphere of the camps. Springtime had come to the woods and ravines about Shiloh, and the war seemed distant. Peach trees blossomed in a field near Stuart's position on the Hamburg Road, while on the river, where the gunboats *Tyler* and *Lexington* were stationed, a calliope on an army transport blared forth, adding its din to the music of the regimental bands beyond the landing. Infantry pickets discharged their muskets at random; many of them were fascinated by their newly issued weapons. All in all, Shiloh was quite the best camp any of the men could remember.

Confederate troops were witness to this festive panorama. Prodded by Beauregard and urged on by news that Buell was drawing close, Johnston had set his army in motion toward Shiloh on April 3. The march, however, was mismanaged, prompting Johnston to bitter complaints. When the Rebel army at last

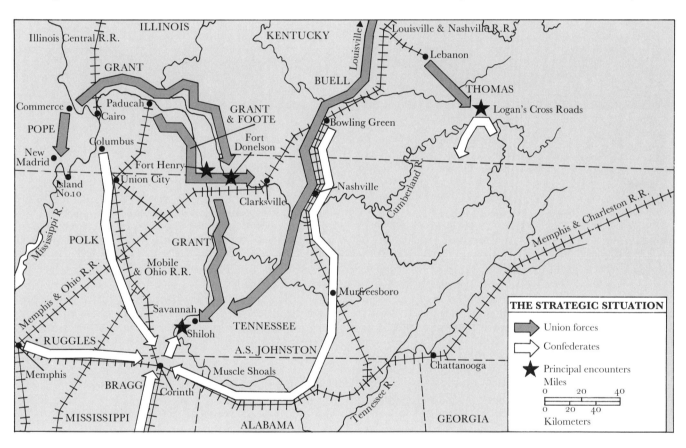

which was still organizing (the men had just drawn their muskets), was bivouacked to Sherman's left and front cross the Ridge Road, but was separated from Sherman's left-flank brigade by a gap of half a mile. The left flank, near the Tennessee, was watched by Stuart's isolated brigade, also of Sherman's division. Behind this line, straggling back toward the landing, were the camps of the three veteran divisions. Major-General John A. McClernand's troops were to Sherman's left and rear along the Purdy Road. General Stephen A. Hurlbut's division, later renowned as the "Fighting Fourth," and General W. H. L. Wallace's command, the army's finest, were tented close by the landing.

Raw troops fighting defensively are most at home in trenches, but Camp Shiloh was not fortified; no one expected an attack. Smith, Sherman, and Grant were of one mind on this matter. Like Howe before Germantown (1777), they believed that entrenching would ruin the army's morale and

sorted itself out three days had elapsed, and the attack, originally scheduled for 3 A.M. on Saturday the 5th, had to be postponed until dawn on the 6th.

Johnston's tactical plan, like his scheme of campaign, was bold. Grant's army was to be overwhelmed by a surprise attack and beaten in detail before Buell's arrival. More particularly, the Confederates would attempt to "turn the left flank of the enemy so as to cut off his line of retreat to the Tennessee River and force him back on Owl Creek, where he will be obliged to surrender." Surprise was the key element in this plan, but frequent skirmishes between the pickets on the 5th seemed to reduce the chances of taking the Union army unawares. In the light of this, both Bragg and Beauregard argued that the attack should be called off. Johnston, however, was unmoved. "I would fight them," he said, "if they were a million."

As the bright dawn on Sunday the 6th lit up the woodland around Shiloh, 40,000 Confederate

# THE COMMANDERS

General Ulysses S. Grant, USA

General Albert Sidney Johnston, CSA

Ulysses Simpson Grant (1822-85) was 39 years old at Shiloh. The man who would one day deliver final victory to the North had begun the war a virtual unknown—a failure plagued by self-doubt and troubled by his addiction to alcohol.

The son of a tanner, Grant graduated from West Point in 1843, his one distinction being a First in horsemanship. After service in Mexico, where he was twice cited for gallantry, Grant rose to the rank of captain in the Fourth Infantry, then drifted into depression and alcoholism when a posting to an obscure frontier fort separated him from his family. His enforced resignation followed inevitably, in 1854. Rejoining his family, he tried his hand at farming and real estate in Missouri but failed in both, and at one point was reduced to selling firewood in the streets of St. Louis. Just prior to the outbreak of war, he was rescued from near-oblivion by the offer of a clerkship in the family harness shop in Galena, Illinois.

With the advent of civil war, Grant received an entirely unexpected commission as colonel of volunteers from Governor Yates of Illinois. Not only for Sam Grant, as his old army friends knew him, but for the nation as well, the commission was a blessing. The new colonel, it transpired, knew how to wage war. Though thoroughly unpretentious and almost naïvely uncomplicated, Grant, once he had conquered his own fears and dispelled the demons of earlier failures, won battles. For two years he molded the course of the war in the West, delivering a succession of decisive victories that broke the back of the Confederacy. Brought to the eastern theater in 1864, he was made General in Chief of the Union armies and directed the final hammering campaigns that sealed the fate of the rebellion.

In the wake of his near-defeat at Shiloh, there were many who called for Grant's removal. But Lincoln was not to be persuaded, saying, "I can't spare this man. He fights!"

Albert Sidney Johnston (1803-62), the Confederate commander, was 59 years old at Shiloh, his first and last great battle. At 6 feet 1 inch and 200 pounds, he was a vigorous man with an imposing physical presence. Though gifted intellectually, Johnston was not a cerebral soldier. He lacked mental discipline, and he was inclined at times to allow his passions to rule his mind. Thus, piqued by criticism of his role in the fiasco of Forts Henry and Donelson, he gambled all on a rash counterstroke at Shiloh.

In appearance Johnston was noble, the archetypal Southern aristocrat; he had, besides, a powerful and attractive personality. At the same time, he shared with Grant, his opponent at Shiloh, an embarrassing slowness of speech, a defect he tended to conceal by remaining aloof and distant in the company of strangers. He was, above all, dashing and brave; under his last autograph, signed on the flap of his pocket map of Tennessee just three days before his death, he had written the phrase *en avant*.

Johnston's appearance and personality helped his career. Before the war he had the reputation of being one of America's greatest living soldiers. Like Lee, he was covertly offered a high command in the Union Army; but he declined the offer and followed his adopted state, Texas, into secession. Jefferson Davis, who appointed him commander of the vast Western Department, prized his services as equivalent to a force of 10,000 men. Despite the promise he showed, however, Johnston failed as the department commander. His worst error was dividing his field army during the Henry and Donelson campaign, a mistake which led to the loss of about 15,000 Confederate troops.

Strangely enough, Johnston's reputation has remained remarkably intact to this day. In the pantheon of Southern heroes, he occupies a prominent place—a true "swords and roses" character of the order of a Lee or a Jackson.

soldiers, formed in four parallel lines with a front of three miles and a depth of over a mile, moved silently toward the Union camps. Their tactical deployment was extraordinary–more akin to the deep attack columns of medieval warfare than to modern linear formations. Each corps in secession attempted to fill the vast front between Owl Creek in the west and Lick Creek in the east. Hardee's corps, augmented by Gladden's brigade of Bragg's corps, formed the first line; Bragg, Polk, and Breckinridge followed, one behind the other. If in the fight to come, one line faltered or got stalled, the others piling in from the rear would add new mass to the attack, driving the enemy before them by sheer weight. So ran Johnston's theory, at any rate; but the potential for disaster was no less inherent in the scheme. The first resistance would cause the lines to become intermingled, bringing congestion and a loss of command control. In addition, Johnston failed to strengthen his right, which was the crucial attack wing in his tactical plan. Evidently, he meant to shift troops to the right flank once the exact position of the Union advance lines had been established and the attack had begun to develop.

The Confederate avalanche bore down on an unsuspecting Union army. Although there had been plenty of signs that an attack was brewing, Sherman, who held a kind of *de facto* command at Camp Shiloh, had dismissed them out of hand. Only the previous day he had told Grant, "I do not apprehend anything like an attack on our position." Grant, in turn, had dashed off a note to Halleck, telling him, "I have scarcely the faintest idea of an attack." To Brigadier-General William Nelson, the commander of Buell's vanguard, who had expressed his anxiety over the exposed position of the Army of the Tennessee, he wrote, "There's nothing to worry about. Give your men a good night's rest . . . There will be no fight at Pittsburgh Landing. The battle will be at Corinth."

Prentiss, for his part, was less confident. His pickets were reinforced and pushed our farther than Sherman's, and the first clash came on his front in the Fraley and Seay Fields about one and a half miles from the camp. Prentiss's pickets resisted as best they could, but the Confederate masses soon shunted them back toward the camps, where Prentiss and Sherman were hurriedly forming lines of battle to meet the onslaught. The firing served also to alert the other divisions, and McClernand, W. H. L. Wallace, and Hurlbut rushed their men toward the front. At Savannah, too, the dull roar of the cannon was heard, and Grant interrupted his breakfast to steam for Pittsburgh Landing on his headquarters boat, the *Tigress*. On the way he stopped at Crump's Landing and ordered Lew Wallace to hold his division in readiness. Grant was still not convinced he had a battle on his hands.

The unengaged divisions arrived in the nick of time. Hildebrand's brigade, on Sherman's left, gave way almost the moment it was hit, and Prentiss's division, attacked on both front and flank, dissolved in fragments at about the same time. McClernand's Fort Donelson veterans helped to stabilize Sherman's shaky line along the Purdy Road, and the debris of Prentiss's force passed through the firm ranks of Hurlbut and Wallace, but by 9 A.M. the Confederates had cleared the outer camps and were re-forming for a second push.

Now began one of the epic contests of the Civil War. With Stuart and Hurlbut anchoring the left, Prentiss and Wallace established a new line along an old, eroded farm lane in a patch of scrub and tall oaks about a mile behind Prentiss's camp. The new position was a natural bastion; the sunken road and dense thickets following the crest of a low hill provided cover for the defenders, while the approach was across open fields enfiladed by batteries. The fire here was so hot, the whizzing and buzzing of rifle and shellfire so intense, that the Confederates nicknamed the area the "Hornet's Nest."

The Hornet's Nest fight began about 9.30 A.M. and lasted without let-up until 4.30 P.M. In those seven hours, the fate of the Union army hung in the balance. Johnston had correctly judged that Sherman and McClernand were no longer a factor in the battle, so he began very early to shift troops toward his center and right, where resistance was stiff. The Hornet's Nest and Hurlbut's position in the Peach Orchard became the focus of the renewed Confederate drive. If the Union line gave way, Johnston would be near to achieving his aim of annihilating Grant's army, for these were the only unbroken Federals between his army and the landing; the latter was already crowded with demoralized fugitives.

The Confederate attacks in this quarter were ferocious, but spasmodic and uncoordinated. Neither Bragg, who directed the attacks on the Hornet's Nest, nor Johnston, who personally led his men against Hurlbut, would allow any deviation from the straight-ahead bayonet tactics that had worked so well in the opening phase. Brigade after brigade struggled forward against the Union lines, but each in succession was rent by a deadly cross-fire and forced back. Governor Isham G. Harris of Tennessee, acting as Johnston's aide-de-camp, stated that both sides exchanged "as heavy fire as I ever saw during the war" at close range, and Grant, traversing the area the next day, recalled, "I saw an open field in our possession the second day, over which the Confederates had made repeated charges the day before, so covered with dead that it would have been possible to walk across the clearing, in any direction, stepping on dead bodies, and without a foot touching the ground."

At the Hornet's Nest, Bragg threw in 12 separate attacks, each as fruitless as its predecessor. Hindman's command was cut to pieces, and Gladden's Gibson's, and Anderson's brigades suffered severe losses. The heroism of Gibson's brigade, which charged four times without support, was typical.

On the Confederate right, much the same scene was being enacted. Johnston and Breckinridge launched seven great assaults in their attempt to dislodge Hurlbut from the Peach Orchard. Johnston exposed himself needlessly, leading one charge on horseback. On returning from the fray, in which he received two minor wounds and had his boot clipped by a bullet, Johnston joked with Harris, saying, "Governor, they came very near putting me *hors de combat* in that charge." Later, after Harris had gone on a mission and returned, the Confederate commander suddenly turned pale and swayed in the saddle. Harris, surprised, asked him, "General, are you wounded?" "Yes, and, I fear, seriously," Johnston answered. Not long after, at 2.30 P.M., he died.

Johnston's death-wound, ironically, need not have been fatal. Some minutes after the charge, he had been hit in the bend of the knee by a stray bullet. The bullet tore an artery, and in the excitement of the moment the wound went unnoticed. Johnston continued in the saddle for the better part of an hour, the blood all the while flowing into his boot; among his personal effects, there was a field tourniquet which

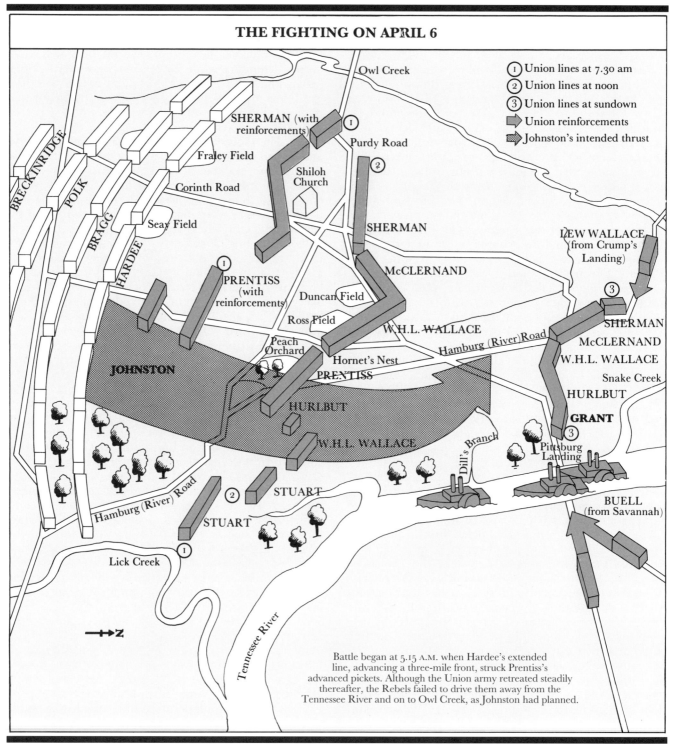

## THE FIGHTING ON APRIL 6

① Union lines at 7.30 am
② Union lines at noon
③ Union lines at sundown
⟹ Union reinforcements
▨ Johnston's intended thrust

Owl Creek

SHERMAN (with reinforcements)

Purdy Road

Fraley Field

Shiloh Church

Corinth Road

Seay Field

SHERMAN

BRECKINRIDGE

POLK

BRAGG

HARDEE

McCLERNAND

LEW WALLACE (from Crump's Landing)

PRENTISS (with reinforcements)

Duncan Field

Ross Field

W. H. L. WALLACE

Hamburg (River) Road

SHERMAN

McCLERNAND

W. H. L. WALLACE

Snake Creek

Peach Orchard

JOHNSTON

Hornet's Nest

PRENTISS

HURLBUT

HURLBUT

GRANT

W. H. L. WALLACE

Dill's Branch

Pittsburg Landing

Hamburg (River) Road

STUART

STUART

BUELL (from Savannah)

Lick Creek

⟶ Z

Tennessee River

Battle began at 5.15 A.M. when Hardee's extended line, advancing a three-mile front, struck Prentiss's advanced pickets. Although the Union army retreated steadily thereafter, the Rebels failed to drive them away from the Tennessee River and on to Owl Creek, as Johnston had planned.

might easily have stemmed the fatal outpouring of blood. Johnston was the highest ranking officer killed in battle during the war.

The popular view of Shiloh is that the Confederate hammering at the Prentiss-Hurlbut line tailed off in the confusion following Johnston's death. This, however, is not so. The Rebels were by no means played out, and vigorous assaults directed by corps and division commanders continued all along the front. News of Johnston's death was kept from the troops and Beauregard assumed overall command, establishing his headquarters at Shiloh Church. Despite his gallantry, Johnston's impact on the course of the battle had been slight; like McDowell at First Bull Run, he had early ignored his duty to command the army, plunging unabashed into the limited role of a brigadier.

At about 3.30 P.M. General Daniel Ruggles, whose division of Bragg's corps was engaged at the Hornet's Nest, massed 62 guns in the Duncan Field

and began to beat down the fire of the defenders. Simultaneously, Confederate troops on the right and left began to make headway, and several brigades slipped through gaps in the Union line and gained a critical foothold in the rear of the Hornet's Nest.

Stuart's inexperienced brigade had earlier fallen apart when hit by 4,200 Confederates of Chalmers's and J. K. Jackson's brigades. The rout was precipitated when the 71st Ohio, led by its absurd colonel (a notable coward weighing some 250 pounds), disgracefully fled without firing a shot. Stuart's retirement uncovered Hurlbut's left, and the Fourth Division was forced to abandon the Peach Orchard position it had so stubbornly defended. Mercifully, the Confederates halted for two hours to draw ammunition, and Prentiss's left, exposed by Hurlbut's fighting withdrawal, was temporarily spared destruction.

Grant, on one of his frequent visits to the front, had asked Prentiss to "hold on at all costs" while he

# THE OPPOSING FORCES

## UNION ARMY
Major-General Ulysses S. Grant

### ARMY OF THE TENNESSEE
Major-General Ulysses S. Grant

First Division (Major-General John A, McClernand):
brigades of Hare, Marsh and Raith.
Second Division (Brigadier-General W. H. L. Wallace):
brigades of Tuttle, McArthur and Sweeny.
Third Division (Major-General Lew Wallace):
brigades of M. L. Smith, Thayer and Whittlesey.
Fourth Division (Brigadier-General Stephen A. Hurlbut):
brigades of Williams, Veatch and Lauman.
Fifth Division (Brigadier-General William T. Sherman):
brigades of McDowell, Stuart, Hildebrand and Buckland.
Sixth Division (Brigadier-General Benjamin A. Prentiss):
brigades of Peabody and Miller.

### ARMY OF THE OHIO
Major-General Don Carlos Buell

Second Division (Brigadier-General Alexander McD.
McCook): brigades of Rousseau, Kirk and Gibson.
Fourth Division (Brigadier-General William Nelson):
brigades of Ammen, Hazen and Bruce.
Fifth Division (Brigadier-General Thomas L. Crittenden):
brigades of Boyle and W. S. Smith.
Sixth Division (Brigadier-General Thomas J. Wood):
brigades of Garfield and Wagner.

### Estimated Totals

It is impossible to determine the exact combat strength
of any Union army at this period of the war. The army
returns list all personnel "present for duty," including the
sick, teamsters, sutlers, and cooks. Thus Grant's Army of
the Tennessee had a "present for duty" strength of
48,894, but as many as 12,000 of this number may have
been non-combatants. Buell stated that he brought
25,000 reinforcements to Grant's aid, but his actual
strength was 17,918. The total "present for duty" strength
of the two Union armies was 66,812 officers and men
and 170 guns (Grant, 134 guns, and Buell, 36.)
Losses: 1,754 killed, 8,408 wounded, and 2,885 captured or
missing. Total: 13,047.

## CONFEDERATE ARMY OF THE MISSISSIPPI
General Albert Sidney Johnston

### I Corps
Major-General Leonidas Polk

First Division (Brigadier-General Charles Clark):
brigades of Russell and Stewart.
Second Division (Major-General B. F. Cheatham):
brigades of Johnson and Stephens.

### II Corps
Major-General Braxton Bragg

First Division (Brigadier-General Daniel Ruggles):
brigades of Gibson, P. Anderson and Pond.
Second Division (Brigadier-General Jones M. Withers):
brigades of Gladden, Chalmers and J K. Jackson.

### III Corps
Major-General William J. Hardee

Brigades of Hindman, Cleburne and S. Wood

### Reserve Corps
Brigadier-General John C. Breckinridge

Brigades of Trabue, Bowen and Statham.

### Estimated Totals

The numbers of infantry and artillery effectives were as
follows I Corps, 9,136; II Corps, 13,589; III Corps,
6,789, and Reserve Corps, 6,439, making a total of
35,953. The cavalry, which was either parceled
out among the divisions or unattached, numbered 4,382.
There were 18 batteries (108 guns) attached to brigades.
The grand total effective strength of the Confederate
army was therefore 40,334 men and 108 guns.
Losses: 1,728 killed, 8,012 wounded, and 959 captured or
missing. Total: 10,699.

---

formed a new line above the landing. Lew Wallace's division, which had been sent for at 8 A.M., and Nelson's division of Buell's army were expected at any time; these reinforcements, added to the remnants of Hurlbut's, Sherman's, and McClernand's divisions, plus stragglers and survivors from the Hornet's Nest, would form the last-ditch defense of the Union army.

By 4.30 P.M., the Hornet's Nest position had become untenable. Yelling Confederates, smelling victory, surged toward the flanks of the Union line and sifted across Prentiss's rear, completing a double envelopment of the embattled Yankees. As Ruggles's massed Rebel battery pounded away, the brigades of Gibson, Hindman, Wood, Anderson, and Stewart rose up and delivered a final frontal assault on the sunken road. Not long after, Prentiss surrendered with 2,200 men. W. H. L. Wallace was mortally wounded leading a breakout to the landing via the ravine of Tillman's Creek. Wallace's men thought they had found a covered way to the rear, but as they

crowded down the ravine, Confederate troops lined the sides and fired indiscriminately into them. The ravine, later known as "Hell's Hollow," became a deadly trap, and hundreds perished before the firing stopped.

Prentiss's and Wallace's divisions had ceased to exist, but their sacrificial fight had saved Grant's army. For the most part, the Confederates paused to re-group and conduct their prisoners to the rear before starting forward again. Two Rebel brigades, however, those of Jackson and Chalmers, had outstripped the main body in their advance and pressed right up to Grant's weakly held line near the landing. There, beginning at 4 P.M., they made the first of several gallant but hopeless assaults against Hurlbut's division and a line of some 20 guns (including four 20-pounder Parrott siege guns) collected by Colonel J. D. Webster of Grant's staff.

The attack of Chalmers's and J. K. Jackson's troops was one of the most desperate offensives of the day. Jackson's men, already out of ammunition, had to cross the ravine of Dill's Branch, a swampy backwater of the Tennessee, before ascending a hill crowned with artillery. Even so, the attempt almost succeeded. The Confederates drove off the gunners but, being armed only with the bayonet, could make no headway against the supporting infantry. Whole regiments huddled under the lip of the hill, unable to advance and unwilling to retreat. During this time they were subjected to a galling flank fire from the big guns of the Union gunboats firing up Dill's Branch. Finally, at 6 P.M., Ammen's brigade, the vanguard of Nelson's division then being ferried across the Tennessee, arrived and drove the Rebels back. The attack at Dill's Branch was the culmination of the day's fighting. Bragg was prevented from launching a last great effort at dusk by an order from Beauregard directing him to retire. The order later became the subject of great controversy, one side maintaining that Beauregard had snatched defeat from the jaws of victory, the other that the Confederate army would have been irreparably shattered by another attack.

During the evening hours, Grant was reinforced by nearly 18,000 men of Buell's army and Lew Wallace's division of his own (which had arrived finally after a remarkably confused march along the dirt roads and tracks north of the battlefield). These reinforcements brought the Federal strength up to 54,592, an advantage of 20,592 men over the estimated 34,000 Confederates (Beauregard later claimed 20,000) arrayed against them. Everything was ready for a Union counterattack.

At dawn on the 7th, the Union army rolled forward, fanning out from the cramped lines covering the landing. The Confederates, who had spent a sleepless night in the Union camps under the unremitting fire of the gunboats, resisted this advance bitterly, contesting every field and ridge line. Union numbers prevailed, however, and by 2.30 P.M., the Confederates had been pushed back to Shiloh Church, where Beauregard ordered a retreat. The Federal troops followed the Confederate withdrawal, but not too far and not too closely.

Thus ended "Bloody Shiloh," the first great battle of the war in the West and one of the fiercest combats in the history of American arms. There were nearly 24,000 casualties, about a quarter of those who had been closely engaged, most of them amateur warriors who had not fired a gun in anger before the morning of April 6.

Though technically a tie, Shiloh was, in its broad effects, a Northern victory of considerable importance. The South lost its last great chance to reestablish the strategic balance in the West; and in the wake of the battle, its leaders were forced virtually to abandon the Mississippi basin. Chattanooga was threatened; Corinth, Island No. 10, and Memphis fell, and Admiral David G. Farragut took New Orleans. On the Mississippi, only the fortresses at Vicksburg and Port Hudson remained in Confederate hands.

The position of Hurlbut's Union division at the Peach Orchard.

Above and left
The battlefield near the Hornet's Nest.
The upper drawing shows the view southward
from the extreme left of Prentiss's position;
the eroded farm lane bisecting the field formed
a natural breastwork for the Union troops.
In the lower picture is a farm near the scene
of Johnston's fatal wounding.

Below
Union defenders in the Hornet's Nest:
they repelled 11 Confederate charges
before they were encircled and forced to surrender.

# GAINES'S MILL

June 27-28, 1862

The Union field hospital at Savage's Station, Virginia. Hcrc 2,500 wounded were abandoned to the Rebels as McClellan withdrew his army during the Peninsular Campaign.

The Confederate States of America did not appear to have much chance of remaining alive when, on May 31, 1862, Robert E. Lee took command of the newly christened Army of Northern Virginia. The Rebels had not won a battle of any importance since First Bull Run, nearly a year before. News of defeats came from the Far West, New Orleans, and the Carolina coast. Most frightening of all, however, were the events of the last two months on the Virginia Peninsula outside Richmond.

Richmond was more than just the capital of the Southern States; it was the new nation's true center. It contained the largest single industrial complex, the only heavy weapons factories, and most of the smaller factories in the sparsely industrialized South. If this city fell, the whole of the South Atlantic tier of states would be deprived of its transportation system, and the Rebels would lose the source of most of their cannon and munitions; such losses would amount to a death blow for the Southern cause.

On April 2, 1862, General George Brinton McClellan, known to some as the "Little Napoleon" and regarded by himself as the savior of the Republic, had landed at the tip of the Peninsula with the vanguard of the largest army yet assembled on the North American continent, the Army of the Potomac. McClellan's force, 130,000 strong, was then less than 60 miles from Richmond.

McClellan had earlier convinced President Lincoln that an advance upon the Rebel armies entrenched at Manassas, barely 10 miles from the Union capital, would be a waste of lives and accomplish nothing of decisive importance. Instead he had worked out a plan to outflank the Confederates by sea. Using the naval advantage at his disposal, he aimed to strike up the unfortified, lightly held Peninsula between the James and York rivers. In one grand stroke, he would decapitate the Confederacy and restore the Union. Lincoln, ever fretful for the safety of his capital, had grudgingly agreed to the plan on condition that Washington remained garrisoned by a large enough force.

Given Lincoln's cautious approval, McClellan had begun moving his well-trained, superbly equipped, and generously supplied host to its appointed base at Fort Monroe. He brought with him over 300 cannon, mostly 12-pound brass Napoleons and 3-inch ordnance rifles, as well as his own favorite weapons–100 heavy siege cannon consisting of 20-pound Parrotts, 32-pound howitzers, Rodman guns, and several batteries from the fleet.

McClellan's army was to take Yorktown, march up the good sandy roads of the Peninsula, set up a base of supplies on the York River, shell Richmond with the heavy artillery, and then storm the battered city–if it had not already surrendered. This push up the long finger of land was to be supported by the powerful gunboats and ironclads of the Navy. With such immense pressure focused on the 12-mile-wide Peninsula, McClellan felt sure that the days of the Confederacy must be numbered.

There was only one drawback to the Union Commander's plan: this was that the move of each pawn in the scheme was linked to that of every other pawn. And, unfortunately for McClellan, things began to go wrong the moment he landed. The day he arrived, he was informed by Flag Officer Goldsborough that the presence of the Rebel ironclad *Merrimack* had made any major naval support impractical, since the Union fleet was preoccupied with trying to keep the *Merrimack* bottled up in Hampton Roads.

The next day, McClellan learned that the maps issued to the army were no use, since the surveyors had marked the roads wrongly. Furthermore, the Southerners, under the flamboyant General "Prince John" Magruder, had dammed up the trickling Warwick River so that it was fordable at only five boggy places; the other crossing points were transformed into impassable lakes. Undeterred, McClellan reckoned that his siege guns would still be able to clear the passages; the old tobacco port of Yorktown, though fortified, would also fall to his guns.

Then it began to rain. The Peninsula, enclosed by two broad rivers and threaded with small streams and swamps throughout its length, flooded. Hitherto good roads became bottomless quagmires in which men, mules, and guns sank and were virtually immobilized. The heavy guns, in particular, could not be moved into position until the rain stopped and the ground dried.

As if rain, the Navy, and the mapmakers had not caused enough trouble, Union staff officers in Washington then discovered that instead of the 70,000 men who, McClellan had promised, would remain to guard the city, there were only 40,000, and these were scattered throughout Northern Virginia. Promptly, Lincoln demanded 30,000 more troops to protect the city. Accordingly, McDowell's corps - the largest and finest body of men in the Army of the Potomac–was ordered to disembark from its transports at Alexandria. This force was detached from McClellan and became the independent Department of the Rappahannock, its task being to guard the southern approaches to Washington. General Banks, in the Shenandoah, and General Wood, who held the Peninsular Campaign's supply base at Fort Monroe, were similarly detached from the command of the "Little Napoleon."

McClellan felt crushed. Even the recruiting offices in the North had been closed, their furniture auctioned, and volunteers turned away. He believed that he had been abandoned by the government and stripped of all power other than that of a local commander. He saw himself betrayed and demoted. The size of the Rebel army began to grow in his mind. Within a few weeks, he believed he was outnumbered, and it took a month before he was ready to begin the bombardment of Yorktown. Lincoln, impatient at the delay, wired McClellan: "You must act." On May 4 McClellan entered the deserted forts of Yorktown. The month he had spent emplacing his guns to pulverize the town had been rendered useless by the Southerners, who had evacuated their position the night before.

McClellan was quick to react, pursuing the Rebels back to the outskirts of Richmond. There, within sight of the spires of the city, his army of 100,000 effectives prepared to dig in. Against this powerful force Joseph Johnston, the Rebel commander, had barely 50,000 men. Although the Confederate President, Jefferson Davis, had earlier pleaded with his general to turn and fight, Johnston had declined. In the face of such odds, he would not risk battle until he was ready.

Johnston and McClellan were a strange match. One would not fight because he did not think he could, the other because he did not think he would have to. Then it started to rain again.

On the Confederate side, Lee tried to instil some urgency. He was the advisor to Davis and the nearest thing the Confederacy had to a chief of staff. He had helped to organize the defenses along the coast when General Ambrose Burnside had landed a small Union force in North Carolina and had planned the movement of troops to aid "Stonewall" Jackson in his Shenandoah Valley Campaign. Now he was constantly seen among the front-line troops, but the immediate benefits of his initiative were slight since Johnston would not confide in him.

Lincoln, equally exasperated with his commander in the Peninsula, came to judge for himself. The roads were like swamps but, he saw, Union engineers had built bridges and corduroy roads wherever they went. Moreover, a railroad had been constructed and was in operation behind the lines, and a huge base had been established on the Pamunkey River at White House, the ancestral home of the Curtis family and at that time the Lee estate. Still, however, McClellan would not move; it was not, apparently, Union weather.

Cannon balls, mortars, and field-guns
arrayed by the waterside at Yorktown, Virginia.
The town was occupied by Union troops on May 4, 1862.

Johnston, after a great deal of prodding by Davis, finally agreed to fight. At this juncture McDowell's 40,000 were marching south; if this army joined McClellan's, Johnston would be trapped and outnumbered by nearly three to one. Confederate reports showed that recent rains had washed away the bridges over the swollen Chickahominy River which divided McClellan's army. The Union general, informed that McDowell would join him by land if he extended his right wing north to meet him, had divided his army unevenly. Less than half faced Richmond on the southern side of the Chickahominy. Johnston chose to attack this weakened portion of the Yankee army.

On May 30 Davis and Lee rode out from Richmond with their entourage to witness what they expected would be the salvation of the city from the blue-clad host. They had, however, picked the wrong man to save them. Johnston had no staff worthy of the name. His maps, even though he had been in the area for several weeks, were incomplete. There was no system of command to fall back on once the first orders were issued. All he could do was order the go-ahead; after that his commanders were on their own, and none of them, not even his nominal second-in-command, Gustavus Smith, knew the overall plan.

The battle at Seven Pines (Fair Oaks) was one of the most mismanaged and bungled actions of a war filled with such disasters. The Rebel army did almost everything wrong. Generals took the wrong roads; regiments attacked on their own without orders, and whole brigades got lost in the woods. The artillery was unable to pass down roads swollen with troops awaiting orders. When Johnston tried to salvage something out of the confusion, he was wounded by musketry and shell fragments. The battle petered out as the sun began to set on the armies and their 11,000 dead and wounded, who had fallen without effecting any change in the Siege of Richmond.

That night, a dejected Confederate President and his general rode back toward the besieged city. The next morning, Lee took command. Few people felt that he had much of a chance.

Lee's first action as commanding general was to order his men to dig in. The Southern soldiers had hitherto regarded digging as beneath their dignity and had only lightly fortified their positions in the three weeks since they had fallen back on Richmond. The only true fortifications were those at Drewry's Bluff, a hill overlooking the James River which the citizens themselves had fortified. The fort proved its value when the garrison (the crew of the scuttled ironclad *Merrimack*) succeeded in turning back a line of Federal gunboats as they steamed upriver to bombard the Confederate city.

As the rains set in again, Lee's men erected a line of gun emplacements and trenches along their front. The Union army had already completed a strong set of works which had been buttressed by four 10-gun redoubts on the south side of the Chickahominy. Once the "King of Spades," as the troops dubbed Lee, had begun his engineering operation, he began to move around the army, trying to inspire some sense of purpose in men weighed down by their earlier defeats and withdrawals. Small details that had been overlooked by Johnston were attended to with great care. Supplies were moved up to the front lines in increasing amounts. The artillery was reorganized and equipped with a better and more mobile system of supply wagons and field forges. Although he still lacked proper staff, Lee was able to make his presence and his orders felt throughout the Army of Northern Virginia.

Lee knew that McClellan's siege batteries would eventually destroy his less numerous and altogether less powerful cannon once they were fully deployed. A Confederate attack was impossible against the four strong Union corps positioned south of the Chickahominy. There remained only one possible weak point at which he could strike–the extended right wing.

McDowell's movement south had been temporarily postponed by Lincoln after "Stonewall" Jackson's troops had outmarched, outmaneuvered, and outfought a collection of Union armies in the Shenandoah Valley. In two months Jackson's "foot cavalry" had marched over 600 miles, fought a dozen actions (four of them full-scale battles), and tied down

Union forces three times as numerous as their own. This campaign had so unnerved the Northern press that Lincoln himself believed Washington to be threatened; hence the postponement. McClellan, on the other hand, still expected support from McDowell and had left a reinforced corps north of the Chickahominy under General Fitz-John Porter to guard his supply base at White House and link up the reinforcing columns.

McClellan's vulnerable right gave birth to a plan of considerable risk in Lee's mind. He sent for the only winning general in the Confederacy–Major-General Thomas "Stonewall" Jackson. Jackson rode 40 miles in a single night to meet with Lee and the divisional commanders of the Richmond front–Ambrose Powell Hill, Daniel Harvey Hill, and James Longstreet–and plan a trap for the "Little Napoleon." According to this plan, Jackson's Valley veterans, masked from Union patrols by J. E. B. Stuart's cavalry, were to move by rail and road to a posi-

even more reason to feel threatened than he knew.

McClellan, under constant pressure from Lincoln, had finally agreed to move. On June 14 he had told the President that he would take up the offensive "as soon as the bridges are completed and the ground fit for artillery to move." After two weeks of satisfactory weather McClellan decided to move cautiously forward. On June 25 he ordered his corps commanders below the Chickahominy to prepare for an advance the next morning. On the 26th he would launch four divisions in a general assault on the town of Old Tavern, which lay at the center of Magruder's line.

Union intelligence, under the direction of the Pinkerton Agency, had consistently supplied McClellan with faulty information, overestimating the numbers of Rebel forces and misapprehending their whereabouts. On this occasion they had estimated Lee's strength at 200,000 men and reported that Richmond was heavily fortified with three dozen

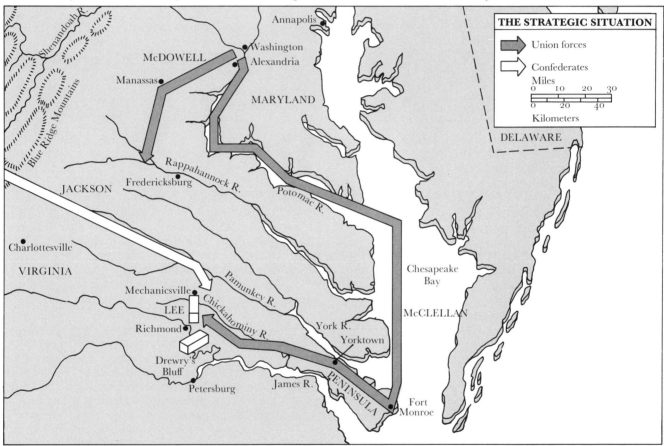

THE STRATEGIC SITUATION

⇒ Union forces

⇒ Confederates

tion behind the lines of Porter's V Corps at Mechanicsville. Once Jackson's 17,000 troops were in position, A. P. Hill's division would cross the Mechanicsville bridges to clear the north bank of the Chickahominy. Longstreet and D. H. Hill would follow over the unmasked bridges below the town and form a line with A. P. Hill. Porter would be crushed against the river, and the Union supply base could be taken at leisure. This would force McClellan either to abandon his lines and fall back to a new base, or to meet Lee in the field.

The main Union army–the four corps of Franklin, Sumner, Heintzelman, and Keyes, totaling 80,000 men–was to be occupied by a demonstration launched by "Prince John" Magruder with 25,000 Rebels. Magruder would be unable to call for reinforcements until Porter was beaten and the bridges in the rear of that corps open to Lee's army. The highly strung Magruder, unsettled by the three-to-one superiority of the Union army facing him, had

strong redoubts and over 200 heavy cannon. Then Pinkerton's agents told the Union commander that Jackson was on the move, and that the Peninsula was his most likely target; thus, finally, the "Secret Service Corps" had reported something correctly. The news gave McClellan another reason to delay. Rather than attack, he chose to do exactly what Lee was doing–to wait for Jackson to arrive.

Lee had massed about 35,000 men at the Mechanicsville bridges to wait for Jackson. Opposite these men, Porter had deployed nearly 20,000, using them to screen, rather than defend, the town. In addition, McCall's division of Pennsylvania Reserves had detachments on picket around Mechanicsville, and a brigade under Meade was detached to guard the siege battery at Doctor Gaines's farm, which controlled the Chickahominy bridges. The remainder of the division was back at Porter's main defensive lines on Beaver Dam Creek.

The Beaver Dam Creek was a natural fortress.

# THE COMMANDERS

Major-General George Brinton McClellan, USA

General Robert E. Lee, CSA

George Brinton McClellan (1826-85) was the man in whom Lincoln placed his hopes for a quick end to the War of the Secession. Born in Philadelphia, he had led his class at West Point, served ably on General Scott's staff in the Mexican War, and had been sent to observe the European way of war in the Crimea by the then-Secretary of War, Jefferson Davis. Most important, however, McClellan, a Conservative Democrat who wanted to wage war only against the armed defenders of the South and not against her people, had in 1861 achieved what no other officer had: a victory. His swift campaign in West Virginia was in itself of only minor importance, but it had catapulted him to the highest military post in the land. As General-in-Chief he now drew on the wealth of the nation to equip, train, and reorganize the finest army in the Western Hemisphere–the Army of the Potomac.

McClellan's vitality and administrative talent infected the army. What had been a ragged, dispirited shambles of a defeated army now cheered him with fierce intensity and pride. His men were ready to do the impossible for him whenever he asked; but he never did. To McClellan, war was a bloodless game of maneuver in which everything had to be just perfect before he would move. Time and again, he refused to throw "these raw men of mine . . . into the teeth of artillery and entrenchments." He fought battles, as one critic said of him, "in tents, on paper, at a table the day before. His enthusiasm was shown as reviews, or before the battle. The battlefield showed him nothing." McClellan, proud and vain, was the administrator the nation needed in the early days of the war, but not the fighter who could end it. Joseph Johnston, his opponent in the Peninsula, knew him well when he said, "Nobody but McClellan would have hesitated to attack." But despite his shortcomings, McClellan was loved by his men and gave the Army of the Potomac the organization and the spirit that would carry it through the years ahead.

Robert E. Lee (1807-70) was a quiet, distinguished Southern aristocrat from the most prestigious of the First Families of Virginia. Like his father, the Revolutionary war hero "Light Horse" Harry Lee, he followed a military career. He saw action with General Winfield Scott in Mexico and was present at the capture of John Brown at Harpers Ferry (1859). As an instructor at West Point, he influenced many of the men who became generals in the Civil War.

Lincoln recognized Lee's talents and offered him the command of the Union Army to crush the rebellion. But Lee, rather than stain his sword with the blood of his native state, resigned from the Regular Army to wear Confederate gray. The Confederacy did not at first appreciate him; he was refused a field command and served as an advisor to President Davis. Although little more than an official spectator, he was able to coordinate the movements of some of the minor Rebel forces.

When Joseph Johnston fell wounded in the Peninsula, Davis offered Lee the command of a dispirited, outnumbered, and materially outclassed army. Twenty years of tiresome duty in the army had taught him a great deal about handling men. He successfully forged the Army of Northern Virginia into a rapier with which to parry and jab at the Union machine. He had the daring and the imagination to take chances that other generals would not have considered, and in five campaigns he outwitted the larger and better equipped armies that Lincoln threw at him. Even when numbers began to tell, Lee held off defeat for nearly two years. His reputation among his men, and his opponents, became one of respect and near-deification.

Lee was not an outstanding tactician. Before the Civil War he had never led troops in combat, and during it he did not try to–he left that to his brilliant lieutenants. He was, though, a master of strategy, the finest America ever produced.

The steep-banked ravines in front of the position formed, with their tangled undergrowth and felled trees, a readymade abatis. The stream was waist deep and would allow the passage of artillery and wagons at only two crossings: Ellerson's Mill and the Mechanicsville Road. The position was further improved by three lines of defensive works: rifle pits on the bank, breastworks along the crest, and battery positions at the top of the hills overlooking the creek. Porter was relying on the firepower of his troops to hold this line: the men were not to advance from their positions to engage the enemy nor to block the field of fire for the artillery. He intended to break the Confederate tide along this barrier.

The Battle of Mechanicsville began on the morning of June 26, 1862, with Magruder's demonstration against the main Union army, the intensity of which soon convinced the Federal corps commanders that they were facing forces superior in number to their own. "Prince John," excitable and terror-stricken though he was, performed admirably on the banks of the Chickahominy. Jackson, however, was far less energetic. Tired and worn from too many months of strain and lack of sleep, "Stonewall" moved with little urgency.

Ambrose Powell Hill, dressed in his red deer-hunting "battle shirt," paced along his side of the river waiting for a signal from Jackson. It was now 3 P.M., and he had heard nothing since before 10 o'clock that morning, when his left-hand brigade, posted upriver at Half Sink, received word that Jackson had been delayed. Hill decided he could not wait any longer and ordered his division across the Chickahominy. Immediately the Light Division, six brigades strong, drove in the Union outposts and uncovered the bridges. Hill then lost control over his command.

The previously well-ordered Confederate ranks crumpled under the fire of massed Union artillery and the men, shattered, took refuge in the rough thickets of the ravine. There, where the Union cannon could not be depressed to fire on them, they stayed, dueling with McCall's Pennsylvania brigades and waiting for Jackson's arrival to extricate them. Meanwhile J. R. Anderson's regiments, strung out to the left to meet Jackson, advanced into the hidden batteries supporting Reynolds's Pennsylvanians. They, too, were forced to take cover in the creek bed.

D. H. Hill, who had spent the last few hours rebuilding the Mechanicsville bridges, sent his lead brigade under Brigadier-General Ripley to turn the Union left wing at Ellerson's Mill. Advancing in thick battalion columns across 400 yards of broken ground into the face of four batteries of rifled cannon, the brigade broke. Pender's brigade, to the left, suffered a similar fate.

Jackson arrived opposite the Union right wing at 5 P.M. He decided that his disordered regiments were in no condition to fight a major battle. The Valley veterans, the key to Lee's attack, bivouacked for the night less than two miles from where A. P. Hill's men were fighting, and dying, in the creek. Eventually, under cover of night and the desultory fire of D. H. Hill's batteries, the Light Division was pulled out, and Lee reformed his troops to prepare for the next day.

During the 26th Lee had been little more than a spectator. With no staff other than a small personal entourage to keep him informed, he had had to ride the lines himself. One consequence was that, lacking guidance from headquarters, the artillery and the engineers–the finest troops in the army–were left idle. Longstreet and Hill, deprived of construction units, lost precious time building their own bridges over the Chickahominy; and while A. P. Hill was being torn apart by the Union guns, the 80-gun Confederate artillery reserve wandered aimlessly behind the army trying to find a place to position itself. Most inexcusable of all, no one had coordinated with Jackson.

On the Union side, McClellan was anything but idle. He had met with Porter on the field that afternoon. Although the latter's corps had held remarkably well, Jackson's presence now caused McClellan to order the corps to withdraw to the next strong position. This was a similar natural fortress along Boatswain's Swamp, just east of Gaines's Mill. McClellan also ordered the evacuation and destruction of the base at the White House; he had already decided to retreat.

Fitz-John Porter was at this stage elated: he had stopped Lee's assault with the cool precision of an experienced fighter facing a stronger but rash challenger. He was confident that he could stop Lee again in the morning, perhaps even force the Confederates back across the Chickahominy. McClellan was less sanguine about the future of his right wing, however. Refusing Lee's challenge to be drawn into a decisive field battle, and distressed over reports that the Rebels were pressing hard against the rest of his army, he gave the order to withdraw.

McClellan's decision was not merely a local, tactical matter, but one of strategic importance. The great supply base at the White House was to be evacuated, all non-movable equipment and stores were to be burned, and the remainder was to be transported by an enormous wagon train which would move across the Union rear toward the James River. The Navy was instructed to bring supplies up the James for the establishment of a new base.

Once the wagons were safe, the Army of the Potomac was to abandon the siege lines and fall back. McClellan, indeed, believed he was trying to save a doomed army. He ordered Porter to protect the bridges over which the wagons must travel. Porter was to entrench his corps on the high ground along the semicircular Boatswain's Swamp. The ground was similar to that of Beaver Dam creek, with breast-high fences dotting the hillsides and a boggy morass in front and to the left of the high ground. The right was a series of ravines and forests which afforded only two access routes for artillery or wagons to be brought forward.

The Union line, despite some reinforcements, had to be thinned out to cover the wide front. The line was further thinned by Porter's insistence that each brigadier should withdraw two of his regiments from the front and place them as a reserve. These regiments were to act as "fire brigades," to contain and destroy any Rebel breakthroughs as well as to relieve the front-line troops if the fighting became too heavy. Slocum's division of Franklin's corps was to be dispatched to consolidate the position, and a portion of Philip St. George Cocke's cavalry division was brought up for support. Most comforting of all, perhaps, to the defenders were the additional batteries from Colonel Hunt's artillery reserve. These extra forces brought Porter's strength to a total of nearly 35,000.

When A. P. Hill began to advance on the morning of June 27, he was met by light resistance. The Rebel infantry, eager to avenge themselves for the defeat they had suffered on the previous day,

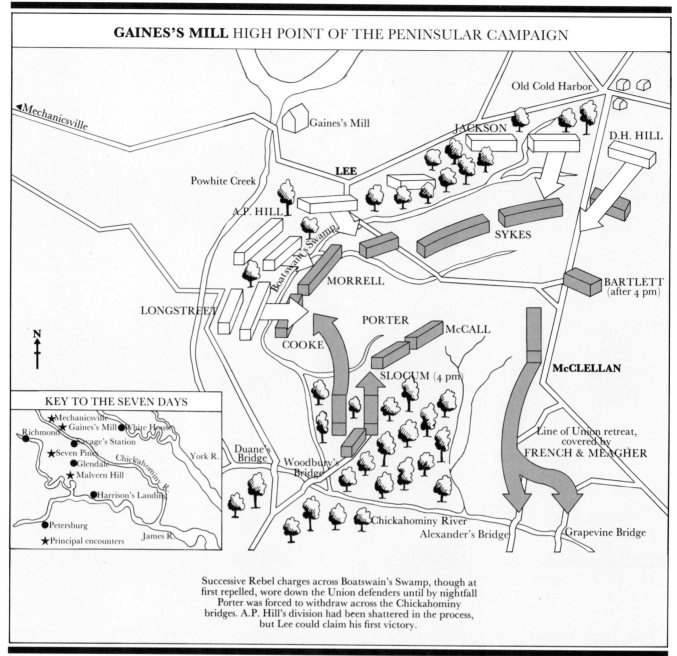

## GAINES'S MILL HIGH POINT OF THE PENINSULAR CAMPAIGN

Successive Rebel charges across Boatswain's Swamp, though at
first repelled, wore down the Union defenders until by nightfall
Porter was forced to withdraw across the Chickahominy
bridges. A.P. Hill's division had been shattered in the process,
but Lee could claim his first victory.

quickly brushed aside Seymour's rearguard brigade
and its supporting horse artillery. Hill's men followed
the withdrawing Union troops, capturing stragglers,
wounded men, and supply wagons. The 9th
Massachusetts Regiment slowed the pursuit near
Gaines's Mill, but by 2 P.M. A. P. Hill was reforming
his division in preparation for an advance on the
heights.

Maxey Gregg, who had led his brigade into the
teeth of the Union army the day before, once again
lost his head in the heat of the pursuit. The Yankee
skirmishers kept withdrawing in front of him, luring
him forward. The Rebels charged through Gaines's
Mill, across the Cold Harbor Road, and through the
fields that led to the slope of Boatswain's Swamp. The
Confederate infantry, weighed down with full equipment, had chased their opponents at a run during the
hottest part of a June day. Thoroughly disorganized,
they came under the brutal fire of the Union batteries. The regiments dissolved into the thickets that
lined the deep, wet ravine, but still they kept moving
–through the marsh, into a line of trees and out again
–and then re-formed. There they kept up a steady fire
on the blue-clad marksmen who lined the hillside.

Without any reconnaisance of the area south of
Gregg, where the ravines were far more treacherous,

A. P. Hill deployed his remaining 10,000 men along a
three-quarter-mile front. Lee rode to meet him and
told him that Longstreet would cover his right and
that Jackson was expected to appear on the far left at
any minute. Hill's Light Division moved to the attack
shortly after 2 P.M. The banks of the ravine where
they charged were almost vertical; a soldier could not
scramble out of them unless he was lifted up by his
comrades. The entire swamp came under the fire of
Porter's redoubtable infantry. Into this death trap
charged an entire Rebel division. It soon fell apart,
and for the second time in as many days Hill's men
were caught in a shooting-gallery war in the tangled
scrub and wood of a Peninsular swamp. The Union
riflemen took a steady toll, but the Southerners held
on.

Porter began to push up fresh regiments along
his center, where Hill had struck. By 4 P.M. the first of
his reinforcements, Slocum's three brigades, had
arrived on the northern bank of the Chickahominy.
One brigade was dispatched into the central battle;
the other two were directed toward the right center
and far right, to brace Sykes's division against the
Rebel assault on that wing. For now Jackson had
arrived on the field,

Lee had earlier instructed Jackson to take a

## THE OPPOSING FORCES *

### UNION ARMY OF THE POTOMAC
Major-General George Brinton McClellan

#### V Corps
Brigadier-General Fitz-John Porter

First Division (Brigadier-General George W. Morell): brigades of Martindale, Griffin and Butterfield.
Second Division (Brigadier-General George Sykes): brigades of Buchanan, Lovell and Warren.
Third Division (Brigadier-General George A. McCall): brigades of Reynolds, Meade and Seymour.
Corps troops: Berdan's Sharpshooters and 4th Pennsylvania Cavalry.
Strength: 37 regiments of infantry, 1 of cavalry and 11 batteries of artillery.

#### Reinforcements

First Division, VI Corps (Brigadier-General Henry Slocum): brigades of Taylor, Bartlett and Newton.
First Division, II Corps (Brigadier-General Israel Richardson): brigades of French and Meagher.
Cavalry Reserve, part (Brigadier-General P. St. George Cooke).
Artillery Reserve, part (Colonel Henry J. Hunt).
Strength: 22 regiments of infantry, parts of 3 cavalry regiments and 9 batteries of artillery.

#### Estimated Totals

McClellan's Army of the Potomac had 59 regiments of infantry, parts of 4 cavalry regiments and 20 batteries of artillery, giving it an approximate total strength of 35,000 men and 124 guns.
Losses: 894 killed, 3,107 wounded, and 2,836 captured or missing; also 22 guns. Total: 6,837 men and 22 guns.

*The forces listed do not represent the full strength of either army, merely those present at Gaines's Mill. In the Peninsular Campaign as a whole, there were an additional 25,000 Confederates and 80,000 Yankees in the respective armies.

### CONFEDERATE ARMY OF NORTHERN VIRGINIA
General Robert E. Lee

#### Jackson's Corps
Major-General Thomas J. Jackson

Whiting's Division (Brigadier-General William H. C. Whiting): brigades of Hood and Law.
Jackson's Division: brigades of Winder, Cunningham, Hampton and Lawton.
Ewell's Division (Brigadier-General Richard S. Ewell): brigades of Elzey, Trimble, Taylor and Johnson.
D. H. Hill's Division (Brigadier-General Daniel H. Hill): brigades of Rodes, G. B. Anderson, Garland, Colquitt and Ripley.
Strength: 68 regiments of infantry and 13 batteries of artillery.

#### Major-General James Longstreet's Command

Longstreet's Division: brigades of R. H. Anderson, Kemper, Pickett, Wilcox, Pryor and Featherston.
Strength: 27 regiments and 7 batteries.

#### Major-General Ambrose Powell Hill's Command

The "Light Division": brigades of Field, Gregg, J. R. Anderson, Archer, Pender and Branch.
Strength: 30 regiments and 7 batteries.

#### Reserve Artillery
Brigadier-General William Pendleton

Strength: 7 batteries

#### Estimated Totals

Lee's Army of Northern Virginia had 125 regiments of infantry and 34 batteries of artillery (only 19 of the latter were engaged), giving it an approximate total strength of 56,000 men and 136 guns (76 engaged).
Losses: approximately 1,400 killed, 6,500 wounded, and 400 captured or missing. Total: approximately 8,300 men.

---

northeast road that would outflank the Union line at Powhite Creek, which is where Lee expected Porter to stand. D. H. Hill would extend the flank and deploy across the Union line of retreat. The rest of the army would drive Porter across the front of this flanking force.

At first Jackson, once again the key to Lee's plan, had cautiously followed an overgrown road which disgorged into a farm clearing at the upper end of the large millpond of Dr. Gaines's four-story mill. Realizing that there was no Union position to be turned there, Jackson struck off into the woods to the northeast, heading back to the Cold Harbor Road. There he fell in behind D. H. Hill's column. Now, instead of four divisions advancing on the Union flank, there was one long, snaking column, thrashing about as it looked for the enemy.

Less than a mile to the east, A P. Hill's men were being butchered, but still the 27,000-strong column marched away to the northeast.

Hill's Light Division was no longer an organized fighting force. By 4 P.M. the regiments, disorganized, low on ammunition, and battered by two hours of fighting, were reduced to a collection of individuals clinging for cover to any tree, rock, or bush they could find. But they stayed to fight.

Lee saw that he had to relieve the pressure on Hill and disengage from the battle. He believed he was now facing McClellan's main force. He dictated an order for Longstreet to make a demonstration on the right. As he did so, General Richard Stoddart Ewell moved onto the field at the head of his Valley troopers.

Ewell began a steady parade advance against Sykes's Regulars. Trimble's brigade, leading the assault on McGhee House, one of the strongpoints along the Union line, passed through the scattered remnants of Gregg's Carolinians, over the rough ground and straight into a sharp Union counterattack. Another of Ewell's brigades, Elzey's Virginians, was pinned down and its leader wounded. Next Dick Taylor (Jefferson Davis's brother-in-law and son of the Mexican War hero Zachary Taylor) sent forward his Louisiana troopers. Taylor's brigade came up against that part of the line where Hill's men had taken such heavy casualties. Within five minutes, most of the front-line officers were dead and the Louisiana infantry, including the famous "Tigers," broke and fled.

D. H. Hill had deployed his men to face Sykes's division. As Ewell's attack began to melt, Hill's fresh men came out of the wooded roads below Old Cold

Harbor and charged across the 400 yards of open ground between them and the Union infantry. By 5.30 P.M. Hill had begun to press back the troops of Brigadier-General George Sykes (his old West Point roommate). Outnumbered, Sykes began to give ground, but did not break. The Yankee cannon kept forcing back the Rebel guns as the latter tried to unlimber in the fields below them. It was a battle of Rebel infantry against Union artillery.

With Ewell still forcing Porter to divert men from the center, Longstreet moved up on A. P. Hill's right. Wilcox's three brigades moved across the fields only to be caught in a crossfire from the guns across the Chickahominy. Pickett came into line, but also drew a tremendous volume of fire. As Whiting's division (another of Jackson's divisions that kept appearing on the field from the woods on the left) was moved behind A. P. Hill, Longstreet prepared to abandon the idea of a diversion, since it would serve no purpose except to slaughter his own men. He decided to attack with all he had.

On the left, Lawton's huge brigade of Enfield-armed riflemen (3,500 strong) came in on the east of the Cold Harbor Road. Although disorganized by the swampy ground, they gave Ewell and D. H. Hill the weight of men and firepower they needed to keep Sykes off-balance. By 7 P.M. a continuous line had been formed from Longstreet to D. H. Hill. After five hours of continuous fighting, the Union infantry were worn down; their guns were so fouled with powder that they had to brace them against trees just to ram down a cartridge. Jackson, whose corps had come on the field at three different times and in three different places, gave his first order of the day: "Tell them this affair must hang in suspense no longer. Sweep the field with the bayonet." Lee had issued a similar order, less rousingly worded, half an hour before.

Longstreet delayed his main attack until all his men were formed. They advanced across the fire zone, a distance of a quarter of a mile, under a steady crossfire from the Union cannoneers. They moved unwaveringly, walking not charging, reloading and firing as they went. Morell's division, which had been in the line all day, responded weakly. The Rebel infantry came up to the creek and, using one another for support, climbed out from the steep embankments and gained the top of the ravine. They went into and came out of Boatswain's Swamp as a division.

Porter was hard-pressed. The extra reinforcements he had requested (French's and Meagher's brigades) had just crossed the bridges and could not yet be placed in his lines. In their absence, Porter pulled men out of the center, where the fighting was less brisk, to slow Longstreet and bolster Sykes. On the Confederate side, Lee at this juncture took command of his center and ordered Whiting, reinforced by the brigades of Law and Hood, to break the center of the Union line.

The Southern infantry moved forward at the run and came quickly upon the Union riflemen. Hood, taking charge of the Confederate assault, held back a little. His old regiment, the 4th Texas, was advancing between Law and Longstreet at the "hunter's slouch," a crouching position used to hunt small game. Hood dismounted and led his men against the Union rifle-pits, ordering them to hold their fire until they were within 10 yards of the defenders' lines. As the tired Northerners began to fall back to the breastworks, Hood opened fire. The effect was devastating: panic flowed back into the line of breastworks, as Hood's men pursued the retreating Yankees hard, followed by Law's 18th Georgia and Jenkins's

South Carolinians.

The defenders began to run. Some groups vainly tried to form up; exhausted and cut off, entire regiments surrendered. The left flank no longer existed. In the Union center Sykes was falling back, but his Regular riflemen contrived to delay the pursuit as, in relatively good order, they gave up their positions. They refused to break.

Porter had set up a 14-gun battery behind his left flank to try and slow the Rebel onslaught. He now hoped to form his broken corps behind these guns, drawing on Sykes and two brigades that McClellan had just sent over the river. Into this confused scene, advancing from low ground on the far left of the Union line, came Philip St. George Cooke with his nearly forgotten cavalry. Cooke had roughly 600 men: two and a half squadrons from the 5th US Cavalry, two from the 1st US, three of Rush's 6th (Pennsylvania) Lancers, and one from Child's 4th Pennsylvania. They fell into line beside the grand battery and faced the Rebel infantry forming on the high ground. Hoping to catch them off balance, Cooke threw his men forward in a charge with sabers, lances, and pistols. He rode through part of the Union battery, which kept firing as he passed, knocking down some of his own men and causing great confusion. As he approached the Confederate infantry, they calmly let loose a volley of terrible power which shattered the first rank of cavalry and brought the second collapsing into it. The horsemen, a few of whom had reached the Confederates, wavered, then streamed in panic to the rear. Their flight carried them through the battery once more, taking the terrified artillery horses along with their own stampeding mounts. The Southerners, following up, seized the wrecked battery. Porter's last line was broken.

The Union corps fell back to the river, collecting itself in the twilight behind the steady ranks of Sykes's Regulars and the brigades of French and Meagher which had been sent to their aid. That night, they withdrew across the bridges. The last to cross were Cooke's battered horsemen. Lee had won his first victory.

The Rebel army, except for the battered brigades of A. P. Hill's Light Division, was in sound fighting shape. On the Union side Porter, although forced back, had given as good as he had got. At a cost of some 4,000 casualties and 3,000 captured, he had inflicted 8,000 killed and wounded on the Confederates (a third of those being in A. P. Hill's division).

McClellan, however, had not lost only men: he had lost so many supplies that it took the Richmond quartermasters three days to work out what had been captured. More important, he had lost the initiative and, with that, what little confidence Abraham Lincoln had left in him.

The siege lifted, Lee tried desperately to chase the Army of the Potomac and destroy it piecemeal. Each time, however, the steady and disciplined Northern infantry threw back the Rebel attack. Lee's whole army did not catch McClellan until July 1. Then, at Malvern Hill, facing Union cannon on high ground, the Rebel infantry was again butchered by grapeshot and canister. After this battle, McClellan reached the James River, and the Peninsular Campaign, with its climax of the Seven Days, was over.

In the course of the Seven Days, some 15,000 Northern soldiers and 20,000 of their Southern compatriots had fallen. The Union defeat determined that there was no longer any chance of a prompt settlement of the rebellion. The South had found her general, and the divisive war would go on.

Above
A view of the action at Gaines's Mill,
painted by the Prince de Joinville,
showing the battlefield
from General Porter's headquarters
behind the Union left.
General Porter (center) points toward
the wood held by Longstreet's Confederates.

Left
The Prince de Joinville (center)
and foreign officers. The Prince,
who later wrote a history of the war,
served on McClellan's staff.

Below
After the Battle of Seven Pines
(Fair Oaks), dead soldiers are buried
and horses burned.

# ANTIETAM

September 17, 1862

Allan Pinkerton, the detective (seated right), and members of his Secret Service staff at their Antietam headquarters, photographed by Mathew Brady. Although successful in the civilian sphere, Pinkerton never grasped the essentials of military work and his reports to McClellan, who appointed him head of Union intelligence, were models of misinformation.

President Abraham Lincoln and his General-in-Chief, Henry Halleck, aided by a collection of bumbling amateur generals, had thoroughly stagnated the Union war effort. In a period of some three months (June–August 1862), they had fared badly in three campaigns and had been held up to ridicule in the army, the press, and by foreign observers.

The first great fiasco had been in the Shenandoah Valley: the Union forces there, commanded by a one-time Western explorer (John C. Fremont), a political sop (Nathaniel P. Banks), and a German professional who could barely utter an order in English (Franz Sigel), had been outgeneraled and fiercely mauled by "Stonewall" Jackson, despite their three-to-one superiority. Major-General George Brinton McClellan was responsible for the second defeat: he had advanced his 100,000-strong Army of the Potomac up the Virginia Peninsula to within sight of the spires of Richmond, only to be ignominiously outmaneuvered and bluffed into defeat during the Seven Days Campaign (see previous chapter). Finally, there was Major-General John Pope. Pompous, a braggart and a liar, he was a constant target for abuse among the soldiers of both sides. On this occasion, at Second Bull Run (Manassas), Pope had led his motley Army of Virginia into a trap cunningly set by Jackson and sprung by Lee.

The entrapment of Pope's army had been unknowingly fostered by Lincoln's thirst for a decisive battle. Disenchanted by McClellan's inactivity and excuses, he had sent a collection of soldiers (rather than a cohesive army) led by an unprepared general hastily imported from the western theater to bring about the desired grand attack. Pope opened his campaign by moving south along the Blue Ridge Mountains to sever the Confederates' rail connections with the fertile Shenandoah. McClellan, meanwhile, was instructed to put pressure on Lee and so facilitate Pope's advance, and eventually to coordinate with the new army for a combined assault on the Rebel capital.

While Pope marched into Virginia, McClellan's Army of the Potomac, operating in the Peninsula, sank deeper in a morass of mud, malady, and misfortune. The "Little Napoleon" cried for reinforcements. But neither Lincoln nor Halleck believed that any number of new men could satisfy the Peninsular commander; so they decided to pull him out. If McClellan would not move on Richmond from the Peninsula, they would put his army where it could do some good: it would be united with Pope's to crush the Rebel capital in a 150,000-man steamroller. McClellan protested loudly, but the War Department had already sent transports to embark the sick and wounded. This Union withdrawal from the Peninsula allowed Lee to take the initiative. With one opposing army temporarily out of the campaign, he planned to gather his forces and fall upon the other army, that of the unsuspecting John Pope.

Pope was not merely a tempting military target: his derisive remarks made in public about the Confederate soldiery and his harshness with the Southern population had made him an emotional target as well. The bumptious Union general inspired Lee's officers as no other Northern soldier ever would; to them he was a bully who must be taught a lesson. Jackson was given first crack at him. The Valley Veterans of "Stonewall's" army mauled Banks's corps at Cedar Mountain on August 9, but were then forced to make a prudent withdrawal after Pope brought up the rest of his powerful 50,000-man force.

Lee and McClellan now raced to reach Pope first. For the Rebels, Longstreet's corps was deputed to watch the Army of Virginia on the Rappahanock River line, while Jackson struck off through the Valley and came out behind the Union army. The hungry Confederates, who had traveled with as little impedimenta as possible, feasted on the miles of supplies they found at Pope's Manassas Junction base. The Union army hurriedly fell back, hoping to catch the elusive Jackson once and for all.

"Stonewall" took up a strong defensive position in an old railroad cutting near the Bull Run battlefield, the site of the Union disaster a year before. Pope threw his army in massed charges against the Rebel defenders; each time the Southern troops threw them back. At one point in the battle, a Confederate regiment was so desperate for ammunition that the men were hurling rocks at the Union infantry. Low on supplies and sorely pressed, Jackson's men slept on their arms during the night that followed (August 29-30).

Pope, elated at having trapped Jackson and reinforced by elements of McClellan's army, prepared to crush the Southern defenders in the morning. Unknown to him, however, Longstreet's Confederate corps had arrived opposite his left flank. Pope was now in the open head of a Rebel "V", and on August 30, when he attacked Jackson, he only succeeded in burying himself deeper into the confluence of the V. That evening, broken and demoralized, the Union army sullenly trod the same road to Washington that their comrades had taken a year earlier after the First Battle of Bull Run.

The capital fell into a despondent mood. Lincoln's armies were in the same positions they had been in a year ago. The streets were choked with wounded men and deserters. On the Potomac, a steamer, with boilers fired, awaited the call to evacuate Lincoln and the Cabinet should Lee advance. The Union President had little choice left but to recall the only general who could revive the broken army–George Brinton McClellan. "If he can't fight himself," remarked Lincoln with little enthusiasm, "he excels in making others ready to fight."

On September 3, McClellan, once again called upon to save an army and a city from the victorious Rebels, rode out to meet the wreckage of what had once been an army. He acted quickly to replace equipment and restore discipline. Washington began to overflow with new recruits as fresh blood was poured into the Union war machine. Halleck ordered the preparation of a field army for an immediate campaign. Within four days, McClellan had seven corps, mostly of veteran units, ready to take the field. In addition to this 90,000-man force, another 70,000 remained in the forts and advance posts around the capital to protect it against any Rebel thrusts. The organizational talents of McClellan had once again saved the Union from despair and almost certain disaster.

As the Union High Command argued over who was to lead the mobile army (McClellan was not trusted by Halleck or the Cabinet), Lee struck. On September 5, with regimental bands playing "Maryland, My Maryland," the Army of Northern Virginia crossed the Potomac to invade the North. The move was a desperate, calculated risk, inspired not so much by military opportunism as by political and economic necessity. The ravages of war had been cruel to the Confederate farmers of Virginia. Given a few weeks' respite, however, they could harvest what remained of their crops and send them to revictual the Southern armies and cities. The North, meanwhile, had been spared the rigors of a campaign on home ground; the rich fields and overflowing larders were unmolested and ripe with the summer's produce. By carrying the war into a land literally flowing with milk and honey, the Rebels could gather supplies and, by bringing the inhabitants a taste of the sword, increase their appetite for peace. More important still, a victory on Northern soil would greatly influence the powers of Europe.

Lee expected it would take McClellan about two weeks before he would be able to interfere in the Confederate invasion. While his army was encamped at Frederick, Maryland, some 40 miles from Washington, he formulated his "Special Order No. 191." According to this, he would separate his already outnumbered army into five major parts: three columns, comprising the divisions of Jackson, McLaws (with R. H. Anderson), and Walker, were to converge upon and trap the Union garrison at Harpers Ferry; Longstreet was to move his troops, along with the artillery park and baggage trains, north past Boonsboro toward the Pennsylvania border to prepare for an advance, while D. H. Hill would be positioned along the South Mountain to cover him and prevent a Union escape from Harpers Ferry. Stuart's cavalry was split among the columns to screen and reconoiter, and, finally, a column of sick and wounded was to return to Virginia.

Each commander mentioned in the plan was to receive a copy of the order. Unfortunately for the Confederates, one copy went astray. Lee, moreover, had underestimated both the resilience of the Army of the Potomac and McClellan's organizational talents. Only days after news of Lee's invasion had come through, the Union general had begun marching northwest to intercept the Confederate columns. Stuart's cavalry and General Pleasanton's mounted Union patrols skirmished in Frederick as the Rebel rearguard marched out in the night of September 12, with the Union infantry close behind.

The welcome received by the Northern soldiers as they paraded through the streets of Frederick the next morning was that of a liberated city greeting her own sons; supplies which the Confederates had been forced either to buy or steal were freely given to the appreciative Yankees. Two men of the 27th Indiana Infantry, resting in the field which had recently been Lee's headquarters, there discovered three cigars wrapped in paper. As they were about to light their new-found treasure, one of the men began to read the wrapping sheet. On it was scrawled "Headquarters, Army of Northern Virginia." The men rushed the note up through the chain of command to McClellan, who was busy entertaining some prominent local merchants. When he read it, McClellan exclaimed, "Here is a paper with which if I cannot whip Bobbie Lee, I will be willing to go home." It was the lost copy of Special Order No. 191.

The next day, the Army of the Potomac marched toward the South Mountain, aiming to split Lee's army and defeat it in detail. South Mountain is the watershed between the Middletown and Cumberland Valleys. The high, rough, wooded mountain offered only four passes over which wagons and guns might travel: the National Road north to Hagerstown; the central passes of Turner's and Fox's Gaps, and the lower route to Harpers Ferry at Cramptons Gap. Major-General William Buel Franklin, with

18,000 men, was to strike through the lower gap and relieve Harpers Ferry, while the main army headed for the middle passes. All that stood between McClellan's 90,000-strong host and Lee's destruction were a handful of J. E. B. Stuart's horsemen and the 5,000 men of D. H. Hill's strung-out division.

While McClellan was moving to catch Lee, the Confederate plan had fallen behind schedule. The columns converging on Harpers Ferry had driven in the Union outposts in the area but had not yet consolidated their hold on the high ground dominating the confluence of the Shenandoah and Potomac rivers.

Lee, meanwhile, had learned of the fate of his lost order and directed Longstreet to fall back to Boonsboro and join Hill at the South Mountain. They were to cover the retreat of the artillery and supply wagons which had already begun their journey toward the Potomac crossing at Sharpsburg. During the night of September 13, the first patrols of Pleasanton's cavalry began to probe the passes. On the

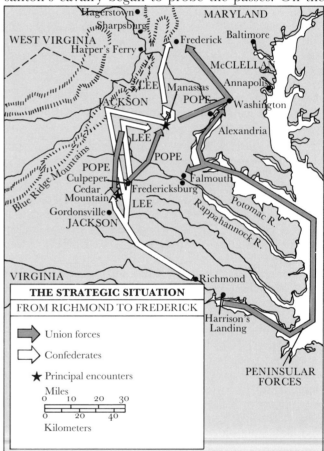

THE STRATEGIC SITUATION
FROM RICHMOND TO FREDERICK

→ Union forces

⇨ Confederates

★ Principal encounters

Miles
0    10    20    30
0        20        40
Kilometers

morning of September 14, Daniel Harvey Hill was gazing across the pastoral Middletown Valley from his perch at Turner's Gap when he saw, unfolding before him like an incoming tide, four corps of the Army of the Potomac. The blue columns covered most of the ground he could see in either direction. Of that sight he later wrote, "I do not remember ever to have experienced a feeling of greater loneliness."

McClellan threw Cox's Kanawha Valley Division against Fox's Gap early in the morning. Colquitt's Georgia brigade fought tenaciously to stop them but to little avail, even when reinforced by Garland's North Carolina infantry. Hill managed to hold out long enough for Longstreet to come up only by bluffing his opponents with a line of cooks, dismounted staff officers, orderlies, and servants, which the Yankees thought was a fresh brigade. The pressure of a full corps at either end of the Confederate line began steadily to drive the defenders back to the summit of the mountain. Cannon could not be brought to bear with any great effect on the defenders, and the broken terrain discouraged any regular battle formations. It was a fight better suited to the Southern country boys than to their Northern city-raised opponents, and they retained their hold on the upper gaps until nightfall, despite the weight of numbers thrown at them. To the south, Franklin had cleared Crampton Gap quickly, but had stopped to wait for further instructions and to face off against parts of McLaws's and Anderson's divisions. Given a little more initiative, the relief of Harpers Ferry could have been effected that night, and, with it, the isolation of the two Rebel divisions on that side of the Ferry. Lee now began a retreat in earnest to the Potomac to enable his army to consolidate with the Harpers Ferry force. The columns stopped for the night around Sharpsburg, just north of the river.

Throughout the night of the 14th, the besieging Rebel infantry at Harpers Ferry hauled their heavy guns up to the heights overlooking the Ferry.

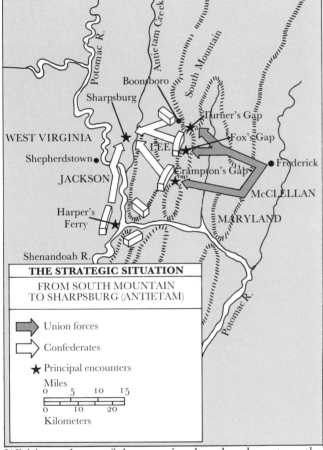

**THE STRATEGIC SITUATION**

FROM SOUTH MOUNTAIN
TO SHARPSBURG (ANTIETAM)

→ Union forces

⇨ Confederates

★ Principal encounters

Miles
0    5    10    15

0    10    20
Kilometers

Within an hour of the opening bombardment on the morning of September 15, the defending guns were silent and the white flags began to appear. Jackson left A. P. Hill's division to take care of the captured men and supplies, and struck north with the other divisions to join Lee.

Still hoping to gain a victory on Northern soil and strengthened by Jackson's promise to meet him at Sharpsburg, Lee decided to stand and face McClellan. He positioned his small 18,000-man force at the bend of the Potomac River which encloses the little Maryland farming community of Sharpsburg, along high ground behind the swift-running Antietam Creek. Both his flanks rested on the swift, muddy Potomac, and the undulating ground of the Sharpsburg ridge afforded his men good concealment from any Union artillery which might be placed to the front. The four-mile-long position was well strengthened by farms, stone walls, and clusters of woods. But, if forced off his line by the enemy, there was only one

ford across the mighty river at his back. From this battleground there could be no successful retreat under enemy pressure.

McClellan arrived on the field at about noon on the 15th. Although he had nearly 75,000 men with him, he believed that it was too late in the day to launch an attack. According to his Pinkerton agents (unreliable as ever), Lee could put at least 100,000 men into the field to oppose him, and McClellan knew all too well what a defeat here would do to the Northern cause. McClellan may not have been the man to win a great battle, but he was certainly the man who could be trusted not to lose one.

Lee, with only 14 of his 39 brigades present, remained calm. On the 16th, Jackson arrived with about 9,000 men and was given command of the left flank. He was to form his lines amid the limestone outcrops, grain fields, and wooded ground north of Dunker Church. Stuart's cavalry and horse artillery would be on his left (near the river) to give him support. D. H. Hill was placed in a natural trench called the Sunken Road, an old farm route which had been worn to well below ground level by traffic and rain. Hill's men set to work tearing apart the fences which lined the lane to form an abatis facing the Union side of the field. Longstreet was responsible for the right and right-center; with him, he had most of the artillery and the divisions of Walker and Jones, their duties being to cover the town and the lower bridge on the creek.

At 2 P.M. McClellan ordered an attack to begin, but there were so many delays that only a desultory artillery engagement took place. The Union general then changed his plans. He would move Hooker's corps across the northern end of the creek (that part farthest from the Rebel lines) and in the morning, with the corps of Sumner and Mansfield standing by, launch a devastating flank assault on Lee's left. Burnside with his corps would attack across the lower bridge on Lee's right flank. Finally, McClellan planned to hold Porter, Franklin, and Pleasanton's cavalry in the center to exploit either wing or drive up the center.

At 6 P.M. the men of General Joseph Hooker's I Corps crossed the Antietam and stumbled into Jackson's skirmish line. A brief engagement took place that served no other purpose than to alert Lee to the movements of the Union right wing. Darkness and steady rain soon ended the fighting. With unnecessary secrecy, McClellan forbade his men to build camp-fires on that rainy night; for supper the wet infantry-men munched on coffee grounds and sugar, uneasily awaiting the dawn.

Lee was prepared to meet whatever McClellan could throw at him. Although he had only 27,000 men deployed on the field, McLaws and Anderson had arrived just before daybreak at his Sharpsburg headquarters with about 10,000 additional troops, and A. P. Hill, though still at Harpers Ferry, was under orders to move up as soon as possible.

McClellan, with 75,000 in battle array and Franklin's corps trudging up the road only a few hours away, let loose with his heavy rifled cannon just after first light. At 6 A.M. Hooker sent his 10 brigades down the Hagerstown Turnpike. The whitewashed walls of the Dunker Church, silhouetted against the dark green backdrop of the West Woods, provided a landmark for the Union attack.

As Doubleday and Ricketts led their divisions forward, Brigadier-General Lawton sent a strong force of Rebel infantry into the Cornfield, which lay

# THE COMMANDERS

Major-General Ambrose E. Burnside, USV

Lieutenant-General Daniel Harvey Hill, CSA

Ambrose Everett Burnside (1824-81) was not one of the luckiest men to wear the uniform of an American major-general. His kindly, unselfish, and gentle nature made him well-liked among his peers, but also offered a tempting target to charlatans, confidence men, and politicians. On his way to the war in Mexico, the newly commissioned Burnside lost his travel money to a Mississippi riverboat gambler. In the 1850s he sank his entire fortune into the development of a breech-loading rifle which was far too expensive for the impoverished US Army to contemplate buying. Perhaps the crowning embarrassment in Burnside's already comic pre-Civil War career was when his fiancée replied in the negative to the minister's final question at the altar.

When war broke out in 1861, Burnside secured himself an independent command in North Carolina, at which he was successful enough to gain some sort of reputation. serving under McClellan, however, Burnside then contrived to fritter away that reputation at South Mountain and Antietam, where the stone bridge he spent the day foolishly fighting for still bears his name.

Lincoln gave command of the Army of the Potomac to Burnside after McClellan was finally fired. Despite Burnside's protestations that he did not feel capable of commanding so vast a force, he took on Lee at Fredericksburg and, though outnumbering him by almost two to one, managed to "snatch defeat from the jaws of victory," as Lincoln acidly put it. He was relieved of his command, suffered further misadventures in the latter part of the war, and resigned his commission in 1865.

Apart from his shortcomings, Ambrose Burnside did leave one thing to glorify his name in posterity. The bushy whiskers which lined his cheeks and became popular throughout the country were named "sideburns" in his honor.

The Fiercest and foulest soldier in Robert E. Lee's army was the learned Daniel Harvey Hill (1821–89), a native of North Carolina. Despite his background as a college professor and his high army rank, "Old Croaker," as Lee dubbed him, rarely had a kind or civil word for anyone. What he lacked in social grace, Harvey Hill more than made up for on the battlefield. He was at his best, as Douglas Southall Freeman wrote of him, "when he had good men on either side of him and was fighting without full responsibility for the field. In that type of combat he had no superior."

Harvey Hill had an almost complete disregard for danger (matched by his intense dislike for the complications of command) and was more often to be found leading a charge than directing it from the rear. He was also the best tactician in the Rebel army. He had little enthusiasm for cavalry, a very healthy respect for Union artillery, and a determined but calculated trust in the power of the infantry to succeed as the arm of decision.

Harvey Hill's inability to get along with others made him a poor choice for high-ranking assignments. Nevertheless, his prowess on the battlefield brought him continually to the fore and made him a constant candidate for promotion. This mixture of conflicting ingredients led to not infrequent explosions that were an undoubted embarrassment to the Confederate high command. One such outburst occurred while Hill was serving in the West under the blustering General Bragg. Finding himself unable to resist telling his commander exactly what he thought of him, he did so and was summarily sacked. Needless (in his case) to say, he was soon reinstated. Fighting generals of his caliber were a rare commodity.

It was perhaps only fitting to his perverse spirit that Harvey Hill should commit innumerable acts of mad bravery, rise to the rank of lieutenant-general, survive the war, and end his days as president of Georgia Military College.

in the path of the Union assault. From his position with the artillery, Hooker could see the sun glint off the bayonets of Lawton's men hidden in the field. His 36 cannon, together with McClellan's heavy batteries across the creek, let loose a hurricane of shot and canister into the field. Hooker later recalled, "Every stalk of corn in the northern and greater part of the field was cut as closely as could have been done with a knife, and the slain lay in rows, precisely as they had stood in their ranks a few moments before. It was never my misfortune to witness a more bloody, dismal battlefield." The surviving Rebels scrambled out of the Cornfield pursued by cheering Yankees. Rickett's men took the East Woods while Doubleday's and Meade's divisions slammed into the West Woods.

Jackson called for more troops; D. H. Hill sent up three of his brigades, and John Bell Hood, who had taken the men of his demi-division out of the line to cook their first hot meal in three days, also came up to meet the Yankee onslaught. Hood's Texans, angry at having their breakfast ruined, headed for the Cornfield and East Woods area. In addition, Stuart's horse artillery on Nicodemus Hill directed their fire with such effect that Union reserves were drawn off to parry any Rebel thrust from that sector.

Jackson's counterattack broke like a great wave on a breakwater. The tiring soldiers of I Corps reeled back in confusion, retreating through the Cornfield and the woods. Hood's Texans unwisely pushed them right up against their own gun line, which retaliated sharply, firing with terrible effect on the over-zealous Confederates. As Hood, with more than half of his division already out of action, recoiled from Hooker's artillery, Mansfield's XII Corps marched onto the field.

At 59 years of age, Major-General Joseph K. F. Mansfield was the oldest general in the Army of the Potomac. His men formed their lines just short of the East Woods. The white-bearded general was riding along the battle line when a stray shot tumbled him from the saddle. Brigadier-General Alpheus Williams took command of the corps and sent the two raw brigades of his own division through the East Woods and back into the blood-soaked Cornfield. Hood's men, retreating to the cover of the West Woods, sucked the inexperienced recruits into a cone of fire from Jackson's hidden riflemen. The new regiments broke and streamed back. Greene's division, the other half of XII Corps, advanced to Dunker Church. There, its offensive power spent, the division remained pinned down for several hours, unable either to advance or fall back.

Lee ordered up Walker and McLaws from the reserve to strengthen the beleaguered left flank. Jackson had stopped the Union attacks, but more than half his own command was now wounded or dead. Captains were commanding brigades; many regiments numbered fewer than a hundred men and others had already ceased to exist.

In the Union center, General Sumner, commanding II Corps, had waited several hours for orders to move across the Antietam. Giving in eventually to impatience, he began to move his three divisions toward the sound of the guns. Sumner's lead division, under Sedgwick, marched blindly in brigade columns into what they believed to be the secure Union rear. The firing had temporarily died down with the repulse of Mansfield's attack, and the thick mass of men unsuspectingly marched on.

"Stonewall" watched the long blue lines approaching and hurriedly scraped together the remains of his command, placing them behind the rocks and trees of the West Woods. When the Union division was only a few yards from the edge of the woods, the Rebel riflemen rose and poured a devastating volley into the parade-order-troops. Then Walker and McLaws reached the field, ensuring the collapse of Sedgwick's flank. In 20 confused and terrible minutes, half the 5,000-man division fell; the frightened remnants raced to the rear.

There were no more attacks that day in the northern sector. Meade–now commanding I Corps after Hooker, mildly wounded in the foot, had left the field–pulled his and Mansfield's men together into a line above the Cornfield. These two corps, along with what remained of Sedgwick's ruined regiments, took no further part in the fighting. Sumner's other two divisions now strayed off to the left, toward the Sunken Road.

D. H. Hill's two weakest brigades, those of Colquitt and Garland, with a handful of Anderson's brigade fallen in beside them, manned this natural trench. A little after 9 A.M. French's division of Sumner's corps moved out past the East Woods, throwing back the Confederate outpost line at the Roulette Farm, and advanced down the slope to the Sunken Road. The front line of the division was at fixed bayonets, the other lines at shoulder arms. A band played as the infantrymen, wearing white ankle gaiters, marched with the precision of a presidential review. Hill held his fire until the opening volley would be sure to hit with devastating effect. That first thunderstorm halted the Union front line, but the division as a whole remained steady, returned the Confederates' fire, and kept on coming. Each time Hill's volleys hit home the line reeled and then reformed.

Longstreet at this point took R. H. Anderson's division and Rodes's fresh division-sized brigade and counterattacked. The 4,000 fresh troops broke through French's thinning ranks, planting their battle flags at the Roulette Farm, 500 yards deep in what had been French's rear. There, flushed with victory, they ran into the Irish Brigade. With their bands drumming, their washerwomen cheering them from behind, and their green flag bearing the golden harp fluttering in the wind, the men of the "Fighting 69th," the pride of the New York regiments, hurled themselves at Longstreet's Alabama and Virginia infantry. Soon their commander, Colonel Thomas Francis Meagher, fed in the rest of his brigade, mostly Irish immigrants raised in New York City. The 88th and 63rd New York and the 29th Massachusetts closed up the gap. The other brigades of Major-General Israel B. Richardson, commanding the last of Sumner's three divisions, passed behind the Irish and also swept toward the Sunken Road,

Disaster befell the Confederates when Gordon's 6th Alabama, acting on a confused order, pulled out of the Sunken Road just as Caldwell's Union brigade was approaching. The advancing Bluecoats straddled the Road and raked the length of Hill's line. Hit from front and flank, the worn-out Southerners fled. The dead Rebels were so thickly spread, it was said, you could walk across the bodies and never touch the ground. The place was christened "Bloody Lane."

With this attack General Richardson brought his division into the heart of Lee's position. Although Richardson himself was mortally wounded at the lip of the Road, his victorious troops charged to within musket range of the town of Sharpsburg. Lee, with all his reserves committed, now set about pulling

# A BATTLE IN THREE PARTS

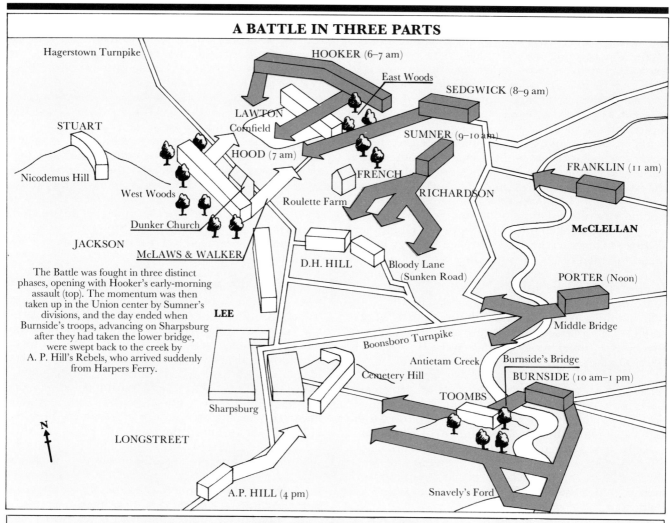

Hagerstown Turnpike

HOOKER (6–7 am)

East Woods

SEDGWICK (8–9 am)

LAWTON
Cornfield

SUMNER (9–10 am)

STUART

FRANKLIN (11 am)

Nicodemus Hill

HOOD (7 am)

FRENCH

RICHARDSON

McCLELLAN

West Woods

Roulette Farm

Dunker Church

JACKSON

McLAWS & WALKER

D.H. HILL

Bloody Lane
(Sunken Road)

PORTER (Noon)

The Battle was fought in three distinct
phases, opening with Hooker's early-morning
assault (top). The momentum was then
taken up in the Union center by Sumner's
divisions, and the day ended when
Burnside's troops, advancing on Sharpsburg
after they had taken the lower bridge,
were swept back to the creek by
A. P. Hill's Rebels, who arrived suddenly
from Harpers Ferry.

LEE

Middle Bridge

Boonsboro Turnpike

Antietam Creek

Burnside's Bridge

Cemetery Hill

BURNSIDE (10 am–1 pm)

Sharpsburg

TOOMBS

N

LONGSTREET

A.P. HILL (4 pm)

Snavely's Ford

---

## THE OPPOSING FORCES

### UNION ARMY OF THE POTOMAC
Major-General George Brinton McClellan

#### I Corps
Major-General Joseph Hooker

First Division (Brigadier-General Abner Doubleday):
brigades of Phelps, Doubleday, Patrick and Gibbon.
Second Division (Brigadier-General James B. Ricketts):
brigades of Duryea, Christian and Hartsuff.
Third Division (Brigadier-General George G. Meade):
brigades of Seymour, Magilton and R. Anderson.
Strength: 43 regiments of infantry and 10 batteries of
artillery.

#### II Corps
Major-General Edwin V. Sumner

First Division (Major-General Israel B. Richardson):
brigades of Caldwell, Meagher and Brooke.
Second Division (Major-General John Sedgwick):
brigades of Gorman, Howard and Dana.
Third Division (Brigadier-General William H. French):
brigades of Kimball, Morris and Weber.
Strength: 37 regiments and 8 batteries.

#### V Corps
Major-General Fitz-John Porter

First Division (Major-General George W. Morell):
brigades of Barnes, Griffin and Stockton.
Second Division (Brigadier-General George Sykes):
brigades of Buchanan, Lovell and Warren.
Strength: 32 regiments and 7 batteries.

#### VI Corps
Major-General William B. Franklin

First Division (Major-General Henry Slocum):
brigadesof Torbert, Bartlett and Newton.
Second Division (Major-General William F. Smith):
brigades of Hancock, Brooks and Irwin.
Strength: 28 regiments and 7 batteries.

#### IX Corps
Major-General Ambrose E. Burnside

First Division (Brigadier-General Orlando B. Willcox):
brigades of Christ and Welsh.
Second Division (Brigadier-General Samuel D. Sturgis):
brigades of Nagle and Ferrero.
Third Division (Brigadier-General Isaac Rodman):
brigades of Fairchild and Harland.
Kanawha Division (Brigadier-General Jacob D. Cox):
brigades of Scammon and Crook.
Strength: 29 regiments and 11 batteries.

#### XII Corps
Major-General Joseph Mansfield

First Division (Brigadier-General Alpheus Williams):
brigades of Crawford and Gordon.
Second Division (Brigadier-General George S. Greene):
brigades of Tyndale, Stainrook and Goodrich.
Strength: 26 regiments and 7 batteries.

#### Cavalry Division
Brigadier-General Alfred Pleasanton

Brigades of Whiting, Farnsworth, Rush, McReynolds and
Davis.

Strength: 14 cavalry regiments and 6 batteries of horse artillery.

Artillery Reserve
Lieutenant-Colonel William Hays

Strength 7 batteries.

Estimated Totals

McClellan's 195 infantry regiments, 14 cavalry regiments, and 63 batteries gave him a total strength of approximately 87,000 men and 378 guns.

Losses: 2,108 killed, 9,549 wounded, and 758 captured or missing. Total: 12,415. On the morning of September 18, McClellan was reinforced by IV Corps and a division of V Corps, giving him 23 more regiments and 6 batteries. Total losses for the Maryland campaign were 2,673 killed, 11,756 wounded, and 13,511 captured or missing. Overall total: 27,940. Of those captured, all were paroled either at Harpers Ferry immediately (nearly 12,000 men) or later from Virginia. These men nevertheless represent a real if temporary loss of manpower to the North since as part of their parole conditions they were not able to serve for an agreed period of time.

## CONFEDERATE ARMY OF NORTHERN VIRGINIA
General Robert E. Lee

Longstreet's Corps
Major-General James Longstreet

McLaws's Division (Major-General Lafayette McLaws): brigades of Kershaw, Cobb, Semmes and Barksdale.
Anderson's Division (Major-General R. H. Anderson): brigades of Wilcox, Mahone, Featherston, Armistead, Pryor and Wright.
D. R. Jones's Division (Brigadier-General David R. Jones): brigades of Toombs, Drayton, Pickett, Kemper, Jenkins and G. T. Anderson.
Walker's Division (Brigadier-General W. H. T. Walker): brigades of Walker and Ransom.
Hood's Division (Brigadier-General John Bell Hood): brigades of Hood and Law.
Evans's Independent Brigade (Brigadier-General N. G. Evans).
Strength: 93 regiments of infantry and 26 batteries of artillery.

Jackson's Corps
Major-General Thomas J. Jackson

Lawton's Division (Brigadier-General A. R. Lawton): brigades of Lawton, Early, Trimble and Hays.
Light Division (Major-General Ambrose Powell Hill): brigades of Branch, Gregg, Field, Archer, Pender and Thomas.

J. R. Jones's Division (Brigadier-General John R. Jones): brigades of Winder, Taliaferro, Jones and Starke.
D. H. Hill's Division (Major-General Daniel H. Hill): brigades of Ripley, Rodes, Garland, G. B. Anderson and Colquitt.
Strength: 93 regiments and 21 batteries.

Reserve artillery
Brigadier-General William Pendleton

Strength: 23 batteries.

Cavalry Division
Major-General J. E. B. Stuart

Brigades of Hampton, Fitzhugh Lee and Robertson
Strength: 15 regiments and 3 batteries of horse artillery.

Estimated Totals

Lee's army of Northern Virginia had 186 regiments of infantry, 15 of cavalry, and 73 batteries of artillery, giving it an approximate total strength of 40,000 men and 292 guns.
Losses: 1,512 killed, 7,816 wounded, and 1,844 captured or missing. Total: 11,172. Lee lost nearly 15,000 men as stragglers during his march to Maryland, most of whom eventually returned to the army, 3,000 on the night of the 17th alone. Total losses for the Maryland campaign were 1,890 killed, 9,770 wounded, and 2,304 captured or missing. Overall total: 13,964.

together all the guns he could find. Longstreet and his staff manned a gun while Hill, a rifle in his hand, led 200 survivors of his division in a desperate charge against the approaching Northerners. Faced by this albeit fragile opposition and with only a light horse artillery battery for support, the tiring Union division opted to halt, so giving Lee some respite.

Lee's left flank, despite being stiffened by reinforcements, was nevertheless perilously close to breaking. In the center, opposite the remnants of Sumner's II Corps, he had only the artillery and a few scattered pockets of rallied men. To exploit this weakness, McClellan moved Porter's corps and Pleasanton's cavalry across the Middle Bridge and prepared to throw these men, along with Franklin, who was advancing on the East Woods, against the denuded Rebel center. As he was about to tip his hat for these 25,000 fresh soldiers to go in, he received an urgent message. It was from Sumner, who had instructed the messenger with these words: "Go back young man and tell General McClellan I have no command! Tell him my command, Banks's command [XII Corps] and Hooker's command are all cut up and demoralized. Tell him General Franklin has the only orga-

nized command on this part of the field."

As he moved up, Porter had also added a note of caution, advising McClellan, "Remember. General, I command the last reserve of the last army of the Republic." With recommendations of this caliber from his most trusted generals, combined with Lee's already staunch defense and reputation for cunning, it is little wonder that George Brinton McClellan suddenly lost his nerve. The order to attack was not given. It was too great a risk for him to take; McClellan would not face Lee without a reserve.

The Army of the Potomac had already fought two battles that day: Hooker and Mansfield in the north, and Sumner in the center. Each attack had come within a hair of cracking the Rebel line. It was now barely past noon, and a third assault was about to be launched, that of Burnside at the lower bridge.

The swift-running Antietam, although difficult to cross, was not an insurmountable obstacle. Along most of the stream, a man could wade across without getting his belt wet. There were two fords, one on either side of the lower bridge; this bridge, on which Burnside's attention became fixed, was the only place where a man could cross dryshod.

Major-General Ambrose Burnside had been in command of an entire wing of the Army of the Potomac in its advance to Antietam. Although only one corps (IX) remained under his command, he was determined to act with the prestige his former responsibility allowed him, and so retained a wing headquarters for himself and left the corps to Brigadier-General Jacob Cox, commander of the Kanawha Division. The instructions McClellan had sent to IX Corps were vague. The corps had been ordered to put pressure on the enemy, but it was not clear whether they were to mount a major attack or a diversion.

At 10 A.M. Cox had directed Crooke's brigade in an ill-fated charge across the bridge. The defending Rebels, Toombs's Georgia brigade, were heavily outnumbered but had clear field of fire from the heights above the bridge, while the only avenue of approach from the Union side, a dirt lane which ran parallel to the creek, was under heavy and accurate artillery fire from Confederate batteries positions on the Cemetery Hill. Several successive assaults were thrown back by the combined fire of the artillery and the riflemen, even though Toombs's 450 men were fighting against 14,000 Federals.

Rodman's division and the other brigade of the Kanawha Division were sent downstream to locate Snavely's Ford, while Crook scouted the right flank to find a local ford reputed to be above the bridge. The purpose of these probes was not to find a crossing point for the corps as a whole, but to bring additional pressure on the Rebel line dominating the bridge. There the fight was taken up by Brigadier-General Samuel D. Sturgis and his New England regiments. Several spirited bayonet charges by the men of his Second Division cleared the zone immediately around the bridge, but the Union infantry could not establish a foothold on the other bank. Eventually two columns under Colonel Edward Ferrero, one of Pennsylvanians, the other the 51st New York, surged across the bloody stones. Arriving on the opposite bank, they peeled off, the Pennsylvanians to the right and the New Yorkers to the left; but the New Yorkers then stopped to return the Rebel fire instead of continuing onward, a mistake that cost them scores of needless casualties.

At the same time, around noon, Rodman and Crook had crossed at the fords on either side of the bridge. The pressure on the handful of Georgians was formidable. With half his men dead or dying, Toombs was finally forced from the heights by the pressure of the Union divisions, and by 1 P.M. the cheering Northerners had gained complete control of the lower Antietam. Sturgis's men, however, were out of ammunition, while Crook's brigade had suffered heavily and was physically worn out. Burnside, crossing the bridge after it had been secured, ordered Sturgis to take his men back across to the supply wagons to draw munitions. Willcox's fresh division was instructed to move up and take their place. This movement, involving the transfer of 10,000 men across a bridge wide enough for only eight men, occupied two precious hours.

Lee took advantage of the delay as best he could. The fighting in the rest of the field had died down, and this allowed him to shift several batteries to reinforce D. R. Jones's 2,400-man division at Sharpsburg. The 25,000 troops of the Union reserve did not move to hinder this shift; it was Burnside's battle and his battle alone. By 3 P.M. the Union IX Corps was ready to advance. Six brigades moved sharply across the fields toward the spires of Sharpsburg.

Some regiments took advantage of the rolling ground, the clumps of trees and the stone fences to cover themselves from the Rebel artillery. Others recklessly charged, opening great gaps between themselves and units advancing more methodically.

The 16th Connecticut, a raw regiment which now held the most advanced position in the Union line, saw a long column of blue-coated infantry approaching up the road from the Shepardstown Ford. The marching troops advanced to within a few dozen yards, Union colors flying, and opened fire. The Connecticut regiment was sent reeling by the first volley: its confused and inexperienced recruits ran back into another Union regiment which had just then begun to fire at the newly arrived column, and the Connecticut men were mown down in the crossfire. Now the still-advancing line of "Bluecoats" rolled up the forward line of Burnside's corps. Ambrose Powell Hill and 3,000 men of his Confederate Light Division had arrived. They had marched 17 miles that afternoon to join the battle.

A few days before, Hill's men had looted the plentiful stores of Harpers Ferry, picking up quantities of blue uniform cloth and coats from the arsenal. The Union flag completed the deception. With this ruthless stroke, Hill succeeded in turning the tide of battle. By 4.30 P.M. Burnside was back to a line just west of the creek, from which he would advance no further. Although a second attack could have cleared the field of Hill's outnumbered and by now exhausted division, Burnside had had the fight knocked out of him. The bloodiest day of battle ever fought in the Western Hemisphere to that date was finally over.

The two armies slept in their battle positions that night, each waiting for the struggle to be renewed in the morning. Lee held a conference with his officers to consider counterattacking the Union right the next day. Despite the arguments of his lieutenants that they should withdraw from the field, Lee was nevertheless determined to stay and fight. He did agree, however, to wait for McClellan to strike first.

McClellan's corps commanders were no more in favor of a renewal of the day's carnage than were Lee's officers. Porter, Sumner, and Franklin cautioned McClellan against committing their divisions against the wily Rebels who, they assumed, had a large reserve waiting to crush the weakened Army of the Potomac. McClellan listened to his generals; he, too, would wait for his opponent to strike in the morning

While the wounded suffered, unattended in the "no-man's land" between the armies, the soldiers on both sides sat and waited for the other to attack. McClellan, with more fresh troops than Lee had soldiers in his whole army, remained cautious. Lee, spoiling for a fight, lacked the manpower to carry the battle to his foe.

During the night of the 18th, Lee reluctantly slipped across the Potomac at Shepardstown, so putting the Maryland campaign behind him. Confederate bands which began to play "Maryland, My Maryland" were cursed and shouted down. The Rebel soldiers only wanted to hear one tune–"Dixie."

President Lincoln, relieved that his army had succeeded in driving Lee from Northern soil, on September 23 announced his Preliminary Emancipation Proclamation. Although the Proclamation would not take effect until January 1, 1863, its declared intent to free all slaves gave moral weight to the Northern war effort and helped to prevent European consciences from siding with the South.

Top
Burnside's Bridge over Antietam Creek. Toombs's outnumbered Georgians occupied the steep wooded slope on the far side.

Above
S. D. Lee's Rebel gunners shell advancing Union infantry near Dunker Church.

Below
A view of the dead on the west side of the Hagerstown Turnpike.

# CHANCELLORSVILLE
## May 1-4, 1863

Skulls and bones of unburied soldiers killed in the fighting that raged along the south side of the Plank Road.

The ill-starred commander of the Army of the Potomac, Major-General George Brinton McClellan, pleading poverty in men, horseflesh, and matériel, had kept his army fettered for nearly two months. Instead of giving chase to General Robert E. Lee's Army of Northern Virginia as it staggered through the Shenandoah Valley after the Antietam Campaign (see previous chapter), McClellan had quietly sat and reorganized his 100,000-strong force. Instead of offering battle, McClellan offered excuses. Lincoln's repeated urgings and personal visits had little appreciable effect upon his over-cautious general. Eventually, on November 5, 1862, Lincoln issued the order for McClellan to be relieved of his command and for Major-General Ambrose E. Burnside to be appointed in his stead. When Lee received the news of his old adversary's dismissal, he reflected, "We always understood each other so well. I fear they may continue to make these changes till they find someone whom I don't understand."

Burnside, full of fire, had his men on the move within two weeks. Restructuring the army into three large Grand Divisions (each of two corps or about 40,000 men), he struck south for the Rappahannock, which he hoped to cross before Lee could react. Although his leading troops outmarched the Rebels to Fredericksburg—the major town on the river, equidistant from Washington and Richmond—the Union pontoon train was delayed for nearly two weeks. While Burnside awaited the means to cross, Lee was able to concentrate his forces on the southern bank of the river.

With over 120,000 men and nearly 300 cannon, facing an army only two-thirds that size, Burnside on December 13, tried to force his way across the swift-flowing river. But the Rebel artillery, so well directed by Major-General Longstreet that "a chicken could not live on that field," held off the unimaginative frontal assaults of the Union commanders. Repeatedly hurled against entrenchments and artillery, Burnside's men were savagely butchered in each of their six major attacks. Some 12,000 Union casualties covered the open ground below the Confederate line on Marye's Heights. The sight of so many bodies in such a small area caused Lee to remark, "It is well that war is so terrible; we should grow too fond of it."

The morale of the Union Army plummeted. An attempt early in January to outflank the Southern lines became so bogged down in the rain-soaked roads that the soldiers christened it the "Mud March." Burnside, his army thoroughly dispirited, his officers near mutiny, was removed from his post on January 25, 1863. The problem of the Union Army was clearly defined by a New York corporal who wrote home, "It has strong limbs to march and meet the foe, stout arms to strike heavy blows, brave hearts to dare. But the brains, the brains - have we no brains to use the arms and limbs and eager hearts with cunning?" Lincoln once again sought a general who could use the North's advantages in men and matériel to win a decisive battle. After some hesitation, he settled on Major-General Joseph Hooker.

Hooker, whose fighting reputation was largely based on a typing error in a dispatch which changed "still fighting–Joe Hooker" to "Fighting-Joe Hooker," was without doubt the loudest and most unabashed wastrel in the Union Army. A drinker and debaucher of such magnitude that his name became a popular synonym for prostitute, Hooker quickly gained the early confidence of the rank-and-file troopers. His reforms, too, designed to improve the sanitary, dietary, and social aspects of he camp, soon reversed the trend toward demoralization within the Army of the Potomac and eased the President's earlier doubts about his new commander's ability to keep "tavern for so large an army." Hooker's Chief of Staff, General Dan Butterfield, introduced a system of corps and division badges to give the men common symbols of which to be proud (and also for quick identification). Mock battles and grand reviews brought back a spirit of efficiency and professionalism to the army.

In addition to his "social" improvements, Hooker gave the army two more lasting reforms: an intelligence service that worked, and a modern cavalry arm. The ineffective and exaggerated reports of the Pinkerton Agency had served McClellan badly. To correct this inadequacy, a network of riders, scouts, spies, and informants was set up under Colonel Sharp both for intelligence gathering and counterintelligence work. In a short time, Hooker had accurate knowledge of the numbers of the Rebel army facing him–an advantage which McClellan had never enjoyed.

Second, the superiority of the Confederate horsemen over the Union cavalry had become so well established that the infantry joked about never having seen a dead cavalryman in Virginia. By pulling in all the detached headquarter guards, pickets, and riders who had been parceled out to individual generals, Hooker collected nearly 12,000 horse-soldiers into a massive mounted corps under Brigadier-General George Stoneman. Within a month, his troopers were doing what no other Union cavalry in the east had yet done: carrying the fight to J. E. B. Stuart and his Virginia horse. Now, his army enlarged, revitalized, well supplied with accurate information, and greatly improved by a modernized if inexperienced cavalry arm, Hooker declared that Lee would have to seek mercy from God, for he would give him none.

On the other side of the Rappahannock, facing Hooker's 130,000-man, 400-gun Army of the Potomac, rested the underfed and ill-supplied men of the Army of Northern Virginia, their numbers reduced to some 60,000. The Confederates nevertheless put on a brave face. Even with their equipment falling apart, their uniforms hardly recognizable as such, and their ranks depleted, they found confidence and courage in the knowledge that they had never been beaten. Indeed, the Rebels' position became stronger every day as they continued to dig and improve upon the trench system that Longstreet and the engineers had devised to cover the 25-mile front from Port Royal to the upper fords of the Rapidan. Mutually supporting, reinforced, and designed to prevent enfilading fire from being directed upon them, this precursor of World War I defensive systems enabled Lee's small force effectively to defend a great expanse of terrain. Furthermore, it allowed Lee to dispatch Longstreet and two divisions south to the Carolinas to gather badly needed supplies and to check secondary Union movements that were threatening Richmond.

The Confederate army made certain organizational improvements in the winter of 1862-63, in particular in the artillery arm. The cannon were reorganized into four four-gun batteries per artillery battalion, with four such battalions attached to each corps, and two in reserve. Although this pattern was adopted so that Lee could mass his outnumbered guns, the battalions were for the most part detailed to individual divisions to provide close fire support. In the forthcoming battle, this attention to organization would shift the balance of firepower in the South's favor.

Lee, secure in the faith that his army was invincible, became increasingly dissatisfied with his defensive stance as the spring thaws began to subside and the roads hardened. He wrote to Richmond of his intention to launch another invasion of the North if Hooker had not moved by the middle of May. "Fighting Joe," however, had plans of his own. Under increasing pressure from Washington to make a move against Lee, the new commander of the Army of the Potomac–the fourth since its creation–prepared for his first great offensive. Like McClellan before him, Hooker proposed to finesse the Rebels out of their strong defensive line rather than to hit it head-on. There were two main possibilities open to him. The country to the southeast of Fredericksburg was open and excellent for maneuvering his large army: but to

ericksburg and the other half of the Union army. To confuse and discomfort still further his as yet unbeaten adversary, Hooker planned for the weight of Stoneman's entire cavalry corps to fall upon the Rebels' only means of supply, the railroad to Richmond.

The cavalry raid, which was scheduled to begin two weeks before the main turning operation (in order to draw off Stuart's command and restrict Lee's ability to patrol his flanks), was stalled by heavy rains which flooded the bridges and fords, making them impassable to the wagons and artillery that accompanied Stoneman's force. Not until April 29, when Hooker's infantry had already been on the march for nearly 72 hours, did the cavalry strike off into the Virginia heartland. Their delayed start severely reduced whatever impact they might have had on Lee's precarious supply lines, and their absence did little more than rob Hooker of patrols, screens, and raiders that he could have used in his Wilderness march.

The Wilderness Church and Hawkins Farm as seen from Howard's headquarters at Dowdall's Tavern on the turnpike. Jackson's attack routed the Union XI Corps and drove them in confusion down this road.

get there he would have to cross on bridges and in boats, as there were few fords. A move to the lower reaches of the river would, moreover, uncover Washington, the defense of which remained Hooker's first concern.

If he marched above the town, he would safely protect his line of communications, but this would mean crossing two rivers, the Rapidan and the Rappahannock, and traversing a primeval forest of trackless bogs, impenetrable thickets, and overgrown trees which the local inhabitants aptly called "The Wilderness." In this untamed country, an army could be quickly thrown into disorder. If well handled, however, it could vanish from the enemy's view, and then, a few miles to the east of Chancellorsville, suddenly emerge immediately to its rear.

Hooker gambled on the element of surprise which the gloomy forest would give him. He proposed to send half his army in a wide sweep behind the Rebel forces, whose attention would be fixed on Fred-

Although Stoneman's cavalry rode to the outskirts of Richmond, burned several railroad and supply depots, and captured several hundred prisoners, the presence of 10,000 well-armed troopers on the battlefields along the Rappahannock would have been much more rewarding to the Union effort.

On April 26, the leading elements of the Union right wing, the corps of Generals Howard, Slocum, and Meade, struck camp and began their march to Kelly's Ford. Once across the Rappahannock, they headed for the crossings of the Rapidan at Ely's and Germanna's Fords and from there pushed into the Wilderness, aiming for Chancellorsville. The march by Howard and Slocum was accomplished with remarkable speed, while Meade, following a wetter, more difficult route, was harried by small parties of Stuart's Confederate horsemen and suffered repeated delays; only after herculean efforts did he reach the designated bivouac area on time. The advance was halted near Chancellorsville on April 30, still deep within the Wilderness, although open ground was barely two miles to the front. The delay allowed Couch's II Corps and Sickles's III Corps to come up in support. There was another reason for the halt: Hooker himself was riding to command the wing, and he did not want his fiery subordinates to enter a battle without him.

The other portion of Hooker's army, under Major-General John Sedgwick, had already crossed the river below Fredericksburg as planned, and was entrenching. Facing Sedgwick was Jackson, who spent the 29th trying to convince Lee to let him attack the Union bridgehead and drive the enemy into the river. Reports from Stuart, however, kept flowing in about large bodies of Union infantry marching through the Wilderness.

It became apparent to Lee that Sedgwick, who was content to dig in under the protection of his cannon on the far bank, had no intention of advancing. The Confederate commander began sending his men

along the turnpike to the left, supported by Couch. Sickle's corps was instructed to remain in the reserve.

Jackson put his force in motion at about the same time, and the two armies collided almost immediately along the wooded roads. The Rebel infantry stalled the Northern columns about halfway between the Tabernacle Church and Chancellorsville, where the two roads are farthest apart. The density of the undergrowth prevented units in either column from coming to the aid of the other, and the fighting was confided to the vicinity of the roads.

Meade, realizing that he could not advance his massive body of men along a narrow wooded track, detached two divisions to follow the River Road to the north, where he hoped they could clear Banks's Ford and thus shorten communications between Hooker and Sedgwick. The thickness of the forest prevented the sound of battle from reaching these divisions, under Humphreys and Griffin, which in due course, though unintentionally, outflanked Jacksons's line.

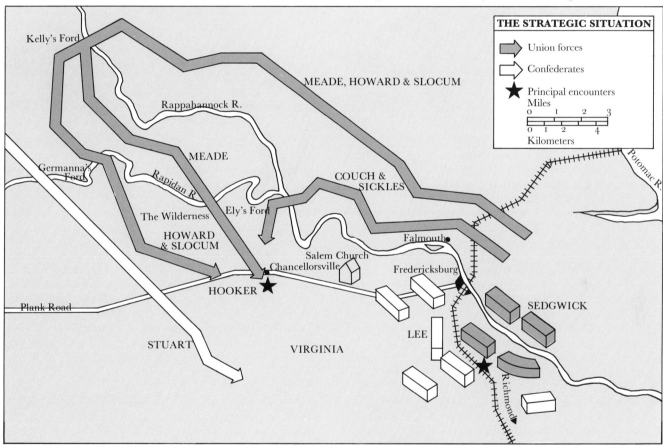

toward the Wilderness with great urgency. He proposed to counterattack the Union sweep before it cleared the brambles and bogs around Chancellorsville. Major-General Jubal Early, with only one reinforced division, remained at Fredericksburg to mask Sedgwick, who by now had only one reinforced corps (he had sent most of his command to join Hooker's march).

The leading division of Longstreet's old corps, that of Major-General Richard H. Anderson, had been skirmishing with the advance guard of Meade's corps since midnight of the 29th. The other division of the Confederate I Corps, under Major-General Lafayette McLaws, joined Anderson at dawn on May 1 and began to entrench. At 8.00 A.M. Jackson arrived with the van of his corps and took command of the line in front of the Tabernacle Church.

The Union army began to advance at 11.00 A.M. in two columns: Slocum moved down the Plank Road on the right flank with Howard in support and Meade

(That evening, they fell back with the rest of V Corps.)

Along the Orange Turnpike, meanwhile, Major-General George Sykes's division of US Regulars found both its flanks overlapped by McLaws's Rebels. After several hours' sharp fighting, Hooker ordered his men to pull back into the Wilderness. Couch, spoiling for a fight, rode back to Hooker's headquarters for permission to continue the battle, while Meade kept sending troops forward. But by the time Hooker finally decided to stand and fight, it was too late: observing his original directive, the Army of the Potomac was already disengaging.

Hooker was not in the least disturbed, however, that his army, having withdrawn, was pinned down in an inhospitable Virginia forest. He was content to have succeeded in his long turning march, and now he sat back to await a Rebel attack. "Fighting Joe" had seen too many troops die in useless assaults against well-defended lines. He had even issued a general order to the army the day before that read, "The

# THE COMMANDERS

Major-General Joseph Hooker, USV

Lieutenant-General Thomas J. Jackson, CSA

"Joe Hooker is our leader, he takes his whiskey strong," proclaimed the balladeers when Major-General "Fighting Joe" Hooker (1814-79) was elevated to the command of the Army of the Potomac in January 1863. Hooker had worked hard for that promotion. The only soldier to be breveted three times during the Mexican War, he had early made a name for himself in the Regular Army. A native of Massachusetts, Hooker then resigned his commission to seek fame and fortune in California, at first as a farmer, then as a surveyor, and quickly rose to command the California militia.

Beginning as a divisional commander in the Civil war, "Fighting Joe" was in all the major–and most minor–engagements fought by the Army of the Potomac. He fought not only Rebels, but his superiors as well, doing so with a frightening ruthlessness. During the Fredericksburg Campaign, Hooker worked hard on the hapless Burnside, ensuring that he would succeed to the command of the Army of the Potomac. He quickly ingratiated himself with the soldiers, and his bluff and bluster made good copy for the newspapers; but his actions worried Lincoln, who complained, "That is the most depressing thing about Hooker, it seems to me he is overconfident."

With tremendous verve, Hooker proceeded to outmaneuver Lee, himself a master of finesse. Then, like a child too pleased at having put together two pieces of a puzzle, he sat down and congratulated himself instead of completing the job. Much to the consternation and frustration of his generals, Hooker became cowardly and inert once Lee began to fight. When asked afterward to explain why he had been so thoroughly trounced, he sadly answered, "I was not hurt by a shell, and I was not drunk. For once I lost confidence in Joe Hooker and that is all there is to it."

In the later years of the war, Hooker served in the West under Generals Thomas and Sherman. There were more tempestuous bouts with his superiors, but he survived them to retire from the Army in 1868.

Major-General Thomas Jonathan Jackson (1824-63) earned his nickname of "Stonewall" at the battle of First Bull Run where his brigade, standing "like a stone wall," formed the rallying point for the wavering Rebel army. That was only the first of many actions in which Jackson, a West Virginian and ex-professor of the Virginia Military Institute, who combined the qualities of a religious mystic with those of a hardened warrior knight, contrived a miraculous victory for an outnumbered Confederate force. In the Shenandoah Valley, with fewer than 20,000 men, he fought half a dozen major battles against an army three times his size, winning every engagement. Marching with such incredible speed that his opponents dubbed his troops "Jackson's foot cavalry," his corps did more to defeat the Union armies in 1862 and 1863 than any comparable body of men in the entire war.

His true value came to light when he began working closely with Robert E. Lee. The calm, resolute, sensitive, and scholarly Lee and the fiery but calculating Jackson formed an almost perfect military team. Jackson's masterpiece came at Chancellorsville where defying every tenet of military science and history, he led an outnumbered army to victory in a flank march that ranks with Frederick the Great's maneuver at Leuthen as one of the greatest actions in martial records. While attempting to exploit his advantage, however, Jackson was mistakenly gunned down by his own men. Although his left arm was amputated, he was expected to recover. His wife traveled to Chandler's Farmhouse at Guiney Station in the Wilderness to help him in his convalescence. Despite early signs of improvement, a fever set in, the most likely cause of which was an undetected internal injury. At the end of a delirious outburst, he became conscious, and said to his wife, "No, no, let us pass over the river and rest under the shade of the trees," and then died at peace. The Confederate cause could never make good the loss of this deeply religious warrior.

operations of the last three days have determined that our enemy must either ingloriously fly or come out from behind his entrenchments and give us battle on our own ground, where certain destruction awaits him." However, to surrender the initiative to Robert E. Lee, a man not noted for his frontal assaults, was to court disaster, even when Lee was outnumbered by two to one.

Stuart's cavalry had spent the first day of the battle watching the movements of the Union army. His scouts, joined by a cartographer, Major Jebediah Hotchkiss, discovered that the Union right flank, which Hooker had considered out of danger because of the dense nature of the terrain, was in fact "up in the air," i.e., exposed and inadequately supported. That night Jackson suggested to Lee that in the morning he should take his corps of Valley veterans, march across Hooker's front, and fall upon the open Union flank. Although he was shocked by the audacity of the plan (which would leave him with hardly 15,000 to contain Hooker's 90,000), Lee assented to it.

Hooker, meanwhile, satisfied with his dispositions, went to bed that night with all the assurance of a victorious general. To the left, Meade's tough V Corps guarded the approach roads; in the center, although projecting forward in a salient, Slocum's XII Corps was entrenched around the commanding Fairview Heights. On Slocum's right, where in Hooker's view there was little chance of action, was XI corps, Major-General Oliver Howard's "Dutchmen" from New York and Pennsylvania. Behind the front line of infantry stood the corps of Couch and Sickles; in addition, Reynold's I Corps was marching from Fredericksburg to join the Union force in the late afternoon. All told, Hooker could count on six corps, nearly 90,000 men, with which to counter any attack by the Confederate infantry, who could muster only half that number. The over-confident Union general was already composing the victory dispatches in his mind.

Major-General Darius Couch, commanding II Corps, did not share his leader's optimism. He later wrote, "To hear from his [Hooker's] own lips that the advantages gained by the successful marches of his lieutenants were to culminate in fighting a defensive battle in that nest of thickets, was too much, and I retired from his presence with the belief that my commanding general was a whipped man." "Stonewall" Jackson would do his best the next day to turn Couch's misgivings into reality.

For the Confederates, the tactic of marching a column of infantry, artillery, and supply trains six miles long across the front of an entrenched enemy of superior strength could turn out to be either a splendid masterpiece of military art, or a disaster reminiscent of the Allied rout at Rossbach in 1757. Lee, with only 32 cannon and two worn divisions, was to annoy and pin a force nearly six times his in size while Jackson, with 50 regiments and 23 batteries (less than 25,000 men in all) marched around the Union army, hoping that it remained immobile, and hit it sharply in the flank.

Throughout the day, Hooker was flooded with reports that the Confederate army was on the move along roads to the south of his positions. Rather than prepare for a possible attack by the Southerners, such as he had been predicting, he assured his own officers that, also true to his predictions, Lee was on the retreat. He added that the heavy rail traffic reported along the Fredericksburg-Richmond line was only further proof of Lee's retrograde movement (evidently Hooker too was successfully taken in by Lee's trick of shuttling empty trains along the line to confuse the Union intelligence service). The spirited efforts of the Rebel troops on his left were also dismissed as a rearguard action intended to keep the Army of the Potomac occupied.

"Fighting Joe" once again sat down to congratulate himself. Instead of sending in the whole army (as Lincoln had repeatedly reminded him to do in his next fight) to tear the long Rebel columns to shreds, he agreed, and then only grudgingly, to Dan Sickles's request to take in his III Corps. One corps, rather than an army, was to pursue the "retreating" Rebels.

In their line of march, Jackson's column had to cross one open stretch of ground, the clearing around Catherine's Furnace, just south of the Union lines at Fairview. The men were ordered to double-time it across the field, the 23rd Georgia Infantry following behind the rest of the Corps to act as rearguard and file-closers: Jackson could not afford any malingerers on this march.

As the tail-end of the Rebel corps passed by his position, Brigadier-General David Birney ordered his supporting artillery to open fire. The rifled cannon tore into the masses of gray-clad soldiers from 1,600 yards. Then Colonel Hiram Berdan's 1st US Sharpshooters moved out to harass the confused Georgians and drive in the pickets, while Birney followed through with his line regiments. A battery of Colonel J. Thompson Brown's Virginia artillery battalion unlimbered to hold off the onrushing Union troops, and a brigade from Anderson's division, under Brigadier-General Carnot Posey, hurried up to their support. At the same time, A. P. Hill countermarched his two tail-end brigades, those of Archer and Thomas, back to the Furnace.

Although by this stage his men had taken a large number of prisoners, many of whom told of Jackson's final destination, Hooker still refused to commit the bulk of his army against the Rebels. Sickles, who now was concentrating the fire of every available gun on the Furnace, was forced to seek reinforcements from Howard's XI Corps and the only cavalry in the entire Union force, Brigadier-General Alfred Pleasanton's brigade. Meanwhile, Couch's corps sat idly in reserve at Chancellorsville, as did most of the Northern artillery. Hooker's complacent attitude is further confirmed by a cable he sent during the afternoon to Major-General John Sedgwick, commanding the Union force at Fredericksburg. "We know that the enemy is fleeing," stated Hooker, " trying to save his trains. Two of Sickles's divisions are among them."

While the two armies sparred at Catherine's Furnace, Jackson was rapidly closing on his prey. Riding with an advance party of cavalry, he spied the main line of the Union left around 3 P.M. He judged that an attack against the trenches of XI Corps would not have enough impact, and so pushed his corps further into the forest, heading toward the Wilderness Tavern. There he turned, straddling the Orange Turnpike less than half a mile from the exposed Union flank. Although by the time he was ready it was about 5 P.M. and there was little daylight left, Jackson was counting on his positional advantage to crush Howard's corps quickly, ruthlessly, and with the minimum of warning.

The morale of XI Corps was remarkably low in the otherwise high-spirited Army of the Potomac. Its soldiers, mainly German immigrants who had been recruited in the Middle Atlantic States, were

# JACKSON'S ATTACK

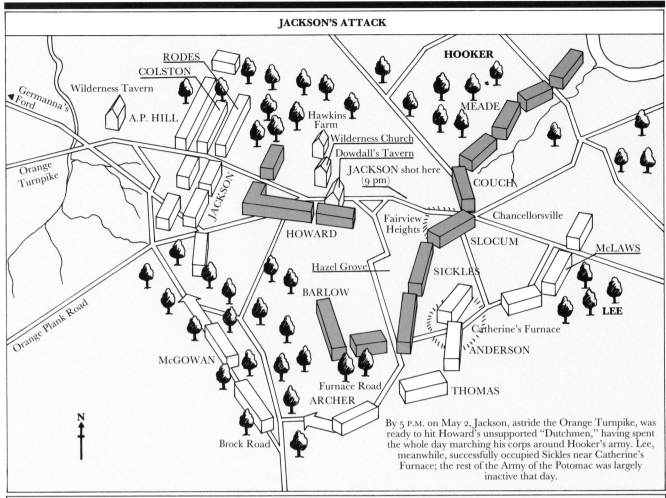

By 5 P.M. on May 2, Jackson, astride the Orange Turnpike, was ready to hit Howard's unsupported "Dutchmen," having spent the whole day marching his corps around Hooker's army. Lee, meanwhile, successfully occupied Sickles near Catherine's Furnace; the rest of the Army of the Potomac was largely inactive that day.

## THE OPPOSING FORCES

### UNION ARMY OF THE POTOMAC
Major-General Joseph Hooker

Headquarters Detachments (Brigadier-General M. R. Patrick): 6 brigades of infantry, 3 of engineers, 2 batteries of artillery, parts of 3 cavalry regiments plus support detachments.
Artillery Reserve (Brigadier-General Henry J. Hunt in nominal command): 12 batteries.

#### I Corps
Major General John F. Reynolds

First Division (Brigadier-General James S. Wadsworth: brigades of Phelps, Cutler, Paul and Meredith.
Second Division (Brigadier-General John C. Robinson): bridgades of Root, Baxter and Leonard.
Third Division (Major-General Abner Doubleday): brigades of Rowley and Stone.
Strength: 39 regiments of infantry and 10 batteries of artillery.

#### II Corps
Major-General Darius N. Couch

First Division (Major-General Winfield S. Hancock): brigades of Caldwell, Meagher, Zook and Brooke.
Second Division (Brigadier-General John Gibbon): brigades of Sully, Owen and Hall.
Third Division (Major-General William H. French): brigades of Carroll, Hays and MacGregor.
Strength: 46 regiments and 8 batteries.

#### III Corps
Major-General Daniel E. Sickles

First Division (Brigadier-General David B. Birney): brigades of Graham, Ward and Hayman.

Second Division (Major-General Hiram G. Berry): brigades of Carr, Revere and Mott.
Third Division (Major-General Amiel W. Whipple): brigades of Franklin, Bowman and Berdan.
Strength: 42 regiments and 11 batteries.

#### V Corps
Major-General George G. Meade

First Division (Brigadier-General Charles Griffin): brigades of Barnes, McQuade and Stockton.
Second Division (Major-General George Sykes): brigades of Ayres, Burbank and O'Rorke.
Third Division (Brigadier-General Andrew A. Humphreys): brigades of Tyler and Allabach.
Strength: 39 regiments and 9 batteries.

#### VI Corps
Major-General John Sedgwick

First Division (Brigadier-General William Brooks): brigades of Brown, Bartlett and Russell.
Second Division (Brigadier-General Albion Howe): brigades of L. Grant and Neill.
Third Division (Major-General John Newton): brigades of Shaler, Browne and Wheaton.
Light Division (Colonel Hiram Burnham): this was a brigade-sized command.
Strength: 47 regiments and 10 batteries.

#### XI Corps
Major-General Oliver O. Howard

First Division (Brigadier-General Charles Devens): brigades of von Gilsa and McLean.
Second Division (Brigadier-General Adolph von Steinwehr): brigades of Buschbeck and Barlow.
Third Division (Major-General Carl Schurz): brigades

of Schimmelfennig and Krzyzanowski.
Strength: 29 regiments and 6 batteries.

## XII Corps
### Major-General Henry Slocum

First Division (Brigadier-General Alpheus S. Williams):
brigades of Knipe, Ross and Ruger.
Second Division (Brigadier-General John W. Geary):
brigades of Candy, Kane and Greene.
Strength: 29 regiments and 5 batteries.

## Cavalry Corps
### Brigadier-General George Stoneman

First Division (Brigadier-General Alfred Pleasanton):
brigades of Davis and Devin.
Second Division (Brigadier-General William Averell):
brigades of Sargent and McIntosh.
Third Division (Brigadier-General David Gregg):
brigades of Kilpatrick and Wyndham.

Reserve Brigade (Brigadier-General John Buford).
Strength: 27 regiments and 6 batteries of horse artillery.

### Estimated Totals

Hooker's Army of the Potomac had 274 regiments of infantry, 27 of cavalry, and 79 batteries of artillery plus detachments, giving it an approximate total of 140,000 men and 404 guns. Although such totals are impressive, a large part of the Union army did not take part in the battle. The entire cavalry corps, except for one brigade, was away on the Richmond raid. Nearly half the troops of Hooker's front line either saw no action at all or for only a brief period of time. The Confederates were rarely opposed by more than two Union corps at a time: most of the Union infantry was either in reserve, marching or countermarching, or was positioned beyond reach of the battle.
Losses: 1,606 killed, 9,762 wounded, and 5,919 captured or missing. Total: 17,287.

# CONFEDERATE ARMY OF NORTHERN VIRGINIA
### General Robert E. Lee

## I Corps (part)

McLaws's Division (Major-General Lafayette McLaws):
brigades of Wofford, Kershaw, Semmes and Barksdale.
Anderson's Division (Major-General R. H. Anderson):
brigades of Wilcox, Posey, Mahone, Wright and Perry.
Corps Artillery (battalions under Colonels Alexander and Walton).
Strength: 40 regiments of infantry and 18 batteries of artillery.

## II Corps
### Lieutenant-General Thomas J. Jackson

Light Division (Major-General A. P. Hill): brigades of Heth, McGowan, Thomas, Lane, Archer and Pender.
D. H. Hill's Division (Brigadier-General R. E. Rodes): brigades of O'Neal, Doles, Iverson, Colquitt and Ramseur.
Early's Division (Major-General Jubal Early): brigades of Gordon, Hoke, Smith and Hays.
Trimble's Division (Brigadier-General R. E. Colston): brigades of Paxton, Jones, Nicholls and Warren.
Corps Artillery (Colonel S. Crutchfield): 6 batteries in battalions under Brown and McIntosh.
Strength: 70 regiments and 27 batteries.

### Reserve Artillery
### Brigadier General William Pendleton

Strength: 6 batteries in battalions under Cutts and Nelson.

### Cavalry Division
### Major-General J. E. B. Stuart

Brigades of Hampton, Fitzhugh Lee, W. H. F. Lee and Jones
Strength: 22 regiments and 4 batteries of horse artillery.

### Estimated Totals

Lee's Army of Northern Virginia had 110 regiments of infantry, 22 of cavalry, and 55 batteries of artillery, giving it an approximate strength of 65,000 men and 232 guns. Most of this army was continually engaged in the fighting. Lee took direct command of I Corps; II Corps was eventually led by J. E. B. Stuart after A. P. Hill and Jackson were wounded. Early's division was detached from II Corps; it remained under his own command.
Losses: 1,581 killed, about 8,700 wounded, and 1,708 captured or missing. Total: approximately 12,000.

dubbed the "Dutchmen" by their comrades, to whom they were culturally, linguistically, and religiously alien. Their commander, the one-armed Major-General Oliver Otis Howard, a native of Maine, had not helped to improve their morale. His distribution of bibles and religious tracts to his men, a large portion of whom were free-thinkers who had left Europe because of pressures from the Church, only widened the gulf between the "foreigners" and their Yankee general.

Howard had placed his three divisions, each in two lines, to cover the two miles of turnpike that ran west from Chancellorsville through Dowdall's Tavern, Hawkins Farm, and the Wilderness Church.

The right flank, under Brigadier-General Charles Devens, Jr., bent slightly to the north of the turnpike and was held by a two-gun section of Captain Julius Dieckmann's 13th New York Light Battery and two regiments–barely 900 men–from Colonel Leopold von Gilsa's brigade. Between those troops and the river to the north were nearly three miles of undefended, unpatroled Wilderness.

The passage of Jackson's corps had not gone unnoticed by the German troops. Many of the officers had served in European armies and had had the foresight to send out advanced posts in front of their positions to warn them of any hostile movement. A "rolling reconnaissance by fire" was initiated by the local commanders in the late afternoon, if only to allow their men to test their weapons and ease their boredom.

In accordance with Jackson's scheme of attack, four brigades from Rodes's division were forced into a single line, brigades abreast. Some 400 yards ahead of them, a line of skirmishers was posted for security reasons and to guide the main body forward. Colston formed up his division a few hundred yards behind Rodes, while A. P. Hill struggled to align his division, most of which was still marching through the woods, in the rear of the corps. Colonel Crutchfield, the corps chief of artillery, lined up his batteries along the narrow road; he kept them still limbered, so that they would be ready to move up in support once the clearings farther along the turnpike were reached.

As the Union infantry were settling down to cook their evening meal, their rifles neatly stacked and their guns unmanned, the Rebel bugles sounded the charge. The noise frightened scores of rabbits, squirrels, and deer who bolted out of the forest toward the Union line, pursued by the Georgia and Carolina infantry. The Southern lines crashed out of the woods that Hooker had thought impenetrable, their nerve-shattering yell screeching from 25,000 throats, and fell upon the unprepared defenders. Overlapped and outweighed, von Gilsa's brigade disappeared. McLean's brigade could fire only three volleys until they, like von Gilsa's men on their right, broke. A Union line, hastily formed 400 yards to their rear, stood for barely 10 minutes against the Southern tide.

The entire right flank collapsed within a quarter of an hour; isolated pockets of resistance were given a wide berth by the racing Confederate infantry and subsequently fell to Crutchfield's well-directed guns. Mobs of frightened, squealing soldiers fled toward Howard's headquarters at Hawkins Farm. Major-General Carl Schurz formed his division across their front to try and rally them. Lieutenant-Colonel Joseph Dickinson, a visitor from Hooker's staff, urged Howard, who had strapped a stand of colors to his body and was vainly trying to rally the mob, "Oh, General, see those men coming down from that hill way off to the right, and there's the enemy after them. Fire, oh, fire at them: you may stop the flight!" To his credit, Howard refused to fire on his own men. The press of fugitives now became too great for Schurz's men to handle, and the mass of broken infantry swept them along with irresistible force.

Hooker, who did not learn of the attack until after 6 P.M. (the thick undergrowth muffled the sounds of battle), began to shift troops to meet the attack. Individual batteries and brigades were turned to the west, the reserve began to move, and Sickles was alerted to the threat in his rear.

Jackson kept his men moving. The leading brigadiers had been told not to stop for any reason until they had advanced to the clearing 1,000 yards down the pike. "They are running too fast for us. We can't keep up with them," one of his officers joked. "They never run too fast for me, sir. Press them, press them!" Jackson retorted, determined to give them no chance to form. "Stonewall" was in excellent spirits. "The Virginia Military Institute will be heard from today!" he repeatedly shouted as he rode the lines.

By 6 P.M. his line had reached its first objective, the Talley plateau, but the attack was almost spent. After marching for eight hours in the humid forest without rest or food, and having charged at the run for nearly an hour through tangled undergrowth, Jackson's left-hand brigades had lost their cohesion. Colquitt, who had turned his brigade to the southeast to face an imaginary threat, had jumbled up the troops behind him on the right flank. To the Confederate front, "Leather Breeches" Dilger, a former artillery officer from Baden, Germany, skillfully handled his single Union battery to frustrate and harass Rodes's advance, buying time until a new defensive line could be formed.

A row of unfinished entrenchments, barely knee-high, which ran to the west of Dowdall's Tavern, was manned by Brigadier-General Adolph von Steinwehr's unscathed division and some of the braver men of Devens's and Schurz's commands. Indeed, Steinwehr's 5,000-man force appeared for a time to be the wall behind which Howard's shattered corps might rebuild. However, the Confederate infantry had not lost all momentum. Joined by Bechman's horse-artillery battery, Rodes's men furiously stormed the trench line. Von Steinwehr's division, its flanks turned on both ends, held for less than 20 minutes before the weight of Confederate men and metal forced it to break.

On the heights of Hazel Grove, which commanded Sickles's extended positions and the Chancellorsville zone, Captain Huntingdon had three batteries from III Corps deployed in the direction of the Rebel attacks. Pleasanton, whose Union cavalry command was scattered throughout the area in search of Howard, brought up Martin's horse battery and deployed alongside the gun line. The III Corps mule train, panicked by the battle, stampeded through their positions, followed by several hundred cheering Southerners. However, the fire of 22 well-manned guns threw the disorganized Rebels back into the cover of the woods.

The 8th Pennsylvania Cavalry, sent off to the north to locate Howard's flank, suddenly found itself in the midst of a Confederate brigade. Still in a column of twos, the horsemen drew sabers and pistols in an attempt to cut their way out. "We struck it as a wave strikes a stately ship," a young trooper later wrote, "the ship is staggered, maybe thrown on her beam ends, but the wave is dashed into spray, and the ship sails on as before." Although the action did little to disrupt Rodes's attacks, news of it spread quickly throughout the Rebel corps. "Be alert for enemy horsemen in the woods" ran the word.

At Catherine's Furnace, Sickles tried to extricate himself from what was quickly becoming a pocket. At 9 P.M. he ordered a bayonet attack to force his way back to Hazel Grove, whereupon his two divisions stumbled into both Union and Confederate lines. A three-sided fight developed in the darkness as Sickles's men faced, to the left, the Rebels and, to the right, Slocum's Union infantry. The Union artillery, which kept firing in the direction of the Confederate army all night, also turned its fire on Sickles's beleaguered corps. Caught in an impossible situation, Sickles eventually managed to pull his bruised divisions back to the south.

The rest of the Union line began to settle at about this time. Reynolds's I Corps had arrived in the rear of Hooker's army, after completing its long march from Sedgwick's line to the Rapidan fords. Couch and Slocum sent their corps into line, and quantities of guns were deployed to face Jackson. Unknown though this was to either army, Jackson was overlapped on both flanks, and, had he advanced, would have found himself enclosed by relatively fresh Northern troops.

Except for XI Corps, which had done no worse than any other soldiers might have done in the circumstances, the Army of the Potomac was in excellent fighting form. Hooker had more soldiers who had spent the day in reserve than Lee had in his entire force. If their commander had only possessed a little more courage, they would have been in an excellent position to crush Lee's army. Hooker had lost his nerve, however, and concentrated on a withdrawal to a shorter line, hoping that Sedgwick would storm Fredericksburg and break through the Confederate lines from the rear.

"Stonewall" on the other hand, had not lost his nerve. Despite the lateness of the hour and the confused state of his corps, the brightness of the moon gave him hope of a night attack with which to finish

"Stonewall" Jackson receives his mortal wound from a bullet fired in error by one of his own men.

off the Army of the Potomac. Riding ahead of his lines with several members of his staff, Jackson scouted the new Union positions. As he rode toward his own men, a group of North Carolina infantry on the alert for Union horsemen opened fire on his party. A. P. Hill shouted to the Carolinians to cease firing, but a second volley poured into them, wounding Jackson three times. Although the infantry quickly discovered their error, the firing drew the attention of a Union battery. Jackson was still being carried from the field when canister and shell from the enemy artillery swept the ground, wounding Hill and killing the litter carriers. The wounded generals were sent to the Wilderness Tavern where Dr. Hunter McGuire treated them. Jackson's wounds were serious, but not mortal: although his left arm had to be amputated, it was expected that such a strongly built man would soon recover.

With both Hill and Jackson wounded, J. E. B. Stuart, who had been away on a flank harassing Union cavalry, was given command of the corps. Neither of the injured generals was in any condition to advise him, and it fell to Rodes to explain the situation to him. Stuart then wisely ordered the corps to halt and reform; daylight would be soon enough to renew the attack.

When Sickles tried to withdraw on the morning of May 3, Stuart followed him like a wolf after a herd of sheep, sending in Archer's brigade and Alexander's artillery battalion to secure the high ground at Hazel

Grove as the men of III Corps fell back from it. Some 1,500 yards northeast of the grove was the main Union position. Colonel Alexander put more than 40 guns on the heights and began to enfilade the Federals at Fairview and Chancellorsville.

The bushy crest of Hazel Grove obscured the Confederate gunners from their Union counterparts. The volume and accuracy of Alexander's fire, reinforced by infantry assaults delivered all along the right wing of Hooker's force, began to disrupt the Union line. As his men withdrew around 9.30 A.M., fire from three directions fell upon them. Hooker lost what little courage he had been able to summon, and General Warren of the engineers was directed to prepare a new line to which the beleaguered army could retreat.

A ball from a Confederate cannon shattered a column of Chancellor House while Hooker was leaning on it. Temporarily stunned, Hooker turned over his command to Couch. The fiery commander of II Corps was all in favor of a counterattack, but Hooker retained sufficient control of himself to direct Couch to fall back on Warren's line. Although he still had a large portion of the army free, the Rebel attacks and Hooker's mismanagement had left Couch with little choice other than to retreat. Sickles's corps had crumbled. Two Rebel brigades had wedged themselves into his line in the early morning and could not be dislodged. Brigadier-General Joe Revere, a descendant of the famous Revolutionary War patriot, had pulled his New

York Excelsior Brigade to the rear without orders, and this in turn completely collapsed Berry's division.

Next, Hancock's neighboring division of Couch's corps was put under tremendous pressure. This came about as Anderson's veterans arrived from Catherine's Furnace, sent in by Lee to try to link up with Stuart. Soon, as the Rebel divisions closed on each other, their opponents became trapped in a pocket. Two Union divisions, those of Hancock and Geary, found themselves fighting back to back against the Rebel assaults. Hancock strung out his 11 regiments into two lines, a few hundred yards apart, and fought off attacks from two sides. Geary, steadily being ground down, reported to Couch, "My division can't hold its place. What shall I do?" Couch replied, "I don't know, but do as we are doing; fight it out." Geary's division did just that, for about another 10 minutes, before it was overwhelmed. At 10 A.M. Hancock received permission to withdraw. With the woods on fire all around, roasting the wounded where they lay helpless, Lee and Stuart reunited their army.

As Lee prepared to continue the attack on the battered, reeling, and disorganized Union line, couriers rushed up with the news that Union troops were marching on his rear: Sedgwick had stormed the heights at Fredericksburg.

"Uncle John" Sedgwick, a favorite among the troops and noted for his common sense and courage, had the largest corps in Hooker's army (more than 23,000 men and 54 guns). It was with this force, plus the 4,500 men of Brigadier-General John Gibbon's division, that he had advanced upon Jubal Early's position on Marye's Heights.

Sedgwick, Hooker, and Early had been classmates at West Point, graduating together in 1837. Early was thus well known to Sedgwick, and also respected by him; and although Sedgwick had been spared the slaughter at Fredericksburg in the previous December (he had been recuperating from a wound received at Antietam), he knew how badly Burnside's attack on Marye's Heights had collapsed.

At 5.45 A.M. on May 3, after marching most of the night from his bridgeheads south of the town, Sedgwick began a 20-minute bombardment of Early's lines. Most of the 10,000 men in Early's command were strung out along the Heights, a few being left in reserve. In the night there had been confusion over an order apparently directing Early to send his guns to Lee; but by dawn this had been finally sorted out, and the artillery was being re-emplaced as the Union bombardment began.

Major-General John Newton opened the attack across the Hazel Run on Early's right. Twice his division was thrown back. Gibbon sent his men to turn the Rebel left, but heavy artillery fire stalled him at the canal. Sedgwick had no option but to go in head-on where Burnside's army had been broken in the winter.

Sedgwick figured that all the charges Burnside had made had faltered because the attacking lines had stopped to return fire and had thrown themselves on the ground for cover. This tactic had kept the men under fire longer than necessary. To prevent this, he not only ordered his men not to fire until they reached the Rebel line at the Sunken Road, but sent the front ranks across the open field at the double with unloaded rifles and fixed bayonets! The momentum of this charge carried Newton's men over the walls and up onto the crest, scattering the defenders. Brigadier-General Albion Howe's division captured the heights south of the town and, together with

Newton, forced Early to retreat down the Telegraph Road, where he was struggling to rally his shattered division. At a cost of 1,500 men, Sedgwick had captured Early's line, 15 guns, a stand of colors, and over 1,000 prisoners.

Without cavalry or horse artillery, Sedgwick could not hope to catch the fleeing Rebels; so, leaving Gibbon to secure the field, he moved the rest of his corps toward the Salem Church, hoping to reach Hooker by nightfall. His advance was slowed by Brigadier-General Cadmus Wilcox's Alabama brigade: by leapfrogging from hill to hill, his regiments bluffed and baffled the Union commander until Early could begin to re-form; at the same time, troops of McLaws's and the rest of Anderson's divisions were marching to his aid.

Newton's troops, exhausted from their morning assaults, followed Brooks's division, with Howe bringing up the rear. The advance was rudely stung at the wooded crest of Salem Church Hill, as Brooks's men met those of McLaws. The Union artillery shelled the woods for 20 minutes before Brooks's infantry went into the attack, only to be broken up by heavy Rebel fire. A second wave reached the top of the hill, but a Confederate counterattack chased them off.

As night fell, Sedgwick found his corps strung out in a five-mile-long horseshoe. Early, meanwhile, was reforming below Fredericksburg, and Lee was between him and Hooker. The Army of the Potomac, only a few miles away, was contained by Stuart with only 25,000 troops. Lee was now concentrating against Sedgwick to trap him against the river. The Rebel attacks of May 4 were uncoordinated and did no appreciable damage to Sedgwick, except to cut him off from Gibbon at Fredericksburg. That night a thick fog rolled in from the river, and VI Corps fell back to a pontoon bridge hurriedly constructed by Brigadier-General Benham's engineers. Rebel scouts crept up to the river bank to fire signal rockets for Lee's batteries, but their indirect fire had little effect on the withdrawal. By dawn Sedgwick's entire corps was north of the river. Robbed of his chance to crush Sedgwick, Lee turned back to concentrate on Hooker, whom he planned to attack on May 6.

On the night of May 4, Hooker had summoned a council of war and, despite the contrary views of his generals, directed the army to retreat across the river. The stormy weather almost wrecked the pontoon bridges, but masked the retreat from Confederate scouts. On the morning of May 6, Lee faced only empty trenches and deserted campsites: once again, the Army of the Potomac had been beaten, but not annihilated. Although Chancellorsville ranks as one of the finest battles fought by Confederate arms, it was a decidedly empty victory. Nothing had come of the week-long battle in terms of strategic position or military advantage. The only result was that the casualty lists were increased for both armies: some 13,000 Rebels and 17,000 Yankees had fallen. Outnumbered by two to one, however, Lee could not afford to trade casualties at so close a rate, especially without any offsetting strategic gains.

The North, despite losing a battle in which it had had all the advantages, indirectly gained from the defeat. Not only did Chancellorsville hasten the removal of Hooker from command, it removed from the lists the North's fiercest individual opponent: Thomas "Stonewall" Jackson. Although he had seemed likely to recover, the valiant hero of the Confederacy lapsed into a fever and died on Sunday May 10. His was the one loss the South could never replace.

Above
Hooker's army comes under strenuous Rebel pressure on the third day of the battle.

Below
Sedgwick's pontoon bridges span the Rappahannock at Fredericksburg.

# GETTYSBURG
## July 1-3, 1863

Dead horses at Trostle's House near the Peach Orchard. Here, on the second day of the battle, Bigelow's 9th Massachusetts battery ferociously opposed a sweeping Rebel advance; many of the battery's horses were shot down in the crossfire during the assault.

"Under the leadership of 'Fighting Joe' Hooker, the glorious Army of the Potomac is becoming more slow in its movements, more unwieldy, less confident of itself, more of a football to the enemy and less an honor to the country than any army we have yet raised." So declared the *Chicago Tribune* shortly after the Northern calamity at Chancellorsville in May 1863. The Midwestern newspaper was making an observation shared by much of the war-weary Union. The once-grand army of George Brinton McClellan had declined into a tatterdemalion specter of its former power and glory.

If the instruments of war were in poor condition in the Army of the Potomac, the hands that guided them were even more feeble. A rash of promotions and political reshuffling had played havoc with the higher ranks. Only three of the 19 infantry divisions and none of the seven corps were led by the same men who had commanded them at Antietam, less than a year before. Nearly half the general officers (12 out of 26) were political favorites. Worst of all, however, the army commander had no faith in himself–a view shared by his President, his General-in-Chief, and a good many of his subordinates, including the talented Major-General Darius Couch, who had resigned after the Chancellorsville Campaign.

The morale of the Yankee soldiers who lined the banks of the Rappahannock was even lower than that of their generals. Consistently defeated by the Rebel army, only to be made to bounce back under the leadership of some dandified dreamer who led them into an even larger disaster, the men of the Army of the Potomac had begun to believe themselves incapable of beating Lee's Confederates. The latter, meanwhile, had also begun to think that they were invincible. The morale of the Army of Northern Virginia was flying as high and as proudly as the "Stars and Bars" itself over the capitol in Richmond.

The return of Longstreet and his two divisions from the Carolinas brought Lee to the peak of his strength in manpower, a total of nearly 70,000 tough, veteran "Invincibles." Stuart's cavalry, recently augmented to 10,000 sabers when several Valley and Virginia regiments were gathered under his standard, and the artillery, nearly 300 cannon strong, were also at the height of their proficiency and reputation. However, Lee did have one problem in common with his opponents, that of inexperienced leaders.

The loss of "Stonewall" Jackson in the Chancellorsville campaign had severely crippled Lee's style of warfare; without an *alter ego* whom he could dispatch to manage part of the field, Lee would have to be everywhere if he wished to be sure that his plans were being carried out correctly. The only experienced corps leader left to him was Lieutenant-General James Longstreet; "My Old Warhorse," Lee called him. Although undoubtedly one of the finest officers in the Confederacy, Longstreet's exaltation of the defense was tragically unsuited to Lee's inspired, almost reckless method of conducting a war.

Now that the initiative was temporarily in their hands, the Confederate commanders found themselves at odds over how to proceed. Some, headed by Longstreet, supported the idea of transferring a corps to the West to smash the Union threat there, either in Tennessee or along the Mississippi. Lee, on the other hand, had gone to war not only for the Southern cause as a whole, but in particular for his native Virginia; he would not therefore countenance any such abandonment of his home soil. He argued that if the Army of the Potomac were allowed time to rebuild, it could sweep across Virginia and on to Richmond and once more attempt to capture the Rebel capital. The Virginia countryside was already strained beyond endurance and could not tolerate another Union offensive; in addition, the Confederate army could no longer maintain itself along the devastated Wilderness line in the present pre-harvest season.

So, for the second time in less than a year, Robert E. Lee determined to invade the Union. To Longstreet this plan was an offensive strategy which would be offset by defensive tactics, *i.e.* they would pick a spot somewhere in the North and force Hooker to throw himself at them. To A.P. Hill and Ewell, who had been promoted to command the other two army corps, it was a march of vengeance to teach the Yankees that the South was unconquerable. To the dashing horseman, J.E.B. Stuart, it was another chance to enhance his reputation at the expense of the ponderous Union army. Lee, however, saw it as a means of drawing the Northern wolves away from the Confederacy; he hoped his campaign would force Lincoln to recall his far-flung legions from every theater, from the Carolinas to the Mississippi, to fight one great decisive battle on the fertile soil of Pennsylvania. This battle Lee's "Invincibles" would, as always, win.

Lee slowly shifted his army from the Rappahannock lines to the northwest along the Blue Ridge Mountains, leaving A.P. Hill to man the trenches lest Hooker make a dash for Richmond while he himself was still getting into position for the invasion. To screen Lee's march, Stuart assembled his cavalry at Brandy Station, about 25 miles upstream from Fredericksburg. On June 5 Stuart put on a grandiose review, mainly for the benefit of the local ladies, finishing it off with a mock battle. The show was so impressive that Stuart decided to keep his men together and repeat it for Lee when he arrived on the 8th. Word of Stuart's showmanship also reached Major-General Alfred Pleasanton, however, who set off with 11,000 troopers to "review" Stuart's men and to confirm Hooker's suspicions that Lee was indeed on the move.

On the morning of June 9, 1863, Pleasanton's troopers emerged from the river mist and surged across the Rappahannock fords below Stuart's headquarters. Although initially surprised, Stuart made haste to recall his flank brigades and throw in whatever regiments he could find. Charge and countercharge swept across the river plain and on to the nearby Fleetwood Hill as the cavalry of both sides fought with sabers, pistols, and shotguns in the largest and most traditional cavalry battle of the war. The experience of the Southerners eventually began to tell, and when the leading elements of the Rebel infantry columns began to enter the lists, Pleasanton wisely withdrew. Although they had been beaten, losing twice as many men as the Confederates, the morale of the Union cavalry was substantially raised by this encounter. For once they had taken the initiative and stood up to their tutors; from then on, the US cavalry was no longer just a collection of mounted scouts and couriers, but a cohesive battlefield arm.

His intelligence reports now confirmed, Hooker in desperation wired Halleck for permission to cross the Rappahannock and head for Richmond while Lee was still maneuvering. The commander of the Army of the Potomac was quickly rebuked. Lee's army, not the city of Richmond, was his real target;

above all, the security of Washington was his primary responsibility. Hooker was thus to march parallel to Lee's columns as they moved north, so protecting the capital against any sudden attack. Infuriated and downcast, Hooker ordered his depots to be moved and the infantry to prepare for a series of forced marches northward.

Halleck meanwhile ordered his Valley commander, General Schenck, to withdraw his outposts at Winchester and to prepare for the defense of Harpers Ferry. Schenck twice refused to obey and relented only when Halleck threatened to remove him from his command. By then, however, it was too late. On June 14, Dick Ewell and the Valley Veterans stormed Major-General Robert Milroy's division at Winchester, capturing over half his 10,000 men along with 23 cannon and 200,000 rounds of small arms ammunition.

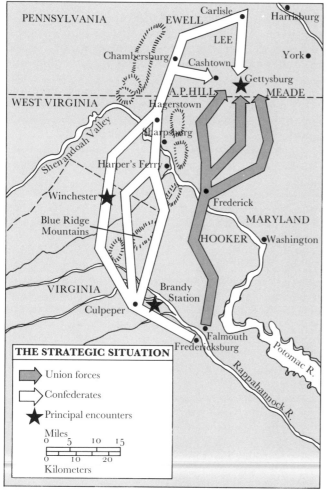

THE STRATEGIC SITUATION

→ Union forces

⇨ Confederates

★ Principal encounters

Miles
0    5    10    15
0    10    20
Kilometers

While Ewell was surging through the Valley, Longstreet and Lee were crossing the Potomac near Sharpsburg. As the Confederates moved forward, Lincoln called for 100,000 volunteers from Maryland, Pennsylvania, and Ohio to meet the crisis. Only some 37,000 men showed up, however, about two-thirds of them from New York militia units deficient in both training and logistical support.

To create confusion among the Union leadership (and, he hoped, to restore his tarnished reputation), Stuart requested that he be allowed to ride around Hooker's army, gathering supplies, destroying supply bases, and collecting information about the Yankee army. Lee, who still controlled over half the Rebel cavalry for army duty, allowed Stuart to take three brigades on the raid, extracting from him a promise to meet the main army at York, deep inside Pennsylvania.

On June 27, when the Union army was at Fred-

erick, Maryland, a courier from Washington arrived to inform General Meade that he was to succeed Hooker to the command of the Army of the Potomac. Once again, Lincoln's patience with a general had been strained to the limit, and a new man had had to be found. Unlike his predecessors, however, Meade was only a simple old soldier and not an ambitious "savior of the Republic."

Meade quickly put his men back on the road, each corps marching within supporting distance of at least one other. As Lee moved north, so did Meade, his columns crossing the Maryland border into the rich, garden-like state of Pennsylvania. Their arrival in this peaceful "Dutch" country considerably brightened the spirits of Meade's soldiers. Here the women and children cheered them as they marched through the towns, giving them food and drink as they passed; many of Pennsylvania's sons were in those long blue columns. Morale improved and the will to fight returned, because, as one soldier put it, "We felt some doubt it was ever going to be our fortune to win a victory in Virginia, but no one admitted the possibility of a defeat north of the Potomac."

In contrast, as his men moved deeper into the Pennsylvania countryside, Lee became increasingly uneasy over the whereabouts of the Union army. With Stuart off on his glory ride (capturing wagon trains and burning bridges) and the rest of his cavalry strung out to cover the mountain passes, the commander of the Army of Northern Virginia was reduced to relying on spies and captured newspaper accounts for intelligence of his enemy. His concern increased when he learned that the ineffective Hooker had been replaced by that solid old regular, George Meade. "General Meade will commit no blunder on my front," remarked Lee, "and if I make one he will make haste to take advantage of it." To deny his new adversary the chance to defeat him in detail, Lee began to concentrate his army around the Cashtown Pass and the asphalt roadway through South Mountain which led to the sleepy college town of Gettysburg, just above the Maryland border.

On June 30, Brigadier-General John Buford had pushed his Union cavalry division to the outskirts of Gettysburg. Encountering a reconnaissance party of Rebel infantry, he obtained assurances from the commander of I Corps, Major-General John Reynolds, that Union foot-soldiers would arrive by late morning, then dismounted his men along McPherson's Ridge to delay any Southern advance.

Major-General Henry Heth, whose men had spied Buford's pickets that afternoon, asked his corps commander, A.P. Hill, for permission to chase away what he assumed were only local militia and head for Gettysburg, where a cache of shoes had been reported. Hill agreed, and on the morning of July 1, Heth's division, led by Brigadier-General James Archer's brigade, headed down the Chambersburg Pike for Gettysburg. Archer's front regiments, deployed in a three-deep cloud of skirmishers, swarmed across the Wiloughby Run at the foot of McPherson's Ridge and ran into Buford's skirmishers: they, armed with breech-loading carbines, kept a steady stream of fire on the advancing Rebels.

The mass of Confederate skirmishers swiftly climbed the slope in the face of the cavalry's fire, gaining momentum as another brigade, under Jefferson Davis's nephew Joseph, came in on their left. As Archer's men reached the crest of the ridge, they met a crashing volley of musketry from the Iron Brigade, the finest unit in Meade's army ("First Brigade, First

Division, First Corps of the First Army of the Republic"). Reynolds had kept his promise. As the Rebel infantry staggered back into the valley, a burly Irish private named Patrick Maloney grabbed Brigadier-General James Archer–the first of Lee's generals ever to be taken prisoner. Maloney proudly presented his prize to Major-General Abner Doubleday. Doubleday, an old army friend of Archer, ran with outstretched hand to greet the newly captured officer. "Archer, I'm glad to see you!" exclaimed the Union general. "Well, I'm not glad to see you by a damn sight," grunted Archer, refusing even to shake his old comrade's hand.

Reynolds, whose attack had gained valuable time for the Union infantry, had been struck by a Rebel sharpshooter's bullet while directing the advance. Doubleday had taken control of the battle; he it was who sent a messenger to notify Meade.

To the north of the Turnpike, Davis's Mississippi brigade was still advancing strongly, despite Archer's repulse. The brigade swept over the ridge, pushing Wadsworth's infantry back into the valley. The leading Confederate units funneled into a deep railroad cutting in an attempt to outflank the withdrawing Union line. Doubleday rushed ahead two regiments which gained the top of the cut, whose sides were too steep to climb, and there captured an entire Confederate regiment. Davis's attack was turned into a rout, and the Union I Corps regained the ridge.

While Heth was re-grouping for a second attack, Howard's "Dutchmen", the discredited survivors of Jackson's attack at Chancellorsville, filed through Gettysburg to take up a line east of the ridge. Leaving his best division, Steinwehr's (the only one which had stood for even a respectable time in the Wilderness fight), on the commanding heights to the south of Gettysburg, Howard linked up with Doubleday to form a line above the town. As Howard was positioning himself, Ewell's leading elements were flooding down the northern thoroughfares onto the plain above the town. Quickly noticing its value, Rebel gunners moved to Oak Hill, above the Yankee line, and began an enfilade of Doubleday's positions. Major-General R.E. Rodes then launched his division at the hinge of the two US corps. Rodes put three of his five brigades into line and advanced haphazardly against Howard's XI Corps. The attack soon miscarried as one brigade drifted wide of the mark and another stalled on the way in. The third brigade was almost destroyed when a Union regiment, springing from cover behind a stone wall, delivered a brutal volley into its flank.

Riding up to Heth's headquarters Lee immediately forbade any further attack until Longstreet and the rest of the army could arrive on the field. Rodes, however, had already launched a second onslaught with his remaining brigades, carrying the stone wall which anchored the junction of the two Union corps. Howard's shaky infantry had begun to give way when Jubal Early's division charged with its full force against their right flank. Brigadier-General Alex Schimmelfennig, a former Prussian officer in command of Howard's Third Division, led his men in a race for the rear, stopping in Gettysburg to hide in a storm cellar, where he remained for the next few days. Indeed, Brigadier-General Gordon, leading Early's attack, had met such feeble resistance that when an officer asked him, "General, where are your dead men?" Gordon replied, "I haven't got any sir, the Almighty has covered my men with his shield and buckler."

Observing the collapse of the Union right, Lee reversed his decision to avoid a battle and ordered Heth's battered division, supported by Pender's which had just come down the turnpike, to launch a frontal assault on McPherson's Ridge. Although the I Corps line was still holding its ground, supported by the corps artillery, which was lined up hub-to-hub across the road, the rout of the "Dutchmen" behind it made any stand suicidal. Brigadier-General Solomon Meredith covered the forced withdrawal of I Corps with his Iron Brigade, taking heavy casualties, as much as 80 percent in one regiment.

As the Union remnants streamed back to the rallying point provided by Steinwehr's men on Cemetery Hill, Major-General Winfield Scott Hancock (commanding II Corps) arrived to take control of the field. The finest tactical commander in the Army of the Potomac, Hancock quickly sized up the terrain and sent his men to defend the wooded summit of Culp's Hill to the east, thus protecting the Baltimore Turnpike. Fresh Union troops, notably those of XII Corps, arrived in the late afternoon to fill in his lines along the Cemetery Ridge, a mild rise of ground that ran south from Cemetery Hill.

Lee was still not anxious to enforce a major engagement: half his army was still absent and only Ewell's troops were in any condition to fight. When his men had finished rounding up the stragglers of XI Corps from the streets of Gettysburg, Ewell reformed his command and marched toward the new Union line. Since his orders from Lee were discretionary, however, and left the decision to attack in his hands, Ewell decided to bivouac his men for the night and consider the advisability of an assault in the morning.

During the night, both sides brought up reinforcements to flesh out the battle lines. Meade arrived late in the night and agreed with Hancock that the position was a good one, allowing him to wage either an offensive or a defensive battle. Lee, too, thought the ground well suited to the offensive. Despite Longstreet's pleadings that they should maneuver around Meade and find a good defensive position, Lee decided to concentrate the entire army there and then, and attack the next afternoon.

By noon on July 2, both armies were almost fully concentrated; only the Union VI Corps and Pickett's Confederate division were still on the road. Even J.E.B. Stuart had at last made his appearance. Lee planned to place Longstreet's two divisions on the far right and to sweep across the Emmitsburg Road in an oblique attack on the Union-held Cemetery Ridge. The brigades were to be launched in succession, gradually building from left to right until the entire length of the Union line was afire with bombarding artillery and the blows of Rebel infantry. Accordingly Longstreet, though himself still unhappy about fighting an offensive battle, slowly moved his two divisions through the covered ground behind the ridges west of the Emmitsburg Road in the hope of surprising the Union defenders.

While Longstreet was shifting his men, Major-General Dan Sickles was chafing at the bit to move ahead. Considering his position along the ridge to be inferior ground when compared to the rise to his front, Sickles prepared to advance into a salient whose apex was at the Peach Orchard. Although a good line, it was too long for his corps to hold; his two divisions were spread so thinly that they could not rest their flanks in line with the rest of the army, either on the Round Top to their left or on the ridge to their right.

# THE COMMANDERS

Major-General George G. Meade, USV

Lieutenant-General James Longstreet, CSA

George Gordon Meade (1815–72) had been an engineer most of his life. Born in Spain, raised in Pennsylvania, and educated at West Point, Meade had "a most soldierly and veteran-like appearance; a grave, stern countenance–somewhat oriental in its dignified expression yet American in its race horse gauntness" (Edwin Coddington, *The Gettysburg Campaign*).

Raised from the rank of brigadier-general of Volunteers to major-general after his success at Fredericksburg, where his Pennsylvania reservists had broken through Jackson's line (the only bright spot that day for the Union), Meade soon took command of a corps. Proving himself a fighter and a capable administrator, Meade rapidly gained the men's support when Lincoln gave him command of the Army of the Potomac. A solid old soldier, he was businesslike and strong on discipline–unlike his more lenient predecessors. He also had the violent impatience of a perfectionist, and although not the general most likely to win a fast-paced, offensive battle, he could be relied on to keep a clear head in a defensive fight.

His caution and attention to detail are what prevented Meade at Gettysburg from sweeping off Cemetery Ridge after Pickett and smashing Lee's army; such a move, many contemporaries and later historians have claimed, would have ended the war. However, a careful consideration of the state of the Union forces after that battle–tired, confused, and still very much in awe of the wily Lee–lends more weight to Meade's decision than to those of his armchair critics.

After Gettysburg, Lincoln retained Meade in command of the Army of the Potomac, even when Grant arrived from the West to take overall command and himself led the Union forces in the field. The hook-nosed old engineer, who had given the Eastern armies their first victory, kept the post to the end of the war. He was thus that army's only long-term commander, and by far its most successful.

James "Old Peter" Longstreet (1821–1904) never wanted to lead men in glorious charges or become a great name in history. Before the Civil War, his ambition was to become chief of the Army Paymaster's Department, in which he was a major.

When his native South Carolina declared itself against the Union, he resigned his blue uniform to wear the Rebel gray, asking for a place in the payroll service. But, like most West Pointers, he could not escape being awarded the responsibility of command.

The slow, plodding qualities most people impart to born accountants were not lacking in Longstreet. Although praised for his tactical common sense, he was strongly disposed toward a defensive style of warfare. "I never like to go to battle with one boot off," he often said when scolded for taking his time.

Longstreet had an overbearing belief that he was always right, even when told otherwise by a commanding officer. Whether that soldier was Beauregard, Bragg, or Lee himself, when he believed them wrong he would tell them, and follow orders so grudgingly that he came within a hair's breadth of insubordination. His constant reluctance to accept any of Lee's plans for the Battle of Gettysburg strained relations between the two men to such a degree that, afterward, Lee gladly sent him and his corps to the West. "Longstreet is a very good fighter when he gets in position and gets everything ready," said Lee of him, "but he is so slow."

Although blessed with several faults which did not make him a popular man to serve with, Longstreet did have his good points. His trench system along the Rappahannock, which presaged those of the Western Front in World War I, was a considerable advance in defensive warfare. Nor did he lack courage, and was often found in the middle of his infantry, edging them on to the fight. Irascible to the end, Longstreet served the Confederacy far better on the battlefield than he would have done in a desk job.

While the fighting rages about them, wounded Rebel prisoners are escorted from the battlefield.

As soon as he realized what Sickles was doing, Meade rode hell-for-leather to stop the maneuver. Sickles, who thought he had the authority to determine where his corps could best fight, was taken aback by Meade's fiery tongue-lashing, but agreed to withdraw his men. Meade then shouted, "I wish to God you could but the enemy won't let you!" and rode off to gather men to support Sickles. By isolating his corps in the salient, Sickles had given the Confederate divisions of John Bell Hood and Lafayette McLaws an excellent opening. Hood began the attack by swinging his right wing around and over the crest of the heavily wooded Round Top. Colonel William Oates, braving the continual fire of Union sharpshooters, brought his Alabamans over the rough ground and began the climb up Little Round Top.

At his signal station on Little Round Top, Brigadier-General Gouverneur K. Warren could see the entire Confederate advance. Sent by Meade to report on the condition of the flank, Warren saw the danger to the army if this natural gun-platform were occupied by Rebel artillery: from Little Round Top, the entire Union line on Cemetery Ridge could be enfiladed. Ordering his signal detachment on the summit to wave their flags excitedly, to suggest great activity and numbers of troops, Warren rode off to find someone to defend the Union left flank.

Colonel Strong Vincent, at 26 the youngest brigade commander in Meade's army, heard one of Warren's couriers tell his divisional commander, James Barnes (First Division, V Corps), that men were needed at the Little Round Top. Without awaiting orders, Vincent rushed his own brigade to the heights, Colonel Joshua Chamberlain's 20th Maine Regiment to the fore. The Northerners hit Oates's Alabama riflemen among the crags and brush at the summit of the Round Top. After a fierce struggle, the exhausted Rebels tumbled back to the valley, leaving the heights to the Union infantry.

The remainder of Law's Alabama brigade rushed up the western face of Little Round Top while Vincent's men were roughing up Oates's command.

Warren, spying his old regiment, Colonel Patrick O'Rorke's 140th New York, flung them at the screaming Confederates just before the gray wave crested the summit. Two guns of Hazlett's battery (V Corps) were hauled up the slopes and, although they could not bear at anything closer than the Devil's Den, a pile of boulders about 100 yards to the west, their reassuring sound greatly aided the New Yorkers. Slowly, and at great cost, the Little Round Top was secured.

The condition of the rest of the Union flank was anything but secure. The Devil's Den constantly changed hands; Meade hurled brigade after brigade into the fray, stuffing seven brigades into the area between the Wheatfield and the Round Tops. Then, just as the Union counterattack seemed about to succeed, Longstreet himself led McLaws's full division in an assault on the Wheatfield and the Peach Orchard. The Union front collapsed, several batteries either overrun by Barksdale's Mississippians or cut down by the heavy fire of Alexander's artillery. On the Union side, Birney's division was isolated, Caldwell's was ruined, and the right-flank division under Brigadier-General Andrew Humphreys was severely hit by Barksdale's Mississippi brigade and then by three brigades from R.H. Anderson's division. The whole Union flank below the Peach Orchard began rolling back to the ridge, with Hood's and McLaws's men fiercely pursuing them.

With the Confederates now gaining the momentum Lee had planned, the Union left flank was in serious danger. Units from six individual corps were jumbled together and had no single commander. Hancock rode down from his position to do what he could. Moving forward with Gibbon's and Hays's divisions, he grabbed the first regiment he came to. "What regiment is this?" Hancock shouted. "First Minnesota," replied its colonel, William Colvill. "Colonel, do you see those colors?" Hancock said, and pointed to the Alabama flag in the center of Anderson's advancing division. "Then take them!"

Although he had only eight companies, 262 men, Colvill charged down the slope of the ridge and

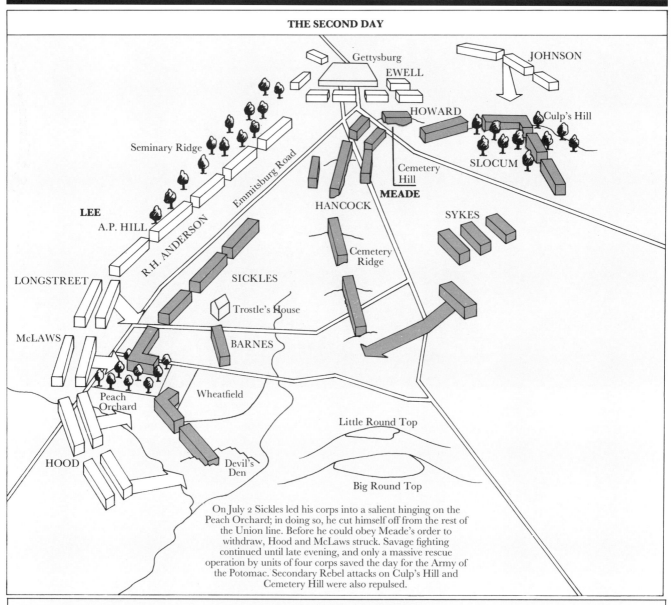

## THE SECOND DAY

On July 2 Sickles led his corps into a salient hinging on the Peach Orchard; in doing so, he cut himself off from the rest of the Union line. Before he could obey Meade's order to withdraw, Hood and McLaws struck. Savage fighting continued until late evening, and only a massive rescue operation by units of four corps saved the day for the Army of the Potomac. Secondary Rebel attacks on Culp's Hill and Cemetery Hill were also repulsed.

## THE OPPOSING FORCES

### UNION ARMY OF THE POTOMAC
Major-General George G. Meade

#### I Corps
Major-General John Reynolds

First Division (Brigadier-General James S. Wadsworth): brigades of Meredith and Cutler.
Second Division (Brigadier-General John C. Robinson): brigades of Paul and Baxter.
Third Division (Major-General Abner Doubleday): brigades of Biddle, Stone and Stannard.
Strength: 32 regiments of infantry and 6 batteries of artillery.

#### II Corps
Major-General Winfield S. Hancock

First Division (Brigadier-General John Caldwell): brigades of Cross, Kelly, Zook and Brooke.
Second Division (Brigadier-General John Gibbon): brigades of Harrow, Webb and Hall.
Third Division (Brigadier-General Alexander Hays): brigades of Carroll, Smyth and Willard.
Strength: 46 regiments and 5 batteries.

#### III Corps
Major-General Daniel Sickles

First Division (Major-General David B. Birney): brigades of Graham, Ward and de Trobriand.
Second Division (Brigadier-General Andrew Humphreys): brigades of Carr, Brewster and Burling.
Strength: 37 regiments and 5 batteries.

#### V Corps
Major-General George Sykes

First Division (Brigadier-General James Barnes): brigades of Tilton, Sweitzer and Vincent.
Second Division (Brigadier-General Roman Ayres): brigades of Day, Surbank and Weed.
Third Division (Brigadier-General Samuel Crawford): brigades of McCandless, Fisher and Martin.
Strength: 35 regiments and 5 batteries.

#### VI Corps
Major-General John Sedgwick

First Division (Brigadier-General Horatio Wright): brigades of Torbert, Bartlett and Russell.
Second Division (Brigadier-General Albion Howe): brigades of Grant and Neill.
Third Division (Major-General John Newton): brigades of Shaler, Eustis and Wheaton.
Strength: 36 regiments and 8 batteries.

## XI Corps
### Major-General Oliver O. Howard

First Division (Brigadier-General Francis Barlow): brigades of von Gilsa and Ames.
Second Division (Brigadier-General Adolph von Steinwehr): brigades of Coster and Smith.
Third Division (Major-General Carl Schurz): brigades of Schimmelfennig and Krzyzanowski.
Strenth: 26 regiments and 5 batteries.

## XII Corps
### Major-General Henry Slocum

First Division (Brigadier-General Alpheus S. Williams): brigades of McDougall, Lockwood and Ruger.
Second Division (Brigadier-General John W. Geary): brigades of Candy, Cobham and Greene.
Strength: 28 regiments and 4 batteries.

## Cavalry Corps
### Major-General Alfred Pleasanton

First Division (Brigadier-General John Buford): brigades of Gamble, Devin and Merritt.

Second Division (Brigadier-General David Gregg): brigades of McIntosh and J. Gregg.
Third Division (Brigadier-General Judson Kilpatrick): brigades of Farnsworth and Custer.
Strength: 31 regiments and 9 batteries of horse artillery.

## Artillery Reserve
### Brigadier-General Robert O. Tyler

Brigades of Ransom, McGilvery, Taft, Huntington and Fitzhugh.
Strength: 24 batteries.

## Estimated Totals

Meade's Army of the Potomac had 240 regiments of infantry, 31 of cavalry, and 71 batteries of artillery, giving it an approximate total of 85,500 men and 370 guns. The overall Chief of Artillery was Brigadier-General Henry Hunt, his command being divided among brigades attached to army corps and the artillery reserve.

Losses: 3,155 killed, 14,529 wounded, and 5,365 captured or missing. Total: approximately 23,049.

# CONFEDERATE ARMY OF NORTHERN VIRGINIA
### General Robert E. Lee

## I Corps
### Lieutenant-General James Longstreet

McLaws's Division (Major-General Lafayette McLaws): brigades of Kershaw, Semmes, Barksdale and Wofford.
Pickett's Division (Major-General George Pickett): brigades of Garnett, Kemper and Armistead.
Hood's Division (Major-General John Bell Hood): brigades of Law, Robertson, Anderson and Benning.
Strength: 52 regiments of infantry and 22 batteries of artillery.

## II Corps
### Lieutenant-General Richard Ewell

Early's Division (Major-General Jubal Early): brigades of Hays, Avery, Smith and Gordon.
Johnson's Division (Major-General Edward Johnson): brigades of Stuart, Williams, Walker and Jones.
Rodes's Division (Major-General R.E. Rodes): brigades of Daniel, Iverson, Doles, Ramseur and O'Neal.
Strength: 59 regiments and 20 batteries.

## III Corps
### Lieutenant-General Ambrose Powell Hill

Anderson's Division (Major-General R.H. Anderson): brigades of Wilcox, Wright, Mahone, Lang and Posey.
Heth's Division (Major-General Henry Heth): brigades of Pettigrew, Archer, Davis and Brockenbrough.
Pender's Division (Major-General William D. Pender): brigades of Perrin, Lane, Thomas and Scales.
Strength: 57 regiments and 20 batteries.

## Cavalry Division
### Major-General J.E.B. Stuart

Brigades of Hampton, Fitzhugh Lee, Robertson, Jenkins, Chambliss and Jones (Brigadier-General John Imboden also commanded a portion of the Rebel horse but did not fight at Gettysburg).
Strength: 27 regiments and 6 batteries of horse artillery.

## Estimated Totals

Lee's Army of Northern Virginia had 168 regiments of infantry, 27 of cavalry, and 68 batteries of artillery, giving it a total strength of approximately 75,000 men and 287 guns.
Losses: about 4,000 killed, 18,000 wounded, and 5,150 captured or missing. Total: approximately 27,000.

into the center of several thousand Confederates. The shock of the charge stalled the masses of Southern infantry for a few precious minutes, time enough for Gibbon's division to come into line on the barren ridge. Fewer than 40 men of the Minnesota regiment came back from the charge, but they brought with them the Alabama flag.

Units from I, II, and XII Corps converged on the left flank to halt the Rebel drive. The commander of VI corps, Major-General John Sedgwick, had kept his men marching all night long and his bands playing continuously while they covered the last 30 miles to Gettysburg; he now led his men into the fight for the lower ridge. The weight of numbers finally began to tell. The Rebel attack, which had reached a peak when Barksdale, his white hair streaming over his shoulders, had led his brigade on to the ridge only to be flung off again, began to fall back. No further support came from Hill's corps, so Longstreet pulled his men back to the Peach Orchard line under the cover

of Alexander's guns. The fighting continued throughout the late evening in the Devil's Den. The Irish Brigade, after being given conditional absolution by its chaplain, Father Corby, joined the scattered regiments of III Corps in a fight in which, according to Shelby Foote in *The Civil War, a Narrative*, "every fellow was his own general. Private soldiers gave commands as loud as the officers; nobody paying attention to either."

With only 11 brigades, eight from his own corps and three from Hill's, Longstreet had fought six full US divisions and innumerable detachments; put more plainly, a little more than 15,000 men had attacked nearly 30,000 and had held their ground admirably. As he was pulling back, Longstreet could hear the sound of Ewell's cannon, announcing the attack by the Confederate II Corps on Culp's Hill and Cemetery Hill.

At 5 P.M. six hidden batteries opened fire on the Union hills. Although subjected to tremendous counterbattery fire by the more numerous and well-emplaced Union guns, the II Corps artillery of Colonel Wainwright continued to give support as the infantry went in. Major-General Edward "Old Clubby" Johnson, brandishing the hickory stick that gave him his nickname, charged up Culp's Hill against the remnants of Wadsworth's division and the Iron Brigade. Faced by the veterans of I Corps, now well dug in, Johnson's men made little progress, but on their right Stuart's Virginia and North Carolina infantry took an abandoned line of trenches and slammed into the five upstate New York regiments of Brigadier-General George Greene. "Pop" Greene, at 62 the oldest brigadier in the Army of the Potomac, was ready for them. A professional engineer, Greene put his 1,300 men behind a traverse of five-inch-thick earth and logs. The Confederates fell back to the deserted trench behind them.

As Johnson was getting mauled, Jubal Early attacked Cemetery Hill. Howard, with the remnants of his XI Corps, held this key position in the Union northern flank. Through the falling darkness and the heavy smoke, two Rebel brigades threw themselves up the hill. Crossing three lines of rifle pits, lunettes, and stone walls, the North Carolina and Louisiana brigades knifed into the "Dutchmen," who, true to form, took to their heels. Howard desperately tried to rally his men, but only a handful, under Colonel Krzyzanowski, stood their ground. Battery I, 1st NY Light Artillery, fought with handspikes, rammers, and fence rails against the men of Early's division. However, the Rebel infantry soon cleaned the hill of Yankees and came down the southern slope. There they saw a body of men: because it was quiet and because they expected that Longstreet would have carried the ridge, they mistook the men for fellow Southerners. As they slowed down, the regiments of the Union II Corps roared into them; gathering darkness was lit by flashes from the Northerners' muskets and the noise of arms was interrupted by the booming voice of their commander, Colonel Samuel S. Carroll. Without support, the near-victorious Rebel infantry withdrew over the crest and settled in the rocks and bushes at the base of the hill.

At his council of war that night, Meade and his subordinates decided to sit and defend for one more day. With both their flanks heavily attacked but still holding, Meade predicted that the point of Lee's next attack would be the center. Brigadier-General John Gibbon, whose division held that portion of the line, recalled, "I expressed the hope that he would, and told General Meade, with confidence, that if he did we would defeat him."

Lee, too, had learned that Meade's flanks were secure, yet he planned to send Ewell back into the fray again in the morning to draw off the Union reserves from the center. While Stuart's cavalry made a wide swing to come in behind the Union army, disordering its rear areas and cramping its movements, Lee proposed to crush Meade's center with the grandest charge of infantry ever made, supported by the greatest cannonade ever heard in the Western Hemisphere. His corps artillery officers assembled 170 guns in a solid mile-and-a-half front in front of Cemetery Ridge. When their fire had sufficiently smothered and confused the defenders, 15,000 Southern infantry would scream the Rebel yell and follow Major-General Pickett up the slopes of Cemetery Ridge and cut the Union army in half.

Longstreet did not share his commander's enthusiasm for this grandiose assault plan. Barely concealing his rage and frustration, the I Corps commander told Lee, "General, I have been a soldier all my life. I have been with soldiers engaged in fights by couples, by squads, companies, regiments, divisions and armies, and should know as well as anyone what soldiers can do. It is my opinion that no 15,000 men ever arrayed for battle can take that position." Despite the vociferous objection of his most experienced officer, the man to whom the overall control of the charge was entrusted, Lee refused to be shaken from his faith in the Rebel infantrymen, a faith which even the previous two days of fierce but inconclusive combat had not marred.

In the morning while Longstreet prepared his units for the attack, Ewell had already begun his assault. Throughout the previous night, the II Corps commander had pushed seven brigades into the cover of the boulders, stone walls, and ravines along his front. At 8 A.M. the attack commenced; its target was the Baltimore Pike on the other side of Culp's Hill.

O'Neal's brigade went forward and was immediately pinned down by the concerted fire of five US batteries. Walker led his brigade to support O'Neal, only to suffer the same result. Johnson then launched the rest of his division, in two lines, up the slopes of Culp's Hill, determined to sweep the defenders

(Major-General Henry Slocum's XII Corps) off the wooded crest. The attack was caught in a crossfire of canister and musketry so violent that, according to the description in Edwin Coddington's *The Gettysburg Campaign,* "the men were mowed down with fearful rapidity . . . the greatest confusion ensued–regiments were reduced to companies and everything mixed up. It came near to being a rout." The Union batteries fired as fast as their gunners could load them, and the riflemen laid down such a heavy fire that the front rankers were continually being sent to the rear to rest and clean their weapons. For over three hours, the Confederates were pounded by fire and metal until

On the third day, the survivors of Pickett's battered division approach to within yards of the Union gun line.
From the Gettysburg Cyclorama, painted by Paul Philippoteaux.

they finally withdrew from the hill.

Soon after 11 A.M., the front began to fall silent. Over the entire battlefield there was an uncertain quiet. Men nervously played cards, dug in, or were drilled by officers anxious to give them something to do. Hancock, in charge of the Union center–a low stone-wall and rail-fence breastwork along the upper section of Cemetery Ridge–put his two divisions in an extended line so that all 5,500 men could bring their fire to the front. From the woods known as Ziegler's Grove, on the right, to the clump of trees some 500 yards to Hancock's left, the infantry of II Corps braced themselves for action in the eerie stillness

pervading the field. The Rebels, too, waited.

At exactly 1 P.M. by his watch, Longstreet told Colonel Alexander to break the silence. Two signal guns barked out the command, letting loose the massed fire of the Confederate batteries. The 75 guns of I Corps, 60 of III Corps, 20 from II Corps on Oak Hill, and a dozen more from the reserve bore down upon Cemetery Ridge. The Union guns, 77 along the ridge, 55 on Cemetery Hill, and six on Little Round Top, took up the challenge–despite the order of the Chief of Artillery, Brigadier-General Henry Hunt, to save their ammunition for the Confederate infantry.

For the better part of two hours, nearly 300 cannon roared across the mile-wide valley. Despite the smoke and the tendency of his gunners to over-shoot (many of their shells landing amid the Union trains, headquarters, and army stragglers behind the ridge), Alexander succeeded in concentrating the bulk of his fire against one Union battery at a time, caus-ing heavy casualties to Hunt's artillery. Eventually, worried over his lack of long-range ammunition, Alexander tried to determine if the Union line was beginning to crack anywhere. Around 3 P.M. 18 guns along Hancock's front were pulled out of line so that fresh guns could move in. Alexander hurriedly dashed off a note to Pickett, "For God's sake come quick. The 18 guns have gone. Come quick or my ammunition will not let me support you properly."

Pickett, the bottom man in his class at West Point, had so far only once seen combat in the war. Coming from a post in the West, he had been wounded early in the fight at Gaines's Mill and so until now had missed his chance for glory. Mounted on a shimmering black horse, dressed in a magnificent new uniform with blue cuffs, gauntlets, and a blue cap resting on a mountain of perfumed hair which hung in dark brown ringlets down to his shoulders, Pickett rode to the front of his men. As if remembering his gallantry of nearly 20 years ago when he was the first man over the ramparts at Chapultepec, the hand-some Virginian roused his men with the words, "Up men and to your posts! Don't forget today that you are from old Virginia!"

Alexander took forward 18 guns (the only ones with more than 15 rounds of long-range ammunition left) to support the Rebel infantry, who came forward in two thick lines on either side of his batteries. Petti-grew's and Trimble's men, six brigades, came down from Seminary Ridge on the left a few minutes ahead of Pickett's three Virginia brigades moving in from the right. Pickett's men obliqued to the north and Pet-tigrew's to the south until the two lines came together about midway along the valley. There, in a slight depression not 500 yards from the Yankee positions, and despite being under fire from Hunt's batteries, the Confederates dressed ranks. Pickett now took con-trol over the whole body of men, aimed the mass toward the clump of trees in Hancock's line, and sent them forward.

The guns of McGilvery's batteries at the lower end of Cemetery Ridge enfiladed the attacking lines, dropping as many as a dozen men with a single shot. Some 300 yards from the ridge, skirmishers began picking off the Rebel officers. Still they came, silent except for the drums beating a steady march. The left flank brigades of Brockenborough and Davis trailed slightly behind the main line. From Cemetery Hill, Major Osborn trained 31 guns of his XI Corps artillery on them. Barely recovered from their pound-ing on the first day, the sad Confederates reeled and were then hit in the flank by the 8th Ohio Regiment, posted out in front of Hays's division. The two brigades broke for the rear.

On the other flank, Pickett was attacked by the Vermont regiments of Brigadier-General George Stannard. The Union brigade advanced out of the line, pivoted 90 degrees to the right, and fired at pistol range into the flank of Kemper's brigade. The Vermont infantry then did an about-face and bore down on the flank of two support brigades from Anderson's division which had lagged behind Pickett and were unable to close up with him. These two brigades, Wilcox's and Perry's, rolled backward to the safety of their gun line.

While Union fire was devastating the flanks of their attack, Pickett's men had tended to pack themselves into a tight mass in the center; in so doing, they achieved the weight of numbers their commander had intended for his final assault. This was about to be launched.

Awaiting the Rebels were the men of Gibbon's and Hays's divisions; only a few raw recruits fired at long range. Brigadier-General Alexander Hays had his troops collect all the loose weapons they could find. After cleaning and loading, some men had as many as four rifles next to them, ready to fire. The 12th New Jersey, armed with old smooth-bores, loaded up with buckshot, so turning their aged muskets into deadly shotguns.

Their pace of 100 yards a minute became even quicker as the Rebels neared the II Corps line; then they broke into a running charge and the Rebel yell sounded from 15,000 throats. A wave of Pender's men led by Major-General Isaac Trimble hit Hays's breastworks, only to be met in the face by four successive lines of fire from rifles, New Jersey "shotguns," and Sharps breech-loaders. The flag of a North Carolina regiment briefly rose over the wall, but the Rebels went no further. Trimble fell, severely wounded. When an aide tried to rally the mob, Trimble told him, "No, the best thing the men can do is to get out of this. Let them go." And go they did, all the way to Seminary Ridge.

To their right, Brigadier-General Lewis Armistead put his hat on his sword and screamed, "Boys, give them cold steel," and led 150 men over the wall. The impetus of the charge and the weight of the men behind them pushed the Southerners through the line of Brigadier-General Alexander Webb's Pennsylvanians. Webb, new to his brigade, grabbed a nearby flag from the standard-bearer of the 72nd Pennsylvania, only to have it torn back by the angry standard-bearer. The men advanced a few feet and fired a scattered volley, but would not charge. Webb ran to the 69th Pennsylvania and tried to get them into the fight, but with a similar lack of success. The men just did not know who this fumbling general was!

Gibbon and Hancock both fell wounded as Colonel Norman Hall led a mixed Confederate brigade into the fight. Then, in what is romantically called the "high water mark" of the Confederacy, Armistead charged with his men into the fire of Cushing's battery, falling mortally wounded by the Union guns. Now the whole Union line was ablaze; even Hunt was riding along and discharging his pistol into the gray masses before him. The noise of the fighting was "strange and terrible, a sound that came from thousands of human throats, yet was not a commingling of shouts and yells but rather like a vast mournful roar"[1] as the men of both armies, rarely in organized units, fell upon each other. Outnumbered and outgunned, Pickett's charge collapsed. Two brigades came forward to cover the retreat, and the Rebel guns fired their last few rounds to give them confidence. The battle was as good as over.

To the east, while Pickett was hurling his division at the Union line, J.E.B. Stuart had reached an open field astride the Hanover Road, some three miles to the rear of Meade's army. As if to announce his presence and to "smell out" any Union horsemen, Stuart unlimbered one of his horse guns and fired several shots. Jenkins's brigade dismounted and formed a skirmish line behind some rail fences, just in case someone answered the shots. The reply was quick in coming: Brigadier-General George Armstrong Custer and his four Michigan regiments rode up, spotted the Rebel horse, and to the general's cry of "Come on you wolverines!" charged the Confederates. Stuart led his men, sabers and pistols drawn, into the swirling *mêlée*. Brigadier-General David Gregg and his Union cavalry division soon arrived and joined in Custer's fight. Both sides quickly broke off the action, the Yankees losing about 250 men, Stuart about 180. Gregg, however, won the field. An embittered Stuart, humiliated twice within a month, rode to rejoin Lee.

Lee had watched the main battle from Seminary Ridge, leaving the fight to Longstreet and Pickett. As the remnants of the grand charge–little more than 5,000 out of the 15,000 that had started–staggered back to the gun line, Lee rode out to meet them. His hat off, a mournful look on his face, he went among his men, asking their forgiveness, praising their gallantry, and urging them to stand against a possible counterattack. He told Pickett to place his men into line, but Pickett replied, "General Lee, I have no division." Lee comfortingly responded, "Come, General Pickett, this has been my fight and upon my shoulders rests the blame."

Despite their fairly light losses that afternoon (fewer than 2,000), the Union army was in no condition to mount a counterattack, least of all against an army which had a solid mile and a half of cannon still plentifully supplied with grapeshot and canister with which to defend itself. The whole Union line, furthermore, was a jumble of units over which no officer had any real control; Hancock, Sickles, and a score of other generals were out of action, and Meade, consequently, had no enthusiasm for a counterattack.

Thus ended the clash at Gettysburg. Both armies faced each other on July 4, Independence Day, refusing to move. That night, however, Lee acknowledged defeat and began moving south, a withdrawal which was steadily, if not brilliantly, followed by Meade. The heavy overall casualties (more than 50,000 altogether) left little taste for battle in either army. The decisive battle sought by Lee had ended in failure, but he had some consolation in that he had stemmed an invasion of Virginia and generally disrupted Union war plans in the east. Although events were turning against the Confederacy, whose cause in the West was doomed by the fall of Vicksburg on July 4, the war was not over. The Union was on top, but not yet victorious.

The spirit of the Southern army was far from broken. As one Rebel survivor of that grand July charge yelled to Lee while he rode the line to rally them, "We'll fight them sir, till hell freezes over, and then we'll fight them on the ice!" They would continue to do so for two more years.

[1] Shelby Foote, *The Civil War, a Narrative* (New York, 1958)

Above
View of the battlefield from the Confederate center looking toward the Union left at the Round Tops (center right).
The Emmitsburg Road (middle distance) and Cemetery Ridge are clearly visible. The ground shown includes the scene
of Longstreet's attacks on July 2 and (foreground) the fields where Pickett's division formed
for its attack on the third day.

Below
Dead of the 1st Minnesota infantry lie gathered for burial near the Wheatfield.

# CHICKAMAUGA

September 19–20, 1863

Johnny Clem (right) and his brother. Clem ran away from home and joined the army at the age of nine. At Chickamauga he shot a Confederate colonel who demanded his surrender. He retired from the army in 1916 with the rank of major-general.

In the summer of 1863, Chattanooga became the focus of one of the war's most savagely contested campaigns. Located in the southeastern portion of the state on a picturesque bend of the Tennessee River, the young city for some time had been spared the ravages of war. Now, as Union armies tightened their grip on the Mississippi Valley and challenged Braxton Bragg's Confederates for control of Middle Tennessee, the conflict edged inexorably closer.

Though difficult of access, in 1863 Chattanooga was possibly the most strategically important point in the Confederacy. It was at the same time a vital rail communications center and the gateway to Georgia and the Deep South; it also dominated the mountainous but fertile region of east Tennessee and northwest Georgia, a vast storehouse of grain, fodder, and livestock coveted by both governments. Additionally, from the Union viewpoint, conquest of the region would give heart to a large oppressed population of Union sympathizers. This consideration was dear to the heart of President Lincoln.

The geography of the Chattanooga region made campaigning difficult, and previously this may have helped protect the city from Union thrusts. The countryside is broken by a succession of parallel ridge lines which, though interrupted frequently by gaps, in those days were a major obstacle to troop movements. The river, which had so assisted Union operations in the spring offensive of 1862, was of little help at Chattanooga: its southwesterly course, conforming to the lay of the ridges, posed yet another obstacle to a Union advance. Moreover, the Northerner's vaunted gunboat fleet could not move upstream beyond the shallows at Muscle Shoals, Alabama, which lies 110 miles downriver from Chattanooga.

To these natural obstacles must be added the problems of logistics. River transport was not available, and the roads of east Tennessee were execrable, which made armies almost entirely dependent on the ramshackle, broken-down rail network of the region. No great force could move far from the rail lines, and campaigns in the area were generally of short duration, with neither side able to stockpile enough food, fodder, and matériel for prolonged operations. Chattanooga was the major Union objective because it sat astride the most important east-west rail connection in the Confederacy.

The first real threat to Chattanooga came when, after six months of methodical preparation, General William S. Rosecrans launched his Tullahoma Campaign (June 23–30, 1863). Rosecrans's 50,000-man Army of the Cumberland swept forward on a broad front from Murfreesboro, Tennessee, and winkled Bragg's numerically smaller Army of Tennessee out of its strong base at Tullahoma. Bragg was thoroughly confused by Rosecrans's complex maneuvering and chose to retire to safer ground south of the Tennessee River. His retreat, however, exposed Chattanooga and alerted Richmond to the imminent danger of a Union offensive toward Atlanta and the Deep South.

Rosecrans's thrust was a serious threat to the Rebel heartland, but at the time there was very little Richmond could do to help Bragg. The Tullahoma campaign was coincident with the great Union victories at Gettysburg and Vicksburg, and the Confederate authorities, anticipating the worst, had no reserves to spare for Tennessee. The news of Rosecrans's almost bloodless triumph caused jubilation in Washington. The Administration now felt that if the Rebels were pressed hard in all theaters, the rebellion would collapse. The Secretary of War, Edwin M. Stanton, reflected this mood when he telegraphed Rosecrans shortly after Tullahoma: ". . . Vicksburg is surrendered to Grant on the 4th of July. Lee's army overthrown, Grant victorious. You and your noble army now have the chance to give the finishing blow to the rebellion. Will you neglect the chance?"

Stanton's anxiety was seen to be justified as Rosecrans developed a McClellan-like case of the "slows," and his great army ground to a halt below Tullahoma. No amount of prodding from Washington could force "Old Rosy" to move before he was quite ready. He was a notoriously stubborn and independent man, but because he had shown that he could accomplish a great deal when he did move, he was tolerated. Finally, in mid-August the Army of the Cumberland, revictualed and reinforced to a strength of nearly 80,000 men (almost double the strength of Bragg's army), rolled forward again. Simultaneously, a small Union army under Ambrose Burnside advanced from Central Kentucky and menaced Knoxville and the Cumberland Gap.

The Confederate house of cards was now indeed on the verge of being tumbled, but the six weeks' respite following Tullahoma and the dissipation of Union pressure elsewhere allowed Richmond just enough time to order reinforcements to Bragg from other, quieter, theaters of operation. The first reinforcements, Simon Bolivar Buckner's command from Knoxville (8,000 men) and John C. Breckinridge's and W.H.T. Walker's divisions of Joe Johnston's Army of Mississippi (11,500 men), arrived before the end of the month, but they were too few to assist Bragg materially in the defense of the river line.

In the initial stages of the campaign, Rosecrans, maneuvering rapidly and decisively, used his superior numbers to deceive Bragg and render Chattanooga untenable. Rosecrans's left flank corps, Major-General Thomas L. Crittenden's, made a demonstration northeast of the town, which led Bragg to believe that the Union army would attempt a crossing of the Tennessee upriver from Chattanooga. When Bragg, in reply, concentrated at Chattanooga, Rosecrans seized the downriver crossings and on August 29 began moving troops over the river in force.

Before Bragg could recover from this blow, the Union corps of Major-Generals George H. Thomas and Alexander McD. McCook were swinging southwest of Chattanooga through gaps in the ridge lines and threatening his long line of communications with Atlanta. It was Tullahoma all over again, and Bragg was once more forced to withdraw. Chattanooga was evacuated, and Crittenden's corps entered the city on September 9, a day behind the retreating Confederates who retired via Rossville toward Lafayette, Georgia.

Bragg's retreat was a military necessity, but it was not nearly as precipitate as Rosecrans believed; he, meanwhile, was concentrating his scattered forces and preparing a devastating counterblow. Rosecrans erroneously believed that Bragg, now in full retreat, would not stop short of Atlanta. Bragg helped foster this delusion by sending scores of sham deserters into the Union lines to spread false stories of Confederate demoralization following the loss of Chattanooga. Unable to obtain proper intelligence of his opponents' whereabouts or intentions, Rosecrans carelessly allowed his three main army corps (a fourth corps, commanded by Major-General Gordon Granger, formed the army reserve) to blunder on into Georgia in the same widely dispersed marching order he had prescribed for the envelopment of Chattanooga. Thus, on September 9, when Bragg decided to assume the offensive, the Confederates at Lafayette were closer in marching time to each of the three Union corps than they were to each other.

From Crittenden on the left, at Chattanooga, to McCook on the right, at Winston's Gap near Alpine, Georgia, Rosecrans's front extended over 40 miles. Thomas, in the center at Stevens's Gap, was roughly equidistant from each flank. Each Union corps was, moreover, separated from its nearest neighbor by several days' hard marching. Bragg, massing opposite Thomas behind Pigeon Mountain, was screened by his active and powerful cavalry corps under Nathan Bedford Forrest and "Fightin' Joe" Wheeler. He had a strategic opportunity similar to that of McClellan on the eve of Antietam; he could, by prompt action, defeat Rosecrans's widely sepa-

attack Crittenden at daybreak on the 13th at Lee & Gordon's Mill on West Chickamauga Creek. But the bishop, to Bragg's chagrin, took a defensive stand and informed his chief that he could hold his position if the Yankees attacked him! When a second, peremptory order failed to move Polk, Bragg abandoned the venture altogether and withdrew his forces to Lafayette, where the army idled for a few precious days while he mulled over the possibilities of further operations against his vulnerable adversary.

The missed chances in McLemore's Cove and against Crittenden were the beginnings of a long string of bad luck for the Army of Tennessee. Rosecrans was now alert to the threat, and he worked hard to reunite his endangered corps, ordering McCook to close on Thomas at Stevens's Gap and directing Crittenden to hold the Rebels in check at Lee & Gordon's Mill until McCook and Thomas joined him.

Strategically, though, Bragg still held the upper hand. On September 11 he had learned that

Chattanooga in 1863, with Lookout Mountain in the distance.

rated columns in detail. Were he to succeed and thereby knock the Army of the Cumberland out of the war altogether, it would be a decisive blow for Confederate independence.

During the next five days (September 9–13), Bragg struggled mightily to achieve his aim. He struck first at Thomas's leading elements, which had advanced from Stevens's Gap into McLemore's Cove, a vast cul-de-sac bounded on three sides by steep ridges and drained on the northeast by West Chickamauga Creek, the Indians' "River of Death." But somehow Bragg's orders miscarried: his subordinates, notably Lieutenant-General D.H. Hill, commanding a corps, and Major-General T.C. Hindman, commanding a division of Buckner's corps, were unable to comprehend his scheme of maneuver and were overcome by a strange paralysis. No attack was made, Thomas withdrew, and Bragg turned next to deal with Crittenden, whose corps was advancing southward along the Chattanooga–Lafayette Road.

The task of crushing Crittenden was entrusted to Lieutenant-General Leonidas Polk, the pusillanimous bishop-general whom Bragg had detested since Shiloh. Polk, with Buckner in support, was ordered to

Longstreet's corps of Lee's Army of Northern Virginia (minus Pickett's depleted division) had been released by President Davis from the Rapidan front and was being hurried by rail to his position. Longstreet's 12,000 men, all seasoned veterans, would give him an advantage rarely enjoyed by Confederate commanders – a numerical superiority over the enemy. Bragg's confidence soared, and on September 14 he decided to move across Crittenden's front and swing around his northern flank to interpose his army between Rosecrans and Chattanooga. That done, he planned to sweep south, driving the Union troops into McLemore's Cove, where they would be destroyed. The Confederate army began to move on September 16, heading for the bridges across West Chickamauga Creek that lay opposite and above Crittenden's position.

Bragg intended to launch his general attack on the 18th, but once again his army proved to be an unwieldy machine, and the entire day was consumed by a leisurely approach march and some lively skirmishing with two Union cavalry brigades which contested the crossings downstream from Lee & Gordon's Mill. In spite of this delay, the Confederates did succeed in seizing their preliminary objectives, Reed's and Alexander's Bridges and the fords below Lee & Gordon's, and managed to push some troops over to the west side of the creek. The initiation of the turning movement, however, had to be deferred until the 19th; its postponement allowed Rosecrans another day in which to gather together his scattered forces. The delay weighed further against Bragg in that, when the battle opened on the 19th, the Union left was nowhere near where he had assumed it to be.

At this point the two armies were operating in Chattanooga–Lafayette Road, the north-south had descended and would not be dispelled until the opposing lines clashed in the woods west of the creek. Although Bragg knew the next day would bring battle, he did not know the true position of the Union army. Rosecrans, who had lately been informed by Washington that Lee was reinforcing Bragg, was not certain he had a battle on his hands, but he knew that he had to strengthen his vulnerable left flank. This

few man-made features of note, the most important being the Chattanooga–Lafayette Road, the north–south route which was the reason the battle was being fought. Most of the fighting was in the vicinity of this road, the Confederate objective being to drive the Union army either along it into McLemore's Cove or across it against the face of Missionary Ridge.

At dawn on the 19th, both armies were on the move. Thomas's corps filed to its post on Rosecrans's left, its leading elements stalking a supposedly isolated Rebel infantry brigade near Reed's Bridge; the Confederates were meanwhile preparing to turn Crittenden's supposedly open flank. The battle began in earnest at 7.30 A.M., when Colonel John T. Croxton's brigade of Brigadier-General John M. Brannan's division, XIV Corps, blundered into the Confederate concentration on the Reed's Bridge Road. Instead of the single unsupported brigade they were hunting, the Union troops ran into Forrest's cavalry and several

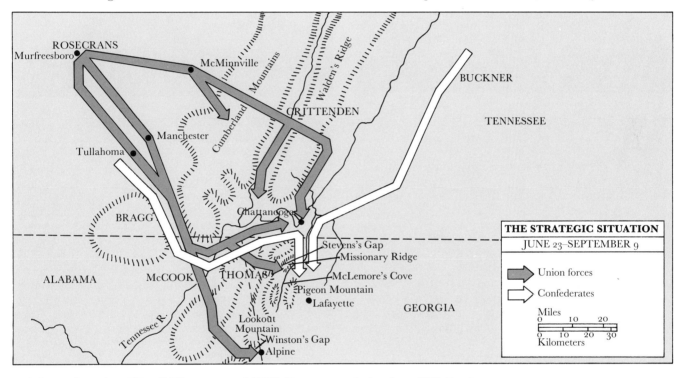

task he assigned to "Pop" Thomas and XIV Corps.

Thomas, with McCook trailing, began to shift north from McLemore's Cove at 4 P.M. on September 18. In 16 hours his corps completed a prodigious forced march that took it across Crittenden's rear by the Dry Valley Road and ended opposite the Confederate bridgehead at Reed's Bridge. McCook, following, replaced Crittenden at Lee & Gordon's, while Crittenden closed to the left and established a link with Thomas, the army's new left. Thus, by sun-up on the 19th Rosecrans had managed to form a fairly compact line of battle six miles long and parallel with the Confederate line near the creek. The maneuver negated Bragg's planned turning movement and meant that the armies would fight head-on in a gigantic engagement as one division after another piled into the fray.

The coming battle would be fought in a vast natural amphitheater hemmed by Missionary Ridge to the west and Pigeon Mountain to the east. The terrain was mostly flat and covered by a dense indigenous forest, broken here and there by farm clearings. Despite the proximity of the creek, there was little water to be found on the field, and the soldiers of both armies were to suffer acutely from thirst. There were

brigades of Walker's corps.

The fighting was at first desultory, following the pattern of the previous day's skirmishing, but then it became severe. The Rebels came on with a yell, driving the Federals back on their supports, and Croxton despatched a wry note to Thomas asking his chief just which one of the four or five brigades he had encountered should he capture? The rumble and rattle of the fight near Reed's Bridge shocked Bragg, who had not expected a battle in that quarter, miles northeast of where he believed the extreme Union right to be. His plans upset, the Confederate commander responded by feeding troops to the front as fast as they could be brought up.

Rosecrans, too, threw in more and more men, and the flame of battle spread south through the woods, consuming constant drafts of men until it burned itself out in a furious late-afternoon fight at the Viniard Farm, a little more than a mile due north of Lee & Gordon's Mill. From the beginning, Thomas's corps fought superbly, beating back numerous attacks on its own front and assisting Crittenden in blunting and repelling the deep penetration of the Union center by Major-General A.P. Stewart's "Little Giant" division–the most serious Rebel threat

# THE COMMANDERS

Major-General William S. Rosecrans, USV

General Braxton Bragg, CSA

**W**illiam Starke Rosecrans (1819-98), a native of Cincinnati, Ohio, had little formal education in his early years. Nonetheless, he gained admittance to West Point (Class of 1842) and there achieved high academic honors. Resigning his army commission in 1853, he returned to Cincinnati, where he became a wealthy and influential businessman. At the outbreak of the war, he helped to train the powerful militia of the State and, with George B. McClellan, a fellow-Ohioan, led it against Robert E. Lee's Confederates in a minor but important campaign that severed the Unionist enclave of West Virginia from Virginia. When McClellan was called to Washington to take over from McDowell after First Bull Run, Rosecrans became the commander of the Department of Western Virginia.

In June 1862 Rosecrans succeeded Pope as commander of the Army of the Mississippi and subsequently won two victories against Rebel forces in Mississippi. In October 1862 he replaced Buell as commander of the Army of the Ohio when the latter was removed for lack of aggressiveness. Rosecrans soon took the offensive with his new command (renamed the Army of the Cumberland) and fought a bruising tactical stand-off with Bragg's Confederates at Stone's River. Next, after months of inactivity, Rosecrans launched his Tullahoma Campaign (June 23-30, 1863), a masterpiece of strategic movement in which he maneuvered Bragg out of Middle Tennessee and across the Tennessee River. But at Chickamauga Rosecrans lost his nerve. His conduct became public knowledge when his Chief-of-Staff indiscreetly leaked the story to the press. Rosecrans was relieved of command and served out the war in Missouri.

Rosecrans was an able commander–energetic, intelligent, and pugnacious. He was solicitous for the welfare of his men, and they loved him like a father. In strategy he preferred the indirect, bloodless approach; tactically, he was a tenacious defender, but he seemed incapable of executing a battlefield offensive.

**O**f those who shared in the glory of Zachary Taylor's Mexican War triumph at Buena Vista (February 23, 1847) Braxton Bragg (1815–76) stood foremost. A young officer of artillery, Bragg was immortalized by Old Zack's crisp order delivered at the crisis of the battle: "A little more grape, Captain Bragg!" The victory catapulted Taylor into the Presidency and made war heroes of Bragg and Jefferson Davis, then a militia colonel commanding the Mississippi Rifles, which supported Bragg's battery. Bragg and Davis subsequently became fast friends. This friendship, remarkable in the sense that the two shared a genius for making enemies and were notoriously difficult to get along with, lasted until Bragg's death.

Both men suffered from a variety of psychosomatic ailments, notably dyspepsia and migraine, and both were stern, imperious taskmasters–perfectionists who demanded, but often did not receive, unquestioning and prompt obedience from inferiors in rank. But, with Bragg, who did not possess Davis's advantages of upbringing, there was no aristocratic veneer to hide these all-too-evident flaws of personality, which seriously undermined his men's confidence in him.

As commander of the Army of Tennessee, Bragg had few friends. His insistence on military routine, on discipline, and doing things "by the book" was probably calculated to relieve his insecurity, but the effect was stultifying. The soldiers feared and despised him. His officers saw him as a pettifogging despot. Thus, although Bragg probably possessed more military aptitude than any other Confederate general, his lack of self-confidence and his dour, unapproachable personality isolated him from his officers and men. He was prone to lose his nerve at the approach of battle and often sunk into indecision during the course of a fight. As a result, his superbly planned battles usually degenerated into bloody slugging matches. No more appropriate military epitaph for Bragg can be found than Nathan Bedford Forrest's lament, "What does he fight battles for?"

of the day. Stewart's proud Shiloh veterans burst from the woods at 2.30 P.M. and wrecked the still-forming battle line of two of Crittenden's divisions near the Chattanooga–Lafayette Road. Supported by Brigadier-General Bushrod Johnson's division on their left, they then pierced the Union center as far as the Glenn–Kelley Road and Rosecrans's headquarters at Widow Glenn's House. But, like a great wave dissipating its force against a beach, the advance of the "Little Giants" wore itself out and lost cohesion with the very depth of its penetration. Disorganized and bereft of support, Stewart's men were easily overwhelmed and pushed back when Thomas organized converging attacks on both of their flanks.

The last of Bragg's blows fell at the Viniard Farm at 4 P.M., about the time Stewart's attack petered out. The attackers were the men of Major-General John Bell Hood's division, heroes of Gettysburg's second day and the fight on Little Round Top. Hood's three brigades were the first of Longstreet's 12,000 to join Bragg. Hurried to the front, Hood's warriors formed on Johnson's left and fell on Rosecrans's shaky right flank. In a furious combat, described by a newspaper correspondent as "fighting front to front, fighting on the flanks, enfilading and cross firing," the Rebels drove deep but suffered the same fate as Stewart's division. Unsupported, they were buffeted back by Union reinforcements.

Hood's offensive was the first firm evidence to reach a hitherto-disbelieving Rosecrans that Lee's Virginia veterans had indeed reinforced Bragg. Rosecrans now knew that the very life of his army, and with it the Union cause, was at stake.

As the sun set and a lull came over the battle at Viniard's, Bragg renewed the combat on the northern flank, and Thomas's embattled men found themselves under attack again, this time by fresh Graycoats from Major-General Patrick R. Cleburne's division supported by Walker's corps. The Irish-born Cleburne, a British Army veteran and sometime lawyer and pharmacist, was one of the South's great offensive-minded soldiers; but, in Thomas, one of the staunchest defenders produced by either side during the war, he had a willing adversary. In a bizarre twilight battle fought in dank thickets overlaid with a murky, sulphurous pall of smoke, Cleburne's men battered back Thomas's line, driving it for a mile or more before they came to a stop, exhausted. Thomas was bent but not broken, and by 7 P.M. the battle flickered to a close all along the line.

Chickamauga's first day had produced some of the most confused, desperate fighting of the war. Both armies had found themselves in a battle they had expected but, for one reason or another, were not well situated to fight. The Union army, trailing on to the field continually from the south, had managed by a strange combination of chance and design to contain and turn back each successive Confederate thrust. Bragg, thwarted in his original design, had been unable to launch the kind of massive, coordinated attack he desired. Thomas, in fact, could hardly believe his good fortune. Normally reticent, he fairly bubbled with excitement in describing his day's work to Rosecrans. "Whenever I touched their flanks they broke, General, they broke," he said. Rosecrans, for his part, never seemed to grasp what was happening tactically, but he had at least accomplished the strategic feat of concentrating his dispersed army on the field of battle.

The lines of battle were now drawn and further marked out by the carnage in the smoldering woods and thickets west of the creek. Neither side had gained an advantage. The armies were battered but not crippled, and both sides looked forward to a renewal of the fray on the 20th. At 11 P.M. Rosecrans convened a council of war at his headquarters. The Widow Glenn's tiny log cabin was jammed with officers, most of them exhausted like Thomas, who catnapped in a corner. Though satisfied with his army's performance, the Union commander recognized that he could not hope to hold an extended six-mile front in the face of renewed Confederate pressure. He therefore ordered a realignment, contracting his front still further and refusing his right flank.

In the new alignment, Thomas still commanded the left, but now, because the Union corps had become intermixed, he held it with two of his own, one of McCook's, and one of Crittenden's divisions. Next, in the center and bending back across the Lafayette Road, were Thomas's two separated divisions (Brannan's and Major-General James S. Negley's). Behind them and in reserve was Crittenden with two divisions (Brigadier-General Horatio Van Cleve's and Brigadier-General Thomas J. Wood's). McCook, with his two remaining divisions (Major-General Jefferson C. Davis's and Major-General Philip H. Sheridan's), was posted on the right covering Widow Glenn's House and the Dry Valley Road, which led through McFarland's Gap and Rossville to Chattanooga.

Having repositioned his command, Rosecrans was confronted with an urgent request from Thomas that Negley be sent from the center to strengthen the left. Thomas was convinced that Bragg would test him again. He had ordered his crescent-shaped line to be strengthened with log and fence-rail barricades, but he needed more men, especially on his vulnerable left flank, where Brigadier-General Absalom Baird's division could not cover the front allotted to it. His faith in Thomas's judgment remaining supreme, Rosecrans assented to the move, ordering Negley to march at about 3 A.M. and directing Crittenden to shift Wood's division into the gap created by Negley's departure.

At Bragg's headquarters, meantime, plans were being laid for a renewal of the offensive on the 20th. Longstreet arrived at 11 P.M., and he and Bragg conferred for an hour while Bragg described his decision to reorganize the army into two wings and attempt once again to attack in echelon from right to left and drive Rosecrans into the McLemore's Cove pocket. Polk, with the right wing (five divisions), was to attack Thomas at dawn and roll up the Union line toward Longstreet's left wing (six divisions), which would join the fray as the battle on the right and center became general.

Dawn broke on Sunday the 20th, but the battle was not resumed as planned. Polk, who imagined himself subordinate only to God, was having second thoughts about his mission. Mainly, he was worried about Granger's Union reserve corps, sitting squarely but thus far passively some two miles north of the Confederate right. Also, Polk had failed to inform Hill of his role in the impending attack. And Hill, even after receiving his orders, moved slowly, because he believed himself Polk's senior. Thus precious hours were lost, and Bragg had to intervene personally to straighten things out. Finally, at 9 A.M., Polk's line heaved forward at Thomas's logworks, and the battle was re-joined.

Polk's men came on with a savage, crunching energy, pressing up to the flaming breastworks and

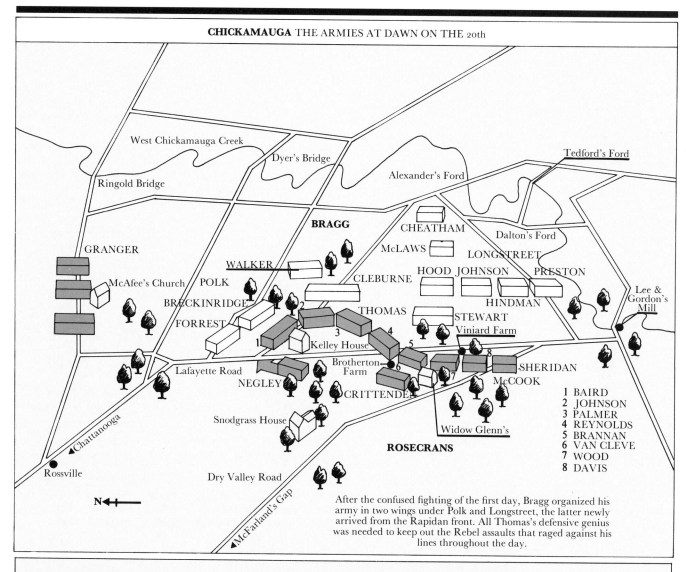

West Chickamauga Creek

Dyer's Bridge

Tedford's Ford

Ringold Bridge

Alexander's Ford

Dalton's Ford

BRAGG

CHEATHAM

McLAWS

LONGSTREET

GRANGER

WALKER

HOOD JOHNSON

PRESTON

McAfee's Church

POLK

CLEBURNE

Lee & Gordon's Mill

BRECKINRIDGE

THOMAS

HINDMAN

FORREST

STEWART
Viniard Farm

Kelley House

SHERIDAN

Lafayette Road

Brotherton Farm

McCOOK

NEGLEY

CRITTENDEN

Snodgrass House

Widow Glenn's

ROSECRANS

1 BAIRD
2 JOHNSON
3 PALMER
4 REYNOLDS
5 BRANNAN
6 VAN CLEVE
7 WOOD
8 DAVIS

Rossville

Dry Valley Road

Chattanooga

N

McFarland's Gap

After the confused fighting of the first day, Bragg organized his army in two wings under Polk and Longstreet, the latter newly arrived from the Rapidan front. All Thomas's defensive genius was needed to keep out the Rebel assaults that raged against his lines throughout the day.

## THE OPPOSING FORCES

### UNION ARMY OF THE CUMBERLAND
Major-General William Rosecrans

#### XIV Corps
Major-General George H. Thomas

First Division (Brigadier-General Absalom Baird): brigades of Scribner, Starkweather and John King.
Second Division (Brigadier-General James S. Negley): brigades of John Beatty, Stanley and Sirwell.
Third Division (Brigadier-General John M. Brannan): brigades of Connell, Croxton and Van Derveer.
Fourth Division (Major-General Joseph J. Reynolds): brigades of Wilder, Edward King and Turchin.
Estimated strength: 20,000 men.

#### XX Corps
Major-General Alexander McD. McCook

First Division (Brigadier-General Jefferson C. Davis): brigades of Carlin and Heg.
Second Division (Brigadier-General Richard W. Johnson): brigades of Willich, Dodge and Baldwin.
Third Division (Major-General Philip H. Sheridan): brigades of Lytle, Laiboldt and Bradley.
Estimated strength: 11,000 men.

#### XXI Corps
Major-General Thomas L. Crittenden

First Division (Brigadier-General Thomas J. Wood): brigades of Buell and Harker.

Second Division (Major-General John M. Palmer): brigades of Cruft, Hazen and Grose.
Third Division (Brigadier-General H. Van Cleve): brigades of Samuel Beatty, Dick and Barnes.
Estimated strength: 12,000 men.

#### Reserve Corps
Major-General Gordon Granger

First Division (Brigadier-General James B. Steedman): brigades of Whitaker and Mitchell.
Second Division (incomplete): brigade of Daniel McCook.
Estimated strength: 4,000 men.

#### Cavalry Corps
Brigadier-General Robert B. Mitchell

First Division (Colonel Edward M. McCook): brigades of Campbell, Ray and Watkins.
Second Division (Brigadier-General George Crook): brigades of Minty and Long.
Estimated strength: 10,000 men.

#### Estimated Totals

The effectives of all arms in Rosecrans's Army of the Cumberland have been estimated at 57,000. The Army also had 150–200 cannon organized in brigades attached to infantry divisions.
Losses: 1,656 killed, 9,749 wounded, and 4,774 captured or missing. Total: 16,179.

## CONFEDERATE ARMY OF TENNESSEE
### General Braxton Bragg

#### RIGHT WING
Lieutenant-General Leonidas Polk

#### Polk's Corps

Cheatham's Division (Major-General B.F. Cheatham): brigades of Jackson, Maney, P. Smith, Wright and Strahl. Hindman's Division (assigned to Longstreet's Left Wing). Estimated strength: 15,000 men.

#### Hill's Corps
Lieutenant-General D.H. Hill

Cleburne's Division (Major-General Patrick Cleburne): brigades of Wood, Lucius Polk and Deshler. Breckinridge's Division (Major-General J.C. Breckinridge): brigades of Helm, Adams and Stovall. Estimated strength: 10,000 men.

#### Reserve Corps
Major-General W.H.T. Walker

Walker's Division (Brigadier-General S.R. Gist): brigades of Gist, Ector and C. Wilson. Liddell's Division (Brigadier-General St John R. Liddell): brigades of Liddell and Walthall. Estimated strength: 9,000 men.

#### LEFT WING
Lieutenant-General James Longstreet

Hindman's Division, (Major-General T.C. Hindman): brigades of J.P. Anderson, Deas and Manigault.

#### Buckner's Corps
Major-General Simon B. Buckner

Stewart's Division (Major-General A.P. Stewart): brigades of Bushrod Johnson, J.C. Brown, Bate and Clayton.

Preston's Division (Brigadier-General William Preston): brigades of Gracie, Trigg and Kelly. Johnson's Division (Brigadier-General Bushrod R. Johnson): brigades of Gregg and McNair. Estimated strength: 12,000 men.

#### Hood's Corps
Major-General John Bell Hood

McLaws's Division (Brigadier-General J.B. Kershaw): brigades of Kershaw and Humphreys. Hood's Division (Brigadier-General E. McIver Law): brigades of Jenkins, Law, Robertson, G.T. Anderson and Benning Estimated strength: 8,000 men.

#### CAVALRY
Major-General Joseph Wheeler

#### Wheeler's Corps

Wharton's Division (Brigadier-General John A. Wharton): brigades of Crews and Harrison. Martin's Division (Brigadier-General William T. Martin): brigades of Morgan, Russell and Roddey.

#### Forrest's Corps
Brigadier-General Nathan Bedford Forrest

Armstrong's Division (Brigadier-General Frank C. Armstrong): brigades of J.T. Wheeler and Dibrell. Pegram's Division (Brigadier-General John Pegram): brigades of Davidson and J.S. Scott. Estimated strength: 15,000 men.

#### Estimated Totals

Bragg's Army of Tennessee numbered 71,551 "present for duty" of all arms, of whom 66,326 were effectives. There were 41 batteries of artillery formed in brigades. The total number of guns is estimated at 175–225. Losses: 2,389 killed, 13,412 wounded, and 2,003 captured or missing. Total: 17,804.

---

overlapping the Union left near the junction of the Lafayette Road and the Alexander's Bridge Road. Breckinridge's division, led by Ben Hardin Helm's brigade, penetrated Thomas's rear in the area of the Kelly Field. Helm, the brother-in-law of President Lincoln's wife, was mortally wounded in the attempt, and his brigade, sheering obliquely along Thomas's refused flank, was fearfully cut up; but Marcellus Stovall's and Daniel W. Adams's brigades arrived at the Lafayette Road virtually untouched. Once there, they swung around astride the road to point south, dressed ranks, and descended yelling into the vacuum behind Thomas's front.

Now Thomas, who had been anxiously awaiting Negley's arrival, faced the first of many crises he would face on the day he earned the sobriquet of "The Rock of Chickamauga." Of Negley's division, only one brigade in fact arrived. The rest, led by its commander, meandered off the field and into Chattanooga, and Thomas was forced to call on Van Cleve, Brannan, and John M. Palmer for help.

Van Cleve, with John Beatty's brigade of Negley's division, arrived just in the nick of time. Stovall and Adams had driven deep into Thomas's rear, pushing the fragmented Federal left before them, and were on the verge of registering a significant victory when they ran into Van Cleve's hurriedly formed line. In the colossal struggle that ensued, the outnumbered Rebels were hurled back with heavy losses, and

Thomas's left was re-established.

Undeterred, Polk now launched Cleburne and, later, Walker's corps and Major-General Benjamin F. Cheatham's big division in repeated assaults on Thomas's front. Here and there, the brave Confederates burst through the barricades, but inevitably they were beaten back by fresh Yankee "fire brigades," rushed to the point of danger. Polk's hammering produced dramatic moments, but the bishop-general committed his men piecemeal, and Thomas counterpunched superbly, containing and breaking up each penetration.

That Thomas was able to do this was a tribute to his defensive genius; nevertheless, he now had well over half the Union army under his command. Rosecrans, determined that Thomas must hold the road to Rossville "if he has to be reinforced by the entire army," had been feeding him troops all morning from the quieter sectors of the field. In doing so, he had seriously neglected his center and right.

During the course of one of these constant shifts and adjustments of the Union line, General Wood in the center received an order from Rosecrans directing him to "close up on Reynolds ((Major-General Joseph J. Reynolds's division)) as fast as possible, and support him." Rosecrans intended for Wood to shift to the left and so fill a gap created earlier when Brannan's reserve brigade had been released to Thomas; instead, Wood pulled his division completely out of the line and passed to the left behind Brannan's remaining brigades. This occurred at 11 A.M., just minutes before Longstreet hurled a massive assault column of 11,000 men into the resulting gap.

Longstreet planned his attack with all the care and ingenuity he was wont to display on the battlefields of the East. Three divisions, those of Johnson, Hood, and McLaws, were stacked one behind the other in a mighty column with a front of half a mile. Deployed parallel to the Lafayette Road in the woods opposite the large open field on the Brotherton Farm, the Graycoats were concealed from their adversaries but poised like a cloaked dagger aimed at the unprotected heart of the Union army. Precisely at 11.15 A.M., shortly after A.P. Stewart on its right took up the rolling battle against Thomas's extreme right (Reynolds and Brannan) and coincident with Wood's fatal withdrawl, the Rebel juggernaut went in.

Infantry, artillery, and mounted men swept forward. The Union center was pierced, and jubilant Rebel soldiers flooded the gap, coursing westward toward Widow Glenn's house and wheeling into the flank of Brannan's surprised division. As Johnson, Hood, and Kershaw pushed on, Major-General Thomas C. Hindman launched his division into the fray on Longstreet's left. Moving abreast of Johnson, Hindman's men widened the gap and routed Davis's and Sheridan's divisions of McCook's corps, completing the destruction of the Union right wing.

Longstreet's Chickamauga attack was probably the single most devastating battlefield offensive of the war—more effective even than Jackson's coup at Chancellorsville. Rosecrans was shattered. He, McCook, Crittenden, and the better part of two corps were swept from the field in rout, making good their retreat to Chattanooga. This portion of the army was later described by one brigadier as "simply a mob." Now Longstreet turned his massed divisions against Thomas, who maintained the fight to cover his chief's retreat to safety. Summoning all his considerable ingenuity, Thomas fashioned a new hook-shaped line on the rutted slopes of Snodgrass Hill, a mile or so west of his still-embattled barricades. The latter served well enough to hold off Polk, but from 2 P.M. the Union line on Snodgrass Hill was subjected to a series of vigorous assaults by Longstreet's wing.

The fighting here was desperate, much of it a struggle at close quarters, and continued until well after dark. The Rebels managed at one point to work their way into the gulleys in the rear of the Union line and seemed to be on the verge of bagging all Thomas's men, but the opportune arrival of Brigadier-General James B. Steedman's division of Granger's corps restored the precarious balance and prevented an otherwise irretrievable disaster.

Finally, at about 6 P.M., Thomas began to withdraw from Polk's front, passing his troops to the north of Snodgrass Hill. Next he evacuated the hill itself, though not without incident—three Union regiments were captured nearly intact by Brigadier-General William Preston's division because they were overlooked when the order to retreat was given. Nonetheless, Thomas's fighting withdrawal was superb. By 8 P.M. the battle had largely ended. Ambrose Bierce, later famous as a short-story writer and journalist, remembered the moment well. Trudging toward McFarland's Gap with Thomas's men, he recalled, "Away to our left and rear some of Bragg's people set up the 'rebel yell.' It was taken up successively and passed round to our front, along our right and in behind us again until it seemed almost to have got to the point whence it started. It was the ugliest sound that any mortal ever heard—even a mortal exhausted and unnerved by two days of hard fighting, without sleep, without rest, without food, and without hope. There was, however, a space somewhere at the back of us across which that horrible yell did not prolong itself—and through that we finally retired in profound silence and dejection, unmolested."

Bragg had gained a victory, but he did not pursue. He was convinced that his army had been entirely used up in the fighting, that it had no fight left in it. Longstreet fumed, and Forrest sent word that "every hour was worth a thousand men," but Bragg was a strange victor; the Union army was soon safely ensconced behind the fortifications of Chattanooga. For the Army of Tennessee, Chickamauga was a hollow triumph. Nearly 18,000 men had fallen; Rosecrans's bold offensive had been blunted, but otherwise nothing had been gained. On the Union side, Rosecrans's army had lost over 16,000 men, but its spirit was unbroken. The men languished for a time under siege in Chattanooga, experiencing near-starvation, but soon Grant came and relieved them, and in due course Joe Hooker arrived by rail with 20,000 Army of the Potomac veterans. A supply line along the river, the Cracker Line, was opened, and the army prepared seriously to throw off the Rebel yoke.

Longstreet's corps departed on November 4, weakening Bragg's cordon, and Grant drove the Confederates off in a series of battles on November 23-25. The Army of the Cumberland redeemed itself in these battles, characterized as "soldiers' battles" because they were not fought according to plan. These actions set the stage for Sherman's Atlanta Campaign and triumphal march to the sea.

After the fight.

Above
Loading and firing: a Confederate
line of battle in the Chickamauga Woods.

Below
The John Ross House at Rossville,
near the gap in Missionary Ridge that leads to Chattanooga.

Bottom
Lee & Gordon's Mill on Chickamauga Creek.

# SPOTSYLVANIA

May 8–19, 1864

A dead soldier of Ewell's corps. War photographers, arriving in the wake of battle, were apt to adjust the positions and attitudes of their subjects–whether men, guns, or horses–if they thought it would make their tableaux more striking.

The new General-in-Chief of the Armies of the United States was so unremarkable in appearance and such a complete stranger to the busy sophisticates of the Federal capital that he slipped into Washington unnoticed. Dressed in plain black civilian clothes and accompanied by his 14-year-old son Fred, Sam Grant detrained at the depot in the late afternoon of March 8, 1864, strode right past an unofficial welcoming committee, and proceeded unescorted to Willard's Hotel, the barracks-like edifice that served as the young city's social center.

At Willard's, Grant asked for lodging, and the registration clerk, not recognizing the rumpled and somewhat undistinguished-looking stranger for what he was, replied that he might have a room on the top floor. This was all right with Grant, who then signed the register: "U.S. Grant and son, Galena, Ill." Scanning the entry, the clerk, heretofore aloof, flushed with embarrassment, and suddenly remembered that a suite had been reserved in the general's name on the second floor. Dutifully, he left his desk and showed the way himself. By dinnertime all Washington knew of Grant's presence, and it was only with difficulty that the general and young Fred managed to partake of a few mouthfuls of food amid a jostling, cheering crowd of fawning admirers in the cavernous hotel dining room. That evening, there was a worse scene at the White House, where Grant attended the President's weekly reception and was nearly mobbed by enthusiastic invitees. It was the kind of treatment that never failed to embarrass Grant, a strikingly unaffected man. The next day, Grant met with the President and assorted Administration grandees, inspected the defenses of Washington, and in a formal ceremony at the White House was invested by Lincoln with the revived rank of lieutenant-general. When this round of activities was completed, the general took his leave of Washington, departing on the 10th for the vast camps of the Army of the Potomac along the Rapidan River.

Grant's tumultuous Washington welcome was indicative of his new status as a national hero. His victories at Vicksburg and Chattanooga had elevated him to the first rank among Union generals, and the New York *Herald* had launched a campaign touting him as "The People's Candidate" for President. (The apolitical Grant quickly squashed this venture; he had, he said, no political ambition beyond one day becoming mayor of his home town of Galena so that he could have the sidewalk repaired between his home and the depot.) He had become, in short, something of a demi-god, the North's man of the hour. Yet Grant had been brought East and made General-in-Chief not because he was the people's choice (a happy coincidence), but because he was a dogged fighter, a grimly determined warrior who would persist in the face of adversity until his object was attained.

The task facing Grant was truly awesome. He had, by his own timetable, eight weeks in which to reorganize the Union war machine for a final, concerted effort that would wreck Confederate resistance. His predecessor as General-in-Chief, Henry Halleck, had presided for a year and a half over hollow victories and near-disasters. He had been wholly discredited, and Lincoln considered him "little more . . . than a first-rate clerk." Under his regime, the Union armies had floundered about as separate entities, operating without relation to one another. Grant's first job, therefore, was to impose order on the

system, to ensure that Union forces would never again operate, as he said, "like a balky team, no two ever pulling together." To do this, he first reorganized the command system, retaining Halleck in the anomalous position of Chief-of-Staff and elevating dependable, trustworthy subordinates whom he had known and worked with in the West. Thus Sherman was given the principal Western command, taking Grant's place as head of the Military Division of the Mississippi. The General-in-Chief himself, who abhorred the idea of becoming desk-bound in Washington, took the field with Meade's Army of the Potomac, which thereafter became known as "Grant's army." The normally irascible Meade, reduced to nominal command of the army he had led to victory at Gettysburg, acquiesced in the whole procedure with remarkably good grace. Another change affecting the Army of the Potomac was the substitution of Phil Sheridan for Alfred Pleasanton as commander of the Army's cavalry corps.

There were, of course, some command changes that Grant might have desired but was powerless to effect. Among these immutables were the positions of the political generals–men whose only qualification for command was their immense influence with certain classes of voters. It had long been recognized, as Halleck stated, that to give such men important commands was "little better than murder," but in a war-weary democracy about to face a crucial presidential election, the voters' goodwill was needed more than ever.

Two of these satraps figured prominently in Grant's plan for the spring campaign: Ben Butler, commander of the 20,000-man Army of the James, and Franz Sigel, whose force of 27,000 men protected the vital Baltimore & Ohio Railroad along its westward course from the Baltimore–Washington vicinity. (A third man, N.P. Banks, might have figured also, but on March 10 he had marched 40,000 veterans right out of the real war by embarking on a disastrous expedition in Lousiana up the Red River.) Butler, whose army was stationed in the Peninsula of Virginia, was important as a prominent war Democrat, and Sigel, a Prussian *émigré*, was the wartime leader of the German immigrant community. Both men were somewhat lacking in talent, and Sigel especially was anything but aggressive, but Grant was determined to use them and their troops as part of his overall scheme to bring pressure to bear all along the line.

Butler's army was reinforced by General Quincy A. Gillmore's 10,000-man force from South Carolina, and Gillmore and General W.F. "Baldy" Smith, both seasoned veterans, became his chief subordinates–military watchdogs put there to see that he carried out his part of the plan without mishap. Sigel was another matter. The German had become so secure in his mountainous Shenandoah fiefdom that he had developed the reprehensible habit of communicating with the War Department through sympathetic congressmen. Just to secure his cooperation in the coming venture would be an achievement, but this Grant did–after reprimanding him for his unseemly breach of military etiquette.

Having reshuffled commands and commanders, Grant turned next to deal with the appaling wastage of manpower that had sapped the campaign strength of Union field forces since the war's beginning. In March, when he took command, there were 860,000 men on the muster rolls of the Union armies, but only 533,000 were available for duty. Of that number, a large fraction were not with the front-line armies; many were on duty in quiet, backwater departments or detached, either in garrisons or guarding supply lines. Typical were the heavy artillery regiments–big, unblooded units whose men were trained as fortress gunners and infantry. These heavy artillerists had been assigned to the forts around Washington and had led an idyllic life, experiencing neither campaign nor combat. Grant ended their halcyon days by ordering 6,000 of them to field service with the Army of the Potomac.

Somehow, Grant broke through the morass of red tape, routine, and prerogative that kept men from the front; in doing so, he ensured a steady supply of reinforcements for the field armies in the coming campaign–an important consideration in view of the twin realities that circumscribed his every action; first, losses were expected to be heavy, and second, the enlistment terms of the three-year men would expire within a few weeks of the campaign's opening. Grant also knew that, as he put it, "the enemy have not got army enough" to resist the kind of coordinated pressure that could be brought to bear if the full manpower resources of the Union were released for the fighting front.

Grant's campaign was uncomplicated, but realistically designed to take advantage of this crushing superiority in men and matériel. Sherman, at Chattanooga, was instructed to "move against Johnston's army, to break it up, and to get into the interior of the enemy's country as far as you can, inflicting all the damage you can . . ." While Sherman brought total war to the Confederate heartland, the Army of the Potomac would operate against Lee's army. Meade was told, "Wherever Lee's army goes, you will go also." By acting in concert and keeping up relentless pressure, the Union forces aimed to prevent any Confederate move to reinforce one army with troops from the other or to unite both their main armies against one of the Union forces.

Complementing these main efforts, there were to be several smaller offensives. In the North, the most important of these would be Butler's advance against Richmond along the south side of the James River, and Sigel's move down the Valley toward Staunton and the tracks of the Virginia & Tennessee Railroad. Both these offensives were designed to threaten or cut Lee's rail communications with the heartland and occupy small secondary Rebel forces which might otherwise reinforce the Army of Northern Virginia. Such was the state of affairs in the Union camp on May 4, 1864, when the spring campaign commenced. The Northern war machine, reworked and brought to peak efficiency by dint of Grant's genius, energy, and perseverance, ground inexorably southward in the war's final push. Grant himself harbored no illusions. He was prepared "to hammer continuously against the armed force of the enemy and his resources until by mere attrition, if in no other way," the rebellion should be crushed.

Since Grant's intention was to go straight at Lee and cling to him, battering all the while, he eschewed maneuver and passed the Rapidan at Germanna's Ford, inviting battle in the tangled thickets of the Wilderness. The two armies had clashed there a year earlier in the epic Battle of Chancellorsville, and bleached skulls and shards of bones, scattered willy-nilly by wild animals–the ghoulish evidence of that fight–were everywhere. Grant's move suited Lee, who bore in from the westward flank, hoping to catch the Union army strung out on the line of march. But Grant had divined Lee's purpose, and turned to meet him. Contact was made on May 5, just west of the Old Wilderness Tavern, the staging area for Jackson's great flank attack of the previous year. Initially, the Northerners held the advantage, since the battle was a meeting engagement and the Rebels had farther to come. In the confused opening sparring, a line of battle was roughed out west of the Brock Road, Grant's axis of advance.

From the outset, Grant sought to pound Lee, launching incessant attacks that careered down the planked turnpikes by which the Confederates were arriving, or floundered about in the smoking undergrowth between the roads. Lee, operating temporarily without Longstreet's corps, counterpunched superbly, but the battle was soon out of control, raging furiously along a five-mile front. On the second day, the Confederate army was seriously imperiled when a massive attack by Hancock's corps crumpled its right flank and routed elements of A.P. Hill's corps along the Orange Plank Road. At this juncture, however, Longstreet's corps arrived and, forming on the run, pitched into the Northerners and drove them back to their starting point.

Having dealt a severe blow to Hancock's corps, Longstreet sought to capitalize on his advantage by organizing a counteroffensive aimed at the Union left on the Brock Road. Had he been successful, he might have duplicated Jackson's feat at Chancellorsville and rolled up Grant's flank, ending the battle in decisive victory for the Confederate cause. This, however, was not to be; luck favored the Union army that morning, for shortly after his troops had driven the enemy in rout back to the Brock Road, Longstreet was severely wounded–shot through the throat in a misdirected volley delivered by some of his own men. It was a crippling loss, one that the Army of Northern Virginia could ill afford, and Lee, arriving on the scene, called off the advance until order could be restored in the hopelessly jumbled ranks of Longstreet's brigades. Five hours later, at 4 P.M., Longstreet's men resumed their attack, overrunning portions of Hancock's breastworks on the Brock Road and coming very close to final victory. Again, however, fortune intervened. The brush caught fire between the lines, and long sections of the earthworks, which were backed with log facings, began to blaze fiercely. An organized advance became impossible along much of the front, and sharp Union counterattacks drove the Rebels from their lodgments.

This repulse effectively ended the Battle of the Wilderness, a bizarre combat fought entirely in a macaber, half-unreal world of blazing thickets crisscrossed by poor country roads. The exact casualties of either army remain unknown, since precise accounting was impossible under the circumstances. Grant reported a loss of 17,666 out of 101,895 engaged (excluding cavalry), and Lee probably lost 8,000 of his 60,000-man force, including, of course, the irreplaceable Longstreet. Hundreds of men, including many of the wounded, were charred beyond recognition by the numerous brush fires.

Lee and his lieutenants believed that they had won a victory in the Wilderness and that the Army of the Potomac, having materialized suddenly in Rebel territory for its obligatory spell of bloodletting, would now turn tail and head north. Certainly, there were many among the rank-and-file of the Northern army who believed the same thing. Used to being led by mediocrities like Burnside and Hooker, they could hope for little more than ignominious retreat, another betrayal. But Grant thought differently. For him the

Wilderness had settled nothing, meant little, and portended less; it had been, however, a fair beginning. Now it was time to get on with the business of bleeding Lee's army. The orders from his headquarters on May 7 were terse but unmistakeably firm: the army was to continue its advance that night, "sidling" (as the men called it) south toward Spotsylvania Court House in a pleasant hamlet fated to become the next great battlefield.

The Union advance along the Brock Road began at 8.30 P.M. that evening: General Gouverneur K. Warren's corps led, filing past the recumbent forms of Hancock's men, who held the breastworks. When the men realized they were, indeed, advancing and not retreating as they had expected, their spirits rose. Haltingly at first, but then with increased fervor, they began to sing, grafting new lyrics onto an old camp ditty. Soon, the dark smoldering woods rang with "Ain't I glad to get out of the Wilderness."

The 7th held nothing but anxiety for Lee. He within the Union lines, which they assumed to be the location of Grant's headquarters, observed a large park of artillery hurriedly decamp. For Lee, this evidence was enough. General Richard H. Anderson, who had taken Longstreet's place, was ordered to prepare his I Corps for a night march to Spotsylvania. The corps was to sift out of line, rest for a period, and get under way at 3 A.M. The rest of the army would follow in order. To expedite this flank march, Lee ordered engineers to cut a trace through the woods from Anderson's right to the Shady Grove Road, which led east to Spotsylvania.

Next there occurred one of those accidents that profoundly affect the course of men's affairs. Anderson, no dawdler, decided that his men could get little rest in the burning woods and that, anyway, the engineers' "road" was so bad that several more hours would have to be added to his marching time; he ordered his two divisions to march at 11 P.M., four hours before the time Lee specified. By chance, those

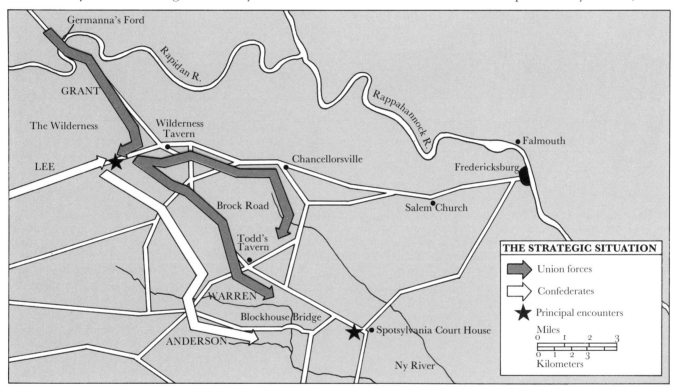

had no clue of Grant's next move, and he knew nothing of the Union commander personally, so he could not engage in his familiar game of founding his own strategy on his opponent's quirks of character. The Army of Northern Virginia itself was but the shadow of the formidable offensive machine it had been a year earlier. The shattering losses sustained by the officer corps at Gettysburg had never been repaired, and this deficiency was accentuated by the sudden loss of two of the army's three corps commanders in the Wilderness (beside the wounded Longstreet, A.P. Hill had reported sick and had been replaced by Jubal Early). The burden of having to intervene personally on the battlefield taxed Lee physically; it was, besides, a role he was uncomfortable with. Increasingly, however, this role was being thrust upon him.

By mid-afternoon on the 7th, the fog of war shielding Grant's intention had begun to dispel. "Jeb" Stuart, Lee's cavalry commander, reported sharp contact with Sheridan's troopers at Todd's Tavern, a crossroads three miles below the extreme Confederate left and just a few miles above Spotsylvania Court House. Sometime later, officers watching a clearing four hours came to represent the slim difference between victory and an early defeat for Lee's army since Anderson, unwittingly, was engaged in a race with Warren for the Spotsylvania crossroads. The Union corps, just then enduring a tiring stop-go march in the wake of Sheridan's cavalry, which was unaccountably fouling the road, would arrive at Spotsylvania soon after dawn. Anderson, thanks to his early start, would now be there in time to help block the way.

"Jeb" Stuart had his hands full, meanwhile. Sheridan's Yankee cavalry, the "Yellowlegs," their Spencer carbines sputtering "seven-forked lightning," were crowding in on Spotsylvania from the north and east, pressing back their gray-clad counterparts by sheer force. Behind the Yankees, dog-tired but willing, the leading elements of Warren's corps filed right and left off the Brock Road and formed into line of battle for the final push that would secure the Spotsylvania crossroads. A Union success here would deliver the campaign to Grant, for Lee would be effectively barred from Richmond. Anxiously, Stuart sent to Anderson for help.

Anderson's men were just then enjoying their

# THE COMMANDERS

Major-General Winfield Scott Hancock, USV

Lieutenant-General Richard S. Ewell, CSA

Winfield Scott Hancock (1824–86) was 38 when the war began, tall, barrel-chested, and handsome. The son of a Pennsylvania lawer, he graduated from West Point in 1844. After combat duty in Mexico and in the Seminole War in Florida, he was made a brigadier-general of volunteers in September 1861 and assisted McClellan in organizing and training the Army of the Potomac. Subsequently, he fought in all the campaigns of the Eastern army (excluding the final one of Appomattox), succeeding to the command of II Corps in May 1863 and leading it from Gettysburg through to the Petersburg campaign. Under his leadership, II Corps became the army's finest fighting force and lost neither a gun nor a color until its defeat at Reams's Station (August 25, 1864), when three regiments refused to fight. This setback broke the exhausted Hancock's spirit, and he was subsequently recalled.

His greatest moments came at Gettysburg and in the desperate fighting of the Wilderness Campaign. At Gettysburg, he virtually directed the fight on the first day, assuming command of the three engaged Union corps, Meade not then being present. On the third day, Hancock's men repelled Pickett's charge and he himself received a terrible wound, from which he never fully recovered. In the Wilderness Campaign, his II Corps bore the brunt of the fighting, smashing Ewell's corps at the "Mule Shoe," but sustaining from first to last an average of 400 casualties a day.

Although he did not rise to command an army and served in a subordinate capacity throughout the war, Hancock was, in Grant's opinion, "the most conspicuous figure of all the general officers who did not exercise a separate command." Loyal, industrious, and brave, he was, like Marlborough's Prince Eugène, one of those rare, self-effacing subordinates, devoid of professional jealousy or destructive ambition, who make good armies function smoothly. His spirit and ability gave force to all the battles of the Army of the Potomac from the Peninsula to Petersburg.

For Richard Stoddert Ewell (1817–72), Jackson's successor as commander of the Second Corps of the Army of Northern Virginia, the Gettysburg Campaign was the beginning of the end of a distinguished military career that had spanned 24 years. At the age of 47, the pop-eyed ex-dragoon was the oldest of Lee's corps commanders, a fading star plagued by indecision, his powers sapped by lingering illnesses, the rigors of campaigning, and the trauma of losing a leg.

Ewell was born in Georgetown, DC, but spent much of his boyhood on the family farm near Bristoe, Virginia, not far from where the Bull Run battles would be fought. Graduating from West Point in 1840, he served with the 1st Dragoons in Mexico and on the frontier. In the Confederate Army he began as a cavalry instructor and then commanded an infantry brigade at First Bull Run. Promoted to major-general on January 23, 1862, he led a division of Jackson's corps until his leg was shattered at Groveton (Second Bull Run) on August 28, 1862.

While convalescing from his wound, "Old Baldhead" acquired a wife, the former Lizinka C. Brown, a widow who seems to have had a profound effect on his temperament. Returning to the army in May 1863, and assuming command of Jackson's old corps, he seemed a changed man. "From a military point of view," wrote a fellow-officer, "the acquisition of a wife did not compensate for the loss of the leg. We were of the opinion that he was not the same soldier he had been when a whole man and a single one."

Ewell's decline as a soldier and consequent fall from Lee's favor began at Gettysburg, where his refusal to press the attack in the late afternoon of the first day created one of the great "what ifs?" of the war. Other failures followed in the Wilderness and at Spotsylvania, whereupon Lee ordered Ewell to relinquish command of his corps and replaced him with Jubal Early. Ewell later took charge of the Richmond defenses; he was captured after the evacuation of the city and imprisoned at Fort Warren.

first real break after six hours of hard marching, cooking bacon slabs for breakfast at Blockhouse Bridge, three miles from Spotsylvania. When Stuart's message arrived, they were fed and rested, and Anderson ordered them post-haste toward the sound of the guns. Anderson's lean, fast-moving infantry arrived just in the nick of time. Fitz Lee's Confederate cavalry division, fighting dismounted behind piles of fence rails, was facing Warren's first assault and desperately needed reinforcing. At the same time, Tom Rosser's Confederate troopers were being chased through the town of Spotsylvania by James H. Wilson's big Union cavalry division. The whole patchwork front–really little more than an umbrella of dismounted skirmishers–that Stuart had fashioned about Spotsylvania was in imminent danger of collapse.

Shortly after 8 A.M., Anderson's leading division, under Brigadier-General Joseph B. Kershaw, relieved Fitz Lee's troopers and beat off a zombie-like attack by Warren's exhausted men. The Yankees were within 50 yards of Lee's improvised breastworks when they received the full force of Kershaw's repeated volleys. The shock was complete, devastating. Warren's troops fell in heaps; the survivors stumbled back, some using their muskets as crutches. Having disposed temporarily of Warren, Anderson shifted two of Kershaw's brigades to Rosser's assistance. At this, Sheridan ordered Wilson to withdraw, and the Yankee threat to the town ended. The day's fighting, however, was not finished. More troops entered the arena, the Confederates angling in from the southwest, the Union troops pushing from the north, along the Brock Road corridor. The lines extended east and west, and Warren, with one division demolished, soon had his other three in action.

When the Confederates were not repelling attacks, they busied themselves with digging in. The new line, with Kershaw astride the Brock Road and Anderson's other division under Major-General Charles W. Field extending nearly to Blockhouse Bridge, occupied high ground on Spotsylvania Ridge and faced generally north. Much of the front was wooded, but there were extensive open areas, especially in Kershaw's sector. The Spotsylvania woods were less dense than those of the Wilderness and consisted mainly of tall stands of oak and pine; farmers' axs had cleared away much of the underbrush.

Lee's trench system at Spotsylvania deserves special mention. Both armies had developed the habit of entrenching immediately on taking up a new position, but the thoroughness of the Confederates astounded Union observers. Colonel Theodore Lyman of Meade's staff noted, "It is a rule that when the Rebels halt, the first day gives them a good rifle pit; the second a regular infantry parapet with artillery in position; and the third a parapet with an abatis in front and entrenched batteries behind. Sometimes they put this three days' work into the first twenty-four hours." These fieldworks followed every dip and roll of the ground, and from a distance very little could be seen of them, often nothing more than a long fresh scar on the surface surmounted by glistening bayonets and red battle flags. They were so elaborate and extensive that they presaged the intricate trench systems of World War I.

The sporadic attacks of Warren's corps did not much disturb the burrowing of the Rebels, and by nightfall it was evident that Lee had frustrated Grant's plan to interpose his troops between the Army of Northern Virginia and Richmond. Nothing now remained but to slug it out on the narrow plateau between the Po and the Ny rivers. During the night, the unengaged troops of both armies arrived and fell into line, expanding the fighting front much beyond the limits of the original engagement. The 9th was relatively quiet and uneventful, but the Union army suffered a grievous loss when Major-General John Sedgwick, the commander of the VI Corps, was killed by a sharpshooter's bullet on the Brock Road. Brigadier-General Horatio G. Wright took his place as commander of the corps. Also, Grant allowed Sheridan to "cut loose" from the army with his 10,000-man cavalry corps to raid Lee's rear (May 9–24). Stuart followed, overhauling the powerful Union force at Yellow Tavern (May 11), where he was mortally wounded. Thus, both armies fought the main battle blindly, without their cavalry to scout and screen.

In its final form, Lee's lines at Spotsylvania resembled an enormous inverted V, the faces running generally southwesterly and almost due south from the apex, which itself was a massive salient projecting northward like an arrowhead into the Union center. This salient, called the "Mule Shoe" by the soldiers, began as an extension of Anderson's line along a ridge commanding the valley of the Ny. When, in the late afternoon of the 8th, Major-General Robert E. Rodes's division (the van of Ewell's corps) took its place on Kershaw's right, its line extended first to the east and then north, following the high ground. That night Major-General Edward Johnson's division filed past Rodes and continued the line toward the Ny, doubling back to the southeast at the point where the ridge fell away toward the low ground occupied by Sedgwick's corps. Brigadier-General John B. Gordon's division completed the projection, occupying its eastern face and constructing a transverse "stop-gap" line across its center. The resulting triangular salient was over a mile long and half a mile wide at its base; its perimeter encompassed over three miles of fortified line, complete with gun platforms, traverses (short barriers at right-angles to the main line to protect against enfilading fire), abatis, and slashing (lines of felled trees).

There was a great deal of concern about this "Mule Shoe," which seemed to be an unnecessarily extensive and vulnerable part of the line, but Ewell, Johnson, and the army's most senior engineers who superintended its construction were convinced it could be held provided it was well stocked with artillery. The most important argument in favor of its retention, however, was that if the Yankees gained possession of the high ground it surrounded, the Confederate army's rear would be exposed to destructive artillery fire. Inevitably, the Mule Shoe became the focal point of the fighting at Spotsylvania. Like all salients, it invited attack, exercising a kind of magnetic attraction. Great battles were fought on the flanks, but the truly decisive combats occurred around and within those few square miles of half-wooded country encompssed by Ewell's earthworks.

The first test of the Mule Shoe took place during the early evening of May 10. All day, Grant had been probing Lee's lines, launching limited offensives and "feeling" for weak spots. One such assault, organized and led by Emory Upton, one of the Union army's most talented young brigadiers, struck the western face of the salient at a portion of the line held by George Doles's Georgia brigade of Rodes's division. The Confederates were surprised by the suddenness of Upton's rush and overwhelmed before they could make much resistance, losing several

# THE MULE SHOE

The diagram shows the Union assaults directed at the Rebels' Mule Shoe salient on May 12. Most successful was that of Hancock's II Corps, which penetrated as far as Gordon's line before the Rebels could mount an effective counterattack. The fighting in the Bloody Angle, on the northwest face, lasted for 18 hours.

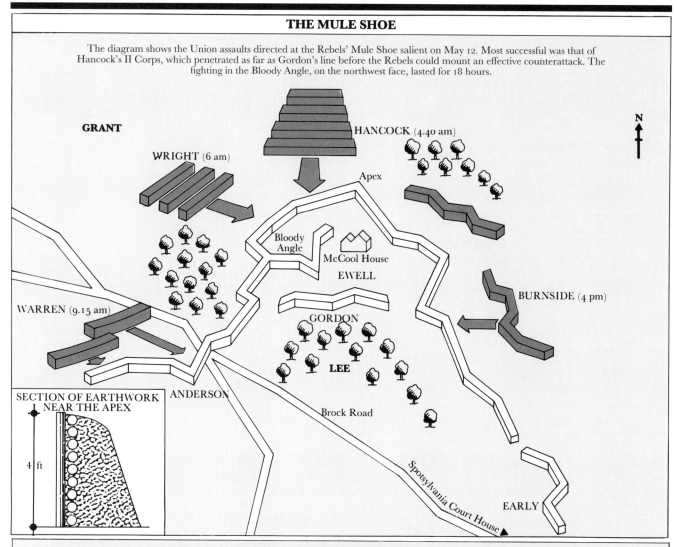

## THE OPPOSING FORCES

### UNION ARMY OF THE POTOMAC

Lieutenent-General Ulysses S. Grant
Major-General George G. Meade

#### II Corps
Major-General Winfield S. Hancock

First Division (Brigadier-General Francis C. Barlow): brigades of Miles, Smyth, Frank and Brooke.
Second Division (Brigadier-General John Gibbon): brigades of Webb, Owen and Carroll.
Third Division (Major-General David Birney): brigades of Ward and Hays.
Fourth Division (Brigadier-General Gershom Mott): brigades of McAllister and Brewster.
Strength: 79 regiments of infantry and 11 batteries of artillery.

#### V Corps
Major-General Gouverneur K. Warren

First Division (Brigadier-General Charles Griffin): brigades of Ayers, Sweitzer and Bartlett.
Second Division (Brigadier-General John C. Robinson): brigades of Leonard, Baxter and Denison.
Third Division (Brigadier-General Samuel W. Crawford): brigades of McCandless and Fisher.
Fourth Division (Brigadier-General James S. Wadsworth, killed; Brigadier-General Lysander Cutler): brigades of Cutler, Rice and Stone.
Strength: 63 regiments and 10 batteries.

#### VI Corps
Major General John Sedgwick, killed;
Major-General Horatio G. Wright

First Division (Wright, succeeded by Brigadier-General David A. Russell): brigades of Penrose, Upton, Eustis and Cross.
Second Division (Brigadier-General Thomas H. Neill): brigades of Wheaton, Lewis Grant, Bidwell and Edwards.
Third Division (Brigadier-General James B. Ricketts): brigades of Truex and Benjamin Smith.
Strength: 52 regiments and 14 batteries.

#### IX Corps
Major-General Ambrose E. Burnside

First Division (Brigadier-General Thomas G. Stevenson, killed; Major-General Thomas L. Crittenden): brigades of Carruth, Sudsburg and Marshall.
Second Division (Brigadier-General Robert B. Potter): brigades of Bliss and Simon G. Griffin.
Third Division (Brigadier-General Orlando B. Willcox): birgades of Hartranft and Christ.
Fourth Division (Brigadier-General Edward Ferrero): brigades of Sigfried and Henry G. Thomas.
Strength: 43 regiments of infantry, 4 of cavalry and 15 batteries.

#### Cavalry Corps
Major-General Philip H. Sheridan

First Division (Brigadier-General A.T.A. Torbert): brigades of Custer, Devin and Merritt.

Men of Hancock's corps storm across the Po River.

Second Division (Brigadier-General David McM. Gregg): brigades of Davies and J. Irvin Gregg.
Third Division (Brigadier-General James H. Wilson): brigades of Bryan and Chapman.
Horse Artillery: brigades of Robertson and Ransom.
Strength: 31 regiments and 18 batteries.

Artillery
Brigadier-General Henry J. Hunt

Artillery Reserve (Colonel Henry S. Burton): brigades of Kitching, John A. Tompkins and Fitzhugh.
Strength: 18 batteries.

Estimated Totals

Grant's Army of the Potomac had 237 regiments of infantry, 35 of calvalry, and 86 batteries of artillery, giving him an approximate total strength of 90,000 men and 274 guns.
Losses: 2,725 killed, 13,416 wounded, and 2,258 captured or missing. Total: 18,399.

## Confederate Army of Northern Virginia

General Robert E. Lee

I Corps
Major-General Richard H. Anderson

Kershaw's Division (Brigadier-General Joseph B. Kershaw): brigades of Kershaw (Henagan), Humphreys, Wofford and Bryan.
Field's Division (Major-General Charles W. Field): brigades of Jenkins (Bratton), George T. Anderson, Law, John Gregg and Benning.
Strength: 43 regiments of infantry and 14 batteries of artillery.

II Corps
Lieutenant-General Richard S. Ewell

Early's Division (Brigadier-General John Brown Gordon): brigades of Pegram, Gordon and Johnston.
Johnson's Division (Major-General Edward Johnson): brigades of James A. Walker (Stonewall Brigade), Steuart, John M. Jones and Hays.
Rodes's Division (Major-General Robert E. Rodes): brigades of Daniel, Ramseur, Doles and Battle.
Strength: 58 regiments and 18 batteries.

III Corps
Major-General Jubal A. Early

Anderson's Division (Brigadier-General William

Mahone): brigades of Perrin, Mahone (Weisiger), Harris, Wright and Perry.
Heth's Division (Major-General Henry Heth): brigades of Joseph R. Davis, Cooke, Kirkland, Henry Walker and Archer.
Wilcox's Division (Major-General Cadmus M. Wilcox): brigades of Lane, Scales, McGowan and Edward L. Thomas.
Strength: 63 regiments and 23 batteries.

Cavalry Corps
Major-General J.E.B. Stuart

Hampton's Division (Major-General Wade Hampton): brigades of Young, Rosser and Butler.
Fitz Lee's Division (Major-General Fitzhugh Lee): brigades of Lomax and Wickham.
W.H.F. Lee's Division (Major-General W.H.F. Lee): brigades of Chambliss and Gordon.
Horse Artillery (Major R.P. Chew): battalion of Breathed.
Strength: 25 regiments and 5 batteries.

Estimated Totals

Lee's Army of Northern Virginia had 164 regiments of infantry, 25 of cavalry, and 60 batteries of artillery, giving him an approximate total strength of 50,000 men and 200 guns.
Losses: some 10,000 men altogether; precise figures are impossible to compute.

hundred men as prisoners. They rallied at a second line, however, and, aided by skillfully directed artillery fire, checked the Union advance. When Upton's supports refused to come up on his flank, Johnson and Gordon counterattacked and drove the Yankees from their lodgment. Upton's success impressed Grant. What had been accomplished on the small scale, he reasoned, might be reproduced with even greater success on the grandest. Without delay, he set about planning a massive assault on the apex of the salient.

The 11th passed without incident as Grant maneuvered three of his four army corps (about 60,000 men) into positions around the Mule Shoe. This movement did not go undetected, but Lee mis-interpreted it. His assumption, supported by the opin-ion of the volatile Early, was that Grant was either retiring on Fredericksburg or preparing again to side-step by the Confederate right. To counter this antic-ipated move, Lee had to have his army prepared to march at a moment's notice. Of particular concern in this connection were the two battalions of artillery in the Mule Shoe—30 guns solidly emplaced but stranded far from good roads. Lee's verbal order to Ewell was to retire most of these guns during the night of the 11th and 12th, preparatory to an evacuation of the Spot-sylvania lines. This order, it transpired, was Lee's cap-ital mistake of the campaign: without the "long arm" of the guns, the salient was untenable.

For the defenders of the Mule Shoe, bereft of their artillery, the hours preceding dawn on the 12th were full of strangely foreboding signs. Bands played within the Union lines, and rhythmic rumblings–rather like the sound of a giant locomo-tive–penetrated the heavy, damp air. "There was," recalled an infantryman, "a nameless something in the air which told every man that there was a crisis at hand." At 4.40 A.M. the storm broke. First, there was a smattering of fire from the Confederate picket northeast of the apex, and then, advancing in massed ranks barely visible in the half-light of the foggy dawn, 20,000 men of Hancock's corps burst like a wave upon Ewell's line. This classic column attack was irresistible and everywhere successful. General Johnson and 2,000 men of his division, including almost the entire "Stonewall Brigade," were captured; the Northerners quickly capitalized on their advantage, penetrating the Mule Shoe as far as Gordon's intermediate line.

At this point Hancock's attack faltered. The assailants crowded the angle at the apex, milling around and mixing with their bewildered prisoners, disorganized as much by their sudden success as by the confined space. Gordon, meantime, organized Con-federate resistance at the second line. With his own and Rodes's divisions, plus Johnson's fragments, he first checked the Union advance and then counter-attacked, driving the Yankees back toward the apex. By mid-morning the battle had become stalemated, the Yankees clinging to the outside face of the captured works and the Confederates holding along Gordon's "stop-gap" line. The fighting had become so fierce and destructive that Campbell Brown, Ewell's stepson and aide, was awed by its magnitude. "I have never before imagined such a struggle to be possible," he wrote, "though I saw Gaines' Mill and Gettysburg."

For Lee, these morning hours presented the spectacle of ultimate defeat–the possibility that his army, already reeling from Hancock's attack, might be torn asunder by Grant's reserves. With calm reso-lution he ordered a counterattack along the west face of the salient, hoping to buy time for a new line to be completed across the base of the Mule Shoe. Grant, on the other hand, sensed victory, and he committed more men to the battle. Wright's VI Corps came in on Hancock's right at 6 A.M., and Major-General Ambrose E. Burnside's IX Corps attacked the north-east face at 4 P.M. Neither Wright nor Burnside had much success, but Hancock's corps fought a titanic combat with Rodes's division and two brigades of Early's corps along the northwest face. This fight, lasting from 10 A.M. on May 12 until 4 A.M. on the 13th, was described by William Swinton, the Army of the Potomac's historian, as "the fiercest and most deadly" struggle of the war. The northwest face and the west angle, known afterward as the "Bloody Angle," were transformed into a frightful rain-soaked and blood-drenched abattoir; according to Swinton, "the woods in front of the salient were one hideous Golgotha."

This desperate battle plugged the gap in Lee's center and allowed the Confederates time to con-struct a new line across the base of the salient. Heavy rains which had begun on the 11th continued through to the 16th, prompting a Rebel artilleryman to com-ment, "It looked as if Heaven were trying to wash up the blood as fast as the civilized barbarians were spilling it." The torrential downpour, so typical of Virginia at that season of the year, imprisoned the armies in a sea of mud and prevented combat, but the first warm, dry day was followed on the 18th by a resumption of Grant's hammering tactics, when Han-cock's depleted corps was hurled against the new line at the base of the salient. This attack broke up in a welter of carnage as the massed ranks of Bluecoats were savaged by musketry and by case and canister from 29 cannon; later Meade admitted ruefully, "We found the enemy so strongly entrenched that even Grant thought it useless to knock our heads against a brick wall."

The last serious fighting at Spotsylvania occurred on the 19th when Ewell took his crippled corps (reduced to 6,000 men, less than the average strength of a Confederate division at the start of the campaign) out of the trenches and around the Union right, searching for evidence of another Yankee side-step. The old Rebel II Corps, operating without its artillery, ran foul of the heavy artillerists Grant had called up from the Washington forts and was forced back in some confusion. This fight ended nearly a fortnight of combat at Spotsylvania. Both armies had suffered severely, though again no accurate records were kept, and estimates vary considerably. Lee's army, fighting for the most part from behind entrenchments, lost fewer men but could ill afford any loss. Grant's tactics of hanging on and battering relentlessly had converted the war into a struggle of attrition which the Confederates were bound to lose despite their *élan*. Lee, as usual, saw this clearly. Speaking to Early in the aftermath of Spotsylvania, he said, "We must destroy this Army of Grant's before he gets to the James River. If he gets there it will become a siege, and then it will be a mere question of time."

Grant, of course, knew this–indeed, his entire campaign was based upon this premise. "The enemy have not got army enough" had been his watchword from the beginning. Sigel was defeated in the Shenan-doah Valley and forced to retreat, and Butler botched his end of the operation below Richmond, but the Army of the Potomac–"army enough"–kept march-ing by its left flank, "sidling" toward the James and Petersburg.

Above
The Battle of the Wilderness, showing the Union position along the Brock Road.
The almost impenetrable barrier of pine and scrub-oak
has been well represented by the artist.

Below
Spotsylvania Court House, center of the hamlet from which the battle took its name.

# ATLANTA
July 20 – September 2, 1864

Mill workers in the "palace of King Cotton." Georgia led the Confederate states in cotton production, and Sherman vowed that his march on the capital, Atlanta, would be lit by the fires of Southern plantations.

In mid-19th century America, cotton was king, and the palace of the king was Georgia. At a rate of over 700,000 bales a year, the red-clay state led the South in producing her basic cash crop; and with the white fiber came the mills to work it and the railroads to transport it. With more rail than any other Southern state except Virginia, Georgia attracted heavy industry. Much of it was centered on Atlanta. Built at the crossroads of the state's four main railroads, the city drew to it large numbers of mechanics, immigrants, and intellectuals, as well as plantation workers. Supply trains from Atlanta sent iron to arm the river and harbor fleets of the Confederacy, food for the far-flung armies in Virginia and Tennessee, and rails for the railroads throughout the young nation. These same railroads carried some 120,000 Georgians into battle. It was Atlanta which kept the rebellion on its feet more than any other region of Jefferson Davis's country.

In late 1863 Braxton Bragg and the Army of Tennessee had been on the offensive, beating the Union army at Chickamauga and then besieging them within the Chattanooga forts. Then Grant arrived to chase Bragg back over the Georgia border. There are only 100 miles between Chattanooga and Atlanta, the same distance that separates Washington from Richmond, and Major-General William Tecumseh Sherman, who replaced Grant when that General moved to direct the war from the East, determined to march on Atlanta–his way lit by the fires of Southern towns and plantations.

Sherman's host of over 100,000 men was unequally divided between three armies: Major-General George Thomas's massive Army of the Cumberland, Major-General John Schofield's Army of the Ohio, and the dashing Major-General James McPherson's Army of the Tennessee. Twenty divisions of infantry, four of cavalry, and over 250 field guns were poised to move on Georgia in a summer campaign. Against this Union colossus, the Confederacy could only scrape together some 42,000 ill-fed, demoralized, and under-equipped soldiers from the Mississippi Basin states. "In this army one hole in the seat of the breeches indicates a captain," wrote one Texan in the Rebel army to his wife, "two holes a lieutenant, and the seat of the pants all out indicates that the individual is a private." Such was the state of the Confederate Army of the Tennessee.

The battering which those men had taken had torn out more than just the seat of their breeches. As Samuel Carter III wrote in *The Siege of Atlanta, 1864*, "The men were deserting by tens and hundreds, and I might say by thousands. The morale of the army was gone. The spirit of the soldiers was crushed." In the hope of restoring some combat value to this horde, President Jefferson Davis grudgingly accepted General Robert E. Lee's recommendation that he should give the army to General Joseph E. Johnston. Almost immediately, Johnston rebuilt the army: an amnesty for deserters who would return to the colors, and a system of furlough to let the men go home and rest, look after their families (and come back well-fed and reclothed) restored morale. Johnston's conscientious attention to the gathering of fresh fruit and vegetables from the countryside to supplement his men's diet, frequent parades, and mock battles all contributed to bringing the army back into fighting shape during the winter and spring. Although exhorted by Davis to take the offensive and reoccupy Tennessee, Johnston had no inclination to waste his outnumbered army in Bragg-style assaults. He would not push against Sherman; he would lead him slowly into Georgia, extending the Union supply lines, picking defensive positions from which the Northerners could only oust him with heavy losses, and generally harassing Sherman into making mistakes. Johnston planned to bleed the North with every step.

Under orders from Grant to coordinate his drive into Georgia with the main Union thrust into Virginia, Sherman prepared to advance on May 3. His well-trained and heavily guarded railroad repair crews had opened the lines from Chattanooga to Ringgold, his front-line camp, and the army began to move forward. After only a short advance, they came to their first obstacle: the 1,400-foot cliffs of the Rocky Face Ridge outside Dalton. The railroad, the only supply route open in this mountainous section of North Georgia, ran through the ridge at Buzzard's Roost. Thomas hurled his men at the Roost to test the Confederate line, only to encounter what Sherman called "a terrible door of death." Quickly learning from his impetuosity, Sherman sent McPherson south to outflank the Rebels via Snake Creek Gap. A single brigade of Southern infantry, barely 4,000 strong, accidentally arrived by rail in time to block the mouth of the gap at Resaca. Imagining it to be the whole Rebel army, McPherson took fright and dug in.

Sherman shifted the whole of his force to the Gap and on May 13 and 14 made a series of massive lunges at the Confederate defenses, now strengthened into a three-mile-long line of trenches and manned by the newly arrived corps of Lieutenant-General Leonidas Polk. Throughout the night, Major-General Joseph Hooker (the former commander of the Army of the Potomac, sent West to redeem his reputation) launched his corps in a series of bayonet charges against the line, only to fail with each assault. The next morning, Hooker again led the way, his men falling like grass beneath a scythe to the hidden batteries and deadly fire of the Southern riflemen. Despite the butchery to their front, the Union assaults began to outflank the Rebel positions, and Johnston abandoned his line, scurrying down the railroad to find a new position.

After Lieutenant-General John Bell Hood bungled a well-laid ambush at Cassville on May 18, Johnston fell back again, seeking the good defensive ground of the Allatoona Range. Rather than assault the high ground along the rail lines, Sherman cut loose from his supply line and struck out overland, to the south, hoping to outflank Johnston. Once again, however, the Confederate general was prepared, and the Yankees found Hood's infantry already entrenched at New Hope Church.

About 6 P.M. on May 25, Hooker threw his corps against the leading division of Hood's corps, that of Major-General Alexander Stewart. In a two-hour battle in what they dubbed the "Hell Hole," the Union troops charged across the muddy ground and over a rain-filled ditch into the fire of 16 field-pieces and nearly 5,000 muskets. Three times Hooker's infantry tried to cross the field, and three times they were hurled back with heavy losses. Both sides brought up their main forces, extending their lines to the east. On the 28th, Major-General Oliver Otis Howard (upon whom Hooker had blamed his disgrace at Chancellorsville), with his IV Corps and Palmer's divison of XIV Corps, advanced in deep columns against Major-General Patrick Cleburne's division. The masses of men, with barely two brigades of frontage, were slaughtered by the well-entrenched

Rebels. Granbury's Texas brigade counterattacked at dusk, capturing the Union wounded still on the field.

Badly bloodied, having lost 3,000 men (10 times his enemy's total), Sherman moved back to the rail lines. His action had forced his opponent to abandon the Allatoona Range, however, and withdraw to the Kennesaw Mountain. The mid-June Georgia rains made the red clay so slippery that it was more like ice than mud. Sherman's advance slowed to a crawl while he positioned his men opposite the twin peaks of Kennesaw. Impatient at the delays and the elusive nature of Johnston's war, Sherman decided to attack the mountain. "Uncle Billy," as his men called him, dug gun positions and parallels to prepare for the assault. At 8 A.M. on June 27, with the sun already bearing down in a 90-degree blaze, 140 Union guns opened up with "a roar as constant as Niagara and as sharp as the crash of thunder with lightning in the edge" (Shelby Foote, *The Civil War, a Narrative*). After an hour's bombardment, the Union infantry stepped out into open ground.

Thomas's Cumberlanders, in two divisional columns, four lines deep, aimed for the center of the Rebel line. Advancing in close order, the Midwesterners made such an easy target for Cleburn's rapid-firing infantry that "every man in our regiment killed from one score to fourscore, yeah, fivescore men," wrote Private Sam Watkins. "All that was necessary was to load and shoot." McPherson's attack on the left made better progress: his men at least climbed to the summit of Little Kennesaw, only to be thrown off by a determined counter-charge. Over 600 dead Yankees carpeted the ground, most of them within 10 yards of the Confederate trenches. The bulk of these two assault divisions fell back, but then became pinned down in the open plain, where the heat rose to a killing 110 degrees.

Only on the far right, where Schofield had launched a feint against Hood, could Sherman claim a measure of success. A small bridgehead over Olley's Creek, barely outflanking the Confederate line, had been established by the Army of the Ohio. As Sherman reinforced his right wing to exploit the bridgehead, Johnston once again slipped away in the night, retiring to a fortified position at Smyrna. Although the Chattahoochee River was to his back, he had numerous pontoon crossings, and his defensive line, which Sherman described as "one of the strongest pieces of field fortification I ever saw," made a Union assault unpromising. Searching for a less costly crossing place, the Union army swung upstream, bridging the "Rubicon of Georgia" at Roswell. On July 9, 1864, Sherman cleared the last natural barrier to Atlanta.

Although he had rebuilt the Army of Tennessee, slowed the advance of an army twice his own in size to barely a mile a day, and inflicted many more casualties than he had lost, the Confederate government did not consider Joe Johnston's campaign to date satisfactory. Having failed to halt the Union army or destroy any major portion of it, Johnston was considered to be a faint-hearted defeatist. Braxton Bragg, once commander of the Army of Tennessee and now military adviser to President Davis, was sent to review the situation in Atlanta. He proposed that a change in command would reverse the Union tide. He put forth the name of the one-armed, one-legged Texan, Lieutenant-General John Bell Hood.

On the night of July 17, with Confederate troops poised along the outer defensive works of Atlanta for a counterattack against Sherman's divided columns, Johnston was formally relieved. Hood, although often critical of his old commander in the past, tried to keep Johnston around to advise him and help him command the army. But Johnston, the burden of the struggle removed from his thin shoulders, would have none of it. Within a day, he would be well on his way out of the Georgia war. Reactions within the Army of Tennessee were gloomy: Johnston was much admired by the men, many of whom viewed his successor with little confidence. Sherman, on the other hand, was delighted. Hood's reputation for fighting was well known, and Sherman felt it to be a welcome change. "This is just what we wanted," he wrote, "viz. to fight in open ground on anything like equal terms, instead of being forced to run up against prepared entrenchments." When trying to find out a little more about Hood's character, Sherman stumbled upon a Kentuckian who knew Hood from the prewar Army days. He told Sherman, "I seed Hood bet $2,500 with nary a pair in

The rail yards at Atlanta Union Depot, meeting-point of Georgia's four main railroads and a prime target for Sherman's summer offensive.

his hands." This was in keeping with Lee's judgment of the man. Consulted by President Davis after Bragg had made his recommendations, Lee had pronounced Hood "a good commander, very industrious on the battlefield, careless off."

The city of Atlanta had been turned into a fortress in the previous year. Colonel L.P. Grant, Chief Engineer of the Department of Georgia, had laid out the 12-mile-long line—studded with 20 redoubts, thousands of rifle pits, and miles of ditches and abatis which surrounded the city. These lines were, as reported by Captain O.M. Poe, Sherman's Chief Engineer, "too strong to assault and too extensive to invest . . . and no assault should be ordered . . . the cost would be too great and success unlikely." Sherman decided that rather than waste any more men against fortifications, he would besiege the city and starve Hood out. The Union armies swung above the city: Schofield and McPherson went to Decatur to destroy that rail line and close in from the east, while Thomas crossed the Peachtree Creek in the north. Although these moves would block any chance of food or men getting into the city and its defenders from the east, a large gap developed between the Union armies. Johnston's plan, which Hood was left to complete, was to maintain this gap by the use of artillery, and to lunge with two corps against the Union center. As Thomas crossed the rough jungle near the Peachtree, Hardee and Stewart would plow into him and drive the Army of the Cumberland into the marshy confluence of the creek and the Chattahoochee. With the main Union army in disarray, the Confederates would swing down upon the other two enemy columns and similarly dispatch them. Thus Sherman's army, drawn into Georgia on a 100-mile, single-track supply line, would find itself beaten and cut off deep in the heart of hostile territory.

Hood, too ill to come to the field, directed that

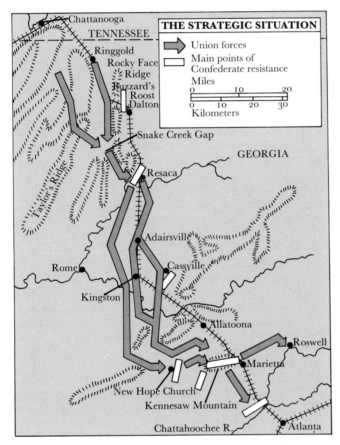

the attack should begin at about noon on July 20. Hardee, a noted intellectual who had written the Army's infantry tactics manual, had difficulty in handling a large number of units. Not satisfied with his noon position, he spent the next three hours sidling back and forth over the rough woodland below Peachtree Creek. Stewart, who was forced to conform to Hardee's line, grew impatient and launched the attack on his own initiative about 3 P.M. Loring's division led the Rebel assault, driving into the gap between the Union right-flank divisions. Initially successful, the attack was slowed by Arthur MacArthur's 24th Wisconsin, and repulsed when Ward's division came up. Farther to the left, the Mississippi and Alabama infantry drove through Collier's Mill, taking the flag of the 33rd New Jersey. Scott's Southern brigade carried through into a ravine below the Mill, only to be slaughtered by Colonel Benjamin Harrison's brigade, which fired down on them from the lip of the cut. O'Neal's brigade of Alabama infantry

suffered a similar fate in another ravine, caught between the murderous fire of Geary's and Williams's Union divisions.

With Stewart's attack shattered, Hardee tried without much vigor to work a division through the heavy thickets and outflank the Union line. Thomas, himself prodding the flanks of the artillery horses with his saber, brought six guns up onto the high ground above the Creek and personally directed their fire, shattering Hardee's assault. This encounter cost the Rebels 4,800 men; Thomas lost barely 1,800. A dispatch from Hood, calling for Cleburne's division of Hardee's corps to march to the eastern front of the Atlanta line, mercifully prevented Hardee from launching a second wave. The Confederate infantry withdrew into the main line of forts during the night, leaving Thomas securely across the Creek.

To the east, Schofield and McPherson were driving down the railroad line from Decatur, bravely delayed by Major-General Joseph Wheeler's cavalry. Lightly armed with pistols and carbines, and heavily outgunned, the Rebel horsemen could do little more than slow the 20,000 Union infantry bearing down upon them. But on the low ridge of Bald Hill, a mile and a half outside the city, Wheeler's troopers twice threw back the Northerners, holding the position until Cleburne's division relieved them at midnight.

On the morning of the 21st, a burial truce was agreed; the heat was so intense that the bodies had already begun to putrefy, and the stench of several hundred corpses was unbearable. By 8 A.M., however, the fighting resumed, and the Union batteries took a frightening toll of the defenders. James A. Smith, one of the brigadiers of Cleburne's command, described the fire from a single battery of 20-pounder Parrotts: "I have never before witnessed such accurate and destructive cannonading. In a few minutes 40 men were killed and over 100 wounded, by this battery alone. In the 18th Texas Cavalry, dismounted, 17 out of 18 men comprising one company were placed *hors de combat* by one shot alone." Leggett directed Force to follow the bombardment and seize the hill. Advancing in two lines "they closed on their colors and swept up over the works precise as on parade," securing the hill, but at a cost of over 40 percent to the brigade. Leggett, quickly renaming the hill after himself, emplaced his guns upon the ridge to shell the city.

Hood, learning of the Union success, prepared a second sortie. Declaring that "the continued use of breastworks during a campaign renders troops timid in a pitched battle," he sent Hardee's corps on a night march to swing wide and hit McPherson's army in the rear. Wheeler's cavalry were to strike the Union supply trains at Decatur, deep in the Union rear area, thus forcing McPherson to fall back on Thomas for support. Cheatham's division would then hit them head on, completing the hoped-for rout. As usual, the unfortunate Army of Tennessee could not do anything on schedule. Hardee's corps did not clear the city until 3 A.M. On dark, narrow, dusty roads, the corps' guns and cavalry became badly entangled with the infantry columns. When at last he reached Cobb's Mill, Hardee divided his men into two columns. He took the mill owner as his guide, and the mill-hand, Case Turner, was told to lead Walker and his two divisions onto the Union flank. Walker, who immediately distrusted his guide, refused to budge from his own bullheaded notion of which was the correct road. When, as the guide warned, he found himself facing a large, unfordable pond, Walker threatened to shoot

# THE COMMANDERS

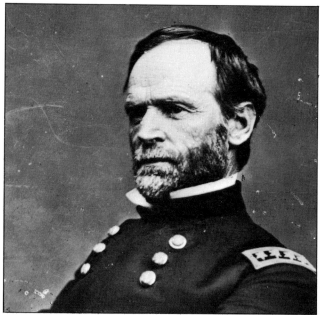

Major-General William T. Sherman, USV

General Joseph E. Johnston, CSA

**B**orn in February 1820 in Ohio, William Tecumseh Sherman had all the gawkiness and clumsiness attributed to an uncivilized hayseed. "He carries his hands in his pockets," wrote John Chapman Gray, "is very awkward in his gait and motion, talks continually and with immense rapidity, and might sit to Punch for the portrait of the ideal Yankee . . . the most American-looking man I ever saw." The tall, ruddy, energetic soldier, who never allowed himself the comforts he denied to his men, was constantly on the move. "A bit of stern open air made up in the image of a man" was Walt Whitman's description of him.

In action Sherman was an attacker. Regardless of the difficulty of the situation, he would first try to breach the enemy lines by pure force; only if that failed would he resort to maneuver. Like Grant, he had begun to "regard the death and mangling of a couple of thousand men as a small affair, a kind of morning dash." He himself wrote, with some prescience, "It may be well that we become hardened. The worst of war is not yet begun." Sherman's blood-lust and destructive drive were not without a purpose. "I believe in fighting in a double sense," he said. "First to gain physical results and next to inspire respect on which to build up our nation's power."

Grant appointed Sherman to the Western command not only because of his courage and determination, but because of another quality which shone out above these traits–his loyalty. As Sherman explained, "Grant stood by me when I was crazy, and I stood by him when he was drunk." Grant's recurrent weakness for the bottle is well known; it is not such common knowledge that Sherman, for all his tough exterior, was prone to nerves and self-doubt, and in 1861 suffered a brief nervous breakdown (the "crazy" episode to which he later referred).

After the fall of Atlanta and his famous "March to the Sea," in 1865 Sherman marched north through the Carolinas and received the surrender of Johnston's Confederates on April 26.

**J**oseph Eggleston Johnston (1820–91) was a professional soldier with a cunning mind. Graduating from West Point in 1839, he served through the Mexican War. In 1861 he resigned to enter the Confederate service, and soon showed that, unlike many of his Civil War counterparts, he possessed a firm grasp of the South's strategic situation. From the first, when he led Confederate troops at First Bull Run and in the early stages of the Peninsular Campaign, Johnston fought like a modern guerrilla. Rather than hurl his outnumbered troops against superior Northern artillery or manpower, he would harry, wait, and strike only when he was sure of victory. Although not the ideal commander in a great decisive battle, he excelled in that most difficult of all military maneuvers, an orderly retreat. Whatever the Confederate High Command thought of it, there is no doubt that his withdrawal to Atlanta was executed with skill and success.

"No officer or soldier who ever served under me will question the generalship of Joseph E. Johnston. His retreats were timely, in good order, and he left nothing behind," said Sherman of his Georgia adversary. Although it is uncertain if "Old Joe" could have triumphed where Hood eventually failed, he would at least have saved the army, and Sherman's "March to the Sea" might never have been completed. In February 1865 Johnston was again appointed to command the Army of Tennessee, which he led until the war's end.

The two opponents of the Georgia campaign respected each other to the last. When Sherman was buried in 1891, Johnston was one of the honorary pall-bearers. In the bitter cold weather outside the Catholic church in New York City where the funeral was held, an American officer urged the pious Johnston, who had uncovered his head when the coffin passed, "General, please put on your hat–you'll get sick in this weather." Johnston retorted, "If I were in there, he'd have his hat off." Five weeks later, Johnston himself died–of pneumonia.

the man. Riding to a small hill to reconnoiter, Walker was felled by a Union sharpshooter.

By noon on the 22nd, rather than at dawn, as planned, the Rebel attack got under way. But now, although they were clear of the pond and briar patches which had blocked their advance, Bate's and Walker's infantry, rather than coming out into an open area behind the Union line, ran up against Greenville Dodge's veterans of XVI Corps. McPherson, who was having a picnic lunch with Sherman and discussing whether or not Hood was preparing to evacuate Atlanta, became aware of the firing and sprang into the saddle. Galloping a little too fast and a few hundred yards too close to the sound of battle, the impetuous young general rode right through his own line and into that of the Confederates, who wasted no time in gunning him down.

Sherman, saddened by his friend's death, angrily ordered a counterattack to regain the corpse. Major-General John A. "Black Jack" Logan was summarily handed command of McPherson's Army of the Tennessee and ordered to hold his ground to the death. The Georgia troops of General Andrew West were about to attack the line. Dodge saw the Rebels coming and held his fire as they advanced. The Confederate divisions, although not coordinated, went up to, over, and through the Yankee line. Cleburne led his division through the gap between Dodge's corps and Bald Hill, and Major-General George Maney threw his men on the flank of the hill. In one of the few well-timed moves he made during the campaign, Hood, strapped to his saddle and watching the fight from the rear of the battle line, sent Cheatham's division head-on at the Union trenches. Brigadier-General D. C. Govan's brigade crawled up the hill and surprised a Union brigade. The Union soldiers quickly threw down their arms, but when someone noticed that they outnumbered the Rebels, they picked them up again. The Southerners then surrendered but, after a quick headcount revealed that the two sides were roughly equal, canceled the capitulation and tore into the Yankees hand-to-hand. (Govan's men eventually won.) The advantage changed hands several times, but by nightfall Logan's men were in command of the hill and Hood, having thrown in all his available troops, called off the attack. More than 8,000 of his men had fallen, taking about 3,700 Northerners with them. The Union left had not been destroyed, as he had hoped, though it had been blunted. Hood still had two rail lines open, to the south and southwest, and that night Atlanta remained a Confederate city.

Sherman now decided to give the task of cutting Hood's rail lines to his cavalry. Three divisions would be sent to tear up the rail lines below the city. McCook was to come in from the west and join Garrad and Stoneman, who would swing in from Decatur and wait for him at Lovejoy Station, well below the city. After destroying the railroad, they would ride to Andersonville Prison Camp and release the 34,000 Union prisoners held there. These men would in effect give Sherman another corps with which to subdue Georgia.

Joe Wheeler, meanwhile, had deployed his Confederate cavalry to prevent just such a raid. When on July 27 Garrard with 4,000 troopers reached Flat Rock, the designated meeting place with Stoneman, he found Wheeler there instead, ready for a fight. Garrard, not the bravest of commanders, let himself be pinned down while he waited for Stoneman. But Stoneman, not wishing to share the glory of rescuing

Andersonville, had gone on ahead with his 2,500 men. Wheeler responded to this development by leaving a brigade to face Garrard, while he sent Iverson and three brigades after Stoneman and took another brigade west to face McCook.

McCook had been steadily advancing and tearing up railroad tracks for several days. He had burned over 1,600 wagons and killed 2,000 mules, all of which were badly needed by Hood, but had not so far met any resistance. Instead of joining up with Stoneman, however, he now found himself being attacked by Wheeler from one side and by W. H. Jackson from the other. In a running fight, the exhausted Union troopers were scattered at Newnan before they could cross the Chattahoochee to the safety of their own lines.

Stoneman was also in danger. Hood had sent a brigade by rail to chase him; Howell Cobb, militia chief of Georgia, was personally leading his Macon militia to close in on Stoneman; and Iverson, with the Confederate cavalry, was in his rear. Caught by the Rebels at Clinton, Stoneman panicked and told two of his brigades to break out in small packets for the Union lines while he held off the pursuers with the third brigade. The next day Stoneman and his 700 men of the rearguard surrendered to Iverson.

Sherman, convinced that his cavalry was worthless and that a move from the east on Atlanta could not succeed, decided to move the Army of the Tennessee from his left to his right. The infantry would cut the railroads and thus seal Atlanta off from food and reinforcements. Logan, who had been only temporarily in command of McPherson's army, was replaced by the one-armed Major-General Oliver Otis Howard, whose corps had been soundly beaten by Jackson at Chancellorsville. Joe Hooker, who had commanded the Union army at that battle and chiefly blamed Howard for his own demotion and disgrace after it, was so incensed by Howard's promotion over him that he resigned. Sherman did not miss him.

As Howard moved around the rear of the Union lines, Hood, through his scouts, learned of the Union general's intentions. S. D. Lee, commanding Hood's corps, was ordered to move west and stop any extension of the Union siege lines. On July 28 Howard reached Ezra Church to the west of Atlanta with the corps of Logan and Blair. Unlike Sherman, he was sure that Hood would still try and fight. As he began to face stiffened opposition from Rebel cavalry, Howard ordered his men to dig in. He could "feel" the Confederate attack coming. The Union infantry tore down the wooden church, erecting hasty barricades along the hills above the Lickskillet Road. Logan's XV Corps faced east and Blair's XVII Corps southeast, hinging on the ruined church. Lee arrived and, without waiting for his own troops to get into full battle order or for Stewart's division to come up on the Union flank, threw his men against the breastworks. At 12.30 P.M. Brown advanced his Rebel division, with three brigades in line and a fourth in reserve, but they became entangled in the briars in front of the Union works. While his men were falling back from the heavy fire, Clayton's division was sent forward. Gibson's brigade of that division moved unsupported against Logan's left and was counterattacked by overwhelming numbers. With his leading units in a panic, Clayton cancelled the attack. Now Lee's men were enfiladed by Union cannon; caught in thickets and heavily outnumbered, they faced disaster. Stewart, arriving at 2 P.M., wisely decided not to launch an all-out assault, but to put enough

# BATTLE OF ATLANTA

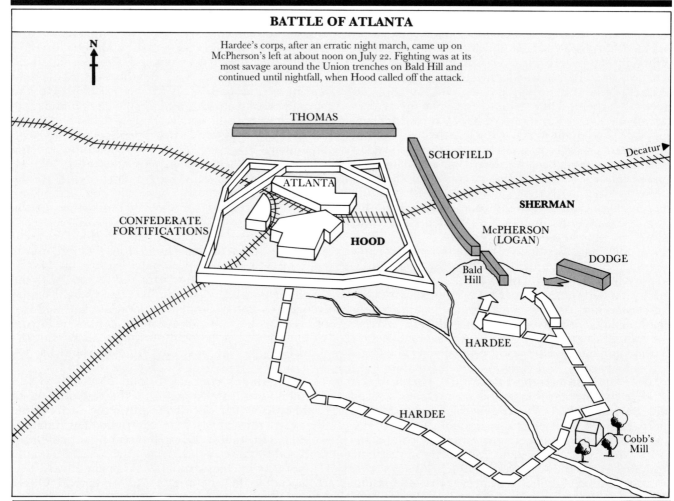

Hardee's corps, after an erratic night march, came up on McPherson's left at about noon on July 22. Fighting was at its most savage around the Union trenches on Bald Hill and continued until nightfall, when Hood called off the attack.

N

THOMAS

SCHOFIELD

Decatur ▶

ATLANTA

SHERMAN

McPHERSON
(LOGAN)

CONFEDERATE
FORTIFICATIONS

DODGE

HOOD

Bald
Hill

HARDEE

HARDEE

Cobb's
Mill

## THE OPPOSING FORCES

**UNION ARMY**
Major-General William T. Sherman

**ARMY OF THE CUMBERLAND**
Major-General George H. Thomas

IV Corps
Major-General Oliver O. Howard

First Division (Major-General David S. Stanley):
brigades of Cruft, Whitaker and Grose.
Second Division (Brigadier-General John Newton):
brigades of Francis Sherman, Wagner and Harker.
Third Division (Brigadier-General Thomas Wood):
brigades of William Gibson, Hazen and Beatty.
Strength: 72 regiments of infantry and 13 batteries.

XIV Corps
Major-General John M. Palmer

First Division (Brigadier-General R. W. Johnson):
brigades of Carlin, King and Scribner.
Second Division (Brigadier-General Jefferson C. Davis):
brigades of Morgan, Mitchell and McCook.
Third Division (Brigadier-General Absalom Baird):
brigades of Turchin, Derveer and Este.
Strength: 64 regiments 13 batteries.

XX Corps
Major-General Joseph Hooker

First Division (Brigadier-General Alpheus Williams):
brigades of Knipe, Ruger and Robinson.
Second Division (Brigadier-General John Geary):
brigades of Candy, Buschbeck and Ireland.
Third Division (Major-General Daniel Butterfield):
brigades of Ward, Ross and Wood.

Strength: 53 regiments and 12 batteries.

Unattached Troops

Colonel Burke's Reserve brigade plus trains.
Strength: 5 regiments.

Cavalry Corps
Brigadier-General Washington Elliot

First Division (Brigadier-General Edward McCook):
brigades of Dorr and La Grange.
Second Division (Brigadier-General Kenner Garrard):
brigades of Minty, Long and Wilder.
Third Division (Brigadier-General Judson Kilpatrick):
birgades of Klein, Charles Smith and Murray.
Strength: 25 regiments and 3 batteries.

**ARMY OF THE TENNESSEE**
Major-General James B. McPherson

XV Corps
Major-General John A. Logan

First Division (Brigadier-General Peter Osterhaus):
brigades of Woods, Williamson and Wangelin.
Second Division (Brigadier-General Morgan Smith):
brigades of Giles Smith and Lightburn.
Fourth Division (Brigadier-General William Harrow):
brigades of Reuben Williams, Walcutt and Oliver.
Strength: 40 regiments and 7 batteries.

XVI Corps
Major-General Greenville Dodge

Second Division (Brigadier-General Thomas Sweeny):
brigades of Rice, Burke and Vanderver.

Fourth Division (Brigadier-General John Fuller):
brigades of Morill, Sprague and Grower.
Strength: 24 regiments and 5 batteries.

## XVII Corps
### Major-General Frank Blair

Third Division (Brigadier-General Mortimer Leggett):
brigades of Force, Robert Scott and Malloy.
Fourth Division (Brigadier-General Walter Gresham):
brigades of Sanderson, Rogers and Hall.
Strength: 24 regiments and 8 batteries.

## ARMY OF THE OHIO (XXIII Corps)
### Major-General John Schofield

First Division (Brigadier-General Alvin Hovey):
brigades of Barter and McQuiston.
Second Division (Brigadier-General Henry Judah):
brigades of McLean, Hascall and Strickland.

Third Division (Brigadier-General Jacob D. Cox):
brigades of Reilly, Manson and McLean.
Cavalry Division (Major-General John Stoneman):
brigades of Garrard, Biddle, Capron and Holeman.
Strength: 37 regiments of infantry, 10 of cavalry and 6 batteries.

### Estimated Totals

For his Atlanta Campaign, Sherman had 319 regiments of infantry, 35 of cavalry, and 67 batteries of artillery, giving him a total of approximately 99,000 men and 254 guns. His peak strength, including reinforcements and deducting casualties, was 112,819, on June 1; by September 1 the total figure was reduced to 81,758. Losses: 4,423 killed, 22,822 wounded, and 4,442 captured or missing.
Total: 31,687 (rising to nearly 40,000 including deserters and stragglers).

## CONFEDERATE ARMY OF TENNESSEE
### General Joseph E. Johnston

#### Hardee's Corps
#### Lieutenant-General William J. Hardee

Cheatham's Division (Major-General B.F. Cheatham):
brigades of Maney, Carter, Strahl and Vaughan.
Cleburn's Division (Major-General Patrick Cleburne):
brigades of Lucius Polk, Lowrey, Govan and Granbury.
Walker's Division (Major-General W.H.T. Walker):
brigades of John Jackson, Gist, Stevens and Mercer.
Bate's Division (Major-General William Bate):
brigades of Lewis, T.B. Smith and Finely.
Strength: 93 regiments of infantry and 15 batteries of artillery.

#### Hood's Corps
#### Lieutenant-General John Bell Hood

Hindman's Division (Major-General T.C. Hindman):
brigades of Deas, Manigault, Tucker and Walthall.
Stevenson's Division (Major-General C.L. Stevenson):
brigades of Brown, Cumming, Reynolds and Pettus.
Stewart's Division (Major-General Alexander Stewart):
brigades of Stovall, Clayton, Baker and Randall Gibson.
Strength: 67 regiments and 12 batteries.

#### Cavalry Corps
#### Major-General Joseph Wheeler

Martin's Division (Major-General W.T. Martin):
brigades of Morgan and Iverson.
Kelly's Division (Brigadier-General J.H. Kelly):
brigades of Allen, Dibrell and Hannon.
Humes's Division (Brigadier-General W.Y.C. Humes):
brigades of Wheeler, Harrison and Grigsby.

Strength: 36 regiments and 5 batteries.

#### Polk's Corps
#### Lieutenant-General Leonidas Polk

Loring's Division (Major-General W. W. Loring):
brigades of Featherston, Adams and Thomas Scott.
French's Division (Major-General Samuel French):
brigades of Ector, Cockrell and Sears.
Cantey's Division (Brigadier-General James Cantey):
brigades of Quarles, Reynolds and O'Neal.
Strength: 55 regiments and 12 batteries.

#### Cavalry Division
#### Brigadier-General W. H. Jackson

Brigades of Armstrong, Ross and Ferguson.
Strength: 13 regiments and 3 batteries.

#### First Division, Georgia Militia
#### Major-General Gustavus Smith

Brigades of Carswell, Phillips, C. D. Anderson and McKay.
Strength: approximately 5,000 men in 7–14 regiments, with some artillery.

### Estimated Totals

Johnston's Army of Tennessee had 215 regiments of infantry, plus militia, 49 of cavalry, and 47 batteries, giving him a maximum total of approximately 62,000 men and 120 guns.
Losses: 3,044 killed, 18,952 wounded, and 12,983 captured or missing. Total: 34,979 (nearly 40,000, like the Unon army, if additional losses are included).

---

pressure on the defenders to allow Lee to pull out.

On August 6 Sherman again tried to extend to his right, sending Schofield against the Rebel lines at Utoy Creek; but Bate's defenders handily repulsed the Army of the Ohio. Sherman now decided that Hood, reduced to barely 36,000 effectives, would have little choice but to remain on the defensive. Rather than accommodate him by launching his troops against the forts of Atlanta, Sherman settled down to a textbook siege operation. He wired Halleck, "I do not deem it prudent to extend anymore to the right, but will push forward daily, by parallels, and will make the inside of Atlanta too hot to be endured." He sent to Chattanooga for two heavy 32-pounder Parrott guns, and on August 9 he began a continuous

bombardment, ordering his artillery officers to "destroy Atlanta and make it a desolation."

The first of several hundred civilians to die from Sherman's guns met her death at the corner of East Ellis and Ivy Streets: a little blonde girl and her dog were obliterated by the undiscriminating cannon shell. Hood complained to Sherman that his lines were a full mile from the town, and that the struggle for Atlanta ought not to take innocent lives. Sherman replied that the object of war was to destroy the enemy's country and that Atlanta, as the chief depot of the manufactures of war for the Confederacy, was hardly a peaceable community of noncombatants.

Mayor James M. Calhoun had meanwhile done his best to turn Atlanta into a fighting city. He demanded that the plantation owners should furnish slaves to build fortifications and repair the railroads, and he pleaded for the citizens to take arms. "All male citizens who are not willing to defend their homes and families are requested to leave the city at their earliest convenience, as their presence only embarrasses the authorities and tends to the demoralization of the others," proclaimed Calhoun.

The population of Atlanta went underground as the bombardment started, retiring to bomb shelters built beneath their homes; the entrance to these shelters was always on the south side, the only quarter from which Sherman's guns could not bear. On August 9, the day that Sherman's firestorm began in earnest, over 5,000 shells fell upon the city (although about two-thirds of them failed to explode). The duel, between 11 Federal and 10 Rebel batteries, went on all day; many of the gunners fell at their posts from sheer exhaustion. The Union gunners kept up a steady rate of fire: each battery was assigned a fixed amount of ammunition which it had to use up in a day. In an attempt to cut off Sherman's supply of ammunition and thus force him to abandon the siege, Hood sent Wheeler's 4,500 troopers off to raid the rail lines. In a month of hard riding, the horsemen tore up 100 miles of Georgia railroad and another 50 in Tennessee; they captured about 1,300 horses and mules and tied down a large garrison on the lines. The raids, however, did little to hamper Sherman and left Hood short on manpower in the crucial month of the campaign.

The unrestricted bombardment did not force Hood either to evacuate the city or to come out and fight, much to Sherman's dissatisfaction. The harassment of the populace produced an effect similar to that of the mass bombing raids of recent history: it gave the people a feeling of participation, unity and, above all, determination to resist the aggressor. Atlanta refused to fall to the guns. On the morning of August 26, no shells fell upon the city. Curious over the unexpected silence, Hood sent out his pickets; they reported that the enemy trenches were abandoned. The cry went through the city: the siege was lifted! For the first time in many weeks the church bells pealed, people came out into the streets, and the bands played "Dixie" throughout the town. Every open building which was not already filled with wounded became a site for a victory ball. Hood was the hero of the Confederacy. But Sherman had not gone away.

More firmly convinced than ever that he had to cut off the two southern rail lines into the city, Sherman prepared a single, massive thrust below the town. Leaving Slocum's XX Corps (Slocum took over from Hooker) to guard the Chattahoochee railroad bridges and keep his communications secure, Sherman and the rest of his army–six full corps–would abandon the siege lines and swing south, cutting the railroads and then swinging up to take Atlanta from its soft underside. Schofield's troops were to be the first to fall upon the railroads: his army aimed at Rough and Ready on the Macon line. Howard was to strike for Jonesboro, farther to the south, with Thomas backing him up.

On August 30 Hood realized what was happening and sent Hardee with 24,000 men to attack Howard, leaving only Stewart and the militia to hold the city. Hardee's force barely made it out of Atlanta: as his last trainload passed Rough and Ready, Schofield made his lunge at the station, quickly overwhelming the garrison. The Confederates detrained at Jonesboro in mid-afternoon on August 31, just as

Howard was crossing the Flint River. The leading Union brigades dug in, and Hardee obligingly charged, but, as Brigadier-General Jacob Cox, one of Howard's officers, observed, "The attack was fierce but neither in weight nor in persistency did it seem equal to the former efforts of the Confederate infantry." Cleburne threw his men at Howard's right, just after S. D. Lee charged the front. The first wave rolled back from the defenders' devastating fire, losing nearly 2,000 men. Cleburne persuaded Lee to go with him to see Hardee, who readily agreed that "success against such odds could at best have been only partial and bloody, while defeat would have meant almost inevitable destruction of the army." Hardee then dug in.

Hood, learning of Schofield's move, recalled Lee's corps for a possible attack on the Army of the Ohio. That was Hood's last message from Atlanta, for the Union troops cut the telegraph wire immediately afterward. On September 1 Sherman threw his whole force against Hardee, who had barely 5,000 men still capable of fighting. Brigadier-General Jefferson C. Davis led three Union divisions against Cleburne at 4 P.M. Repulsed in the first charge, Davis rallied his men and swept the Rebels from their works. Cleburne, the best of the Rebel divisional officers, held up the Union mass with Granbury's Texans, behind whom Hardee reformed. That night, the weakened Confederate corps slipped off to join Hood.

His rail lines ruined, his army bled white, and his position untenable, Hood evacuated Atlanta the same day. His tattered columns moved out, as Stephen Vincent Benet wrote, like "soldiers of retreat beneath a fading star." Soon only the cavalry remained. Their final task was to destroy the rolling mill and the ammunition supply. In a column of fire and thunder, seven locomotives and 18 boxcars filled with ordnance exploded, tearing the guts out of the inner city. This task competed, the horsemen rode down the McDonough Road to join the army. With them went the last vestige of law and order. On the following morning (September 2), Mayor Calhoun rode out with a white flag and surrendered the city to Slocum. Colonel William Cogswell and his 2nd Massachusetts infantry were the first Union troops to enter the town.

Sherman's army occupied Atlanta for two months, resting and rebuilding. During that time Sherman sent Thomas north to Tennessee to protect the Union supply lines, while he himself vainly pursued the elusive Hood around the Georgia and Alabama countryside. After several weeks Sherman abandoned these efforts in favor of a massive sweep through eastern Georgia to Savannah. On November 9 Sherman's army began its "March to the Sea." With Howard on the right and Slocum on the left, the 50,000 Bluecoats marched like a horde of locusts to the Atlantic, cutting a path of devastation 50 miles wide and 300 miles long. The first victim of this holocaust was Atlanta herself. As he paused to watch the smoke clouds gather over the burned-out landscape, a nearby band of XIV Corps played "The Battle Hymn of the Republic," which the marching infantry along the Decatur Road picked up in a hearty chorus of 10,000 voices. "Never before or since," said Sherman, deeply moved, "have I heard a chorus of 'Glory, Glory, Hallelujah' done with more spirit or in better harmony of time or place." Sherman's march culminated at the seaport of Savannah in mid-December. As he had promised, he gave the city to Lincoln as a Christmas present.

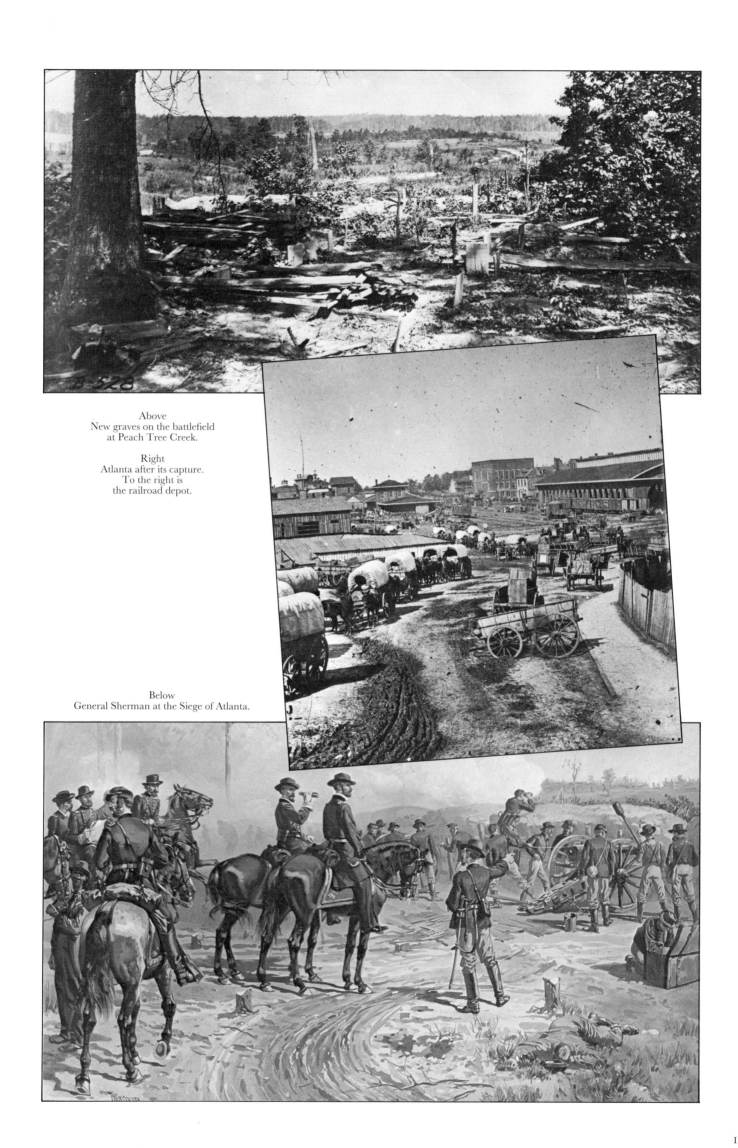

Above
New graves on the battlefield
at Peach Tree Creek.

Right
Atlanta after its capture.
To the right is
the railroad depot.

Below
General Sherman at the Siege of Atlanta.

# MOBILE BAY

## August 5, 1864

After the battle–the shot-pummeled lighthouse beside Fort Morgan, the five-sided Confederate bastion commanding the only deep-water entrance to Mobile Bay.

Next to New Orleans, the cotton-exporting city of Mobile, Alabama, was the most important Gulf Coast port of the Confederacy. Lying at the mouth of the Mobile River, the "Queen of the Gulf" was 150 years old in 1861, a cosmopolitan city grown prosperous on the transportation of cotton, food crops, lumber, and naval stores brought to its wharves from the interior.

Mobile was not at first an important objective of Union naval forces in the Gulf. The establishment of an efficient blockade in the Gulf as a whole, and the capture of the port of New Orleans, were of infinitely more significance to Navy Secretary Gideon Welles's Strategy Board. Even after the fall of New Orleans in April 1862, Washington remained unconvinced of Mobile's importance. Flag Officer David Glasgow Farragut, the commander of the Western Gulf Blockading Squadron, suggested an immediate move against the city, but Lincoln vetoed the proposal, preferring instead to divert the better part of Farragut's fleet up the Mississippi in a frantic dash to assault the Confederate stronghold of Vicksburg.

The Mississippi held little but frustration for Davy Farragut's deep-water ships and salt-water sailors. The Union fleet ran the Vicksburg gauntlet, but as Commander David D. Porter put it, "Ships . . . cannot crawl up hills 300 feet high, and it is that part of Vicksburg which must be taken by the army." Since the army was nowhere in the vicinity, combined operations were impossible and Farragut was forced to return to the Gulf, harried on his way by Confederate guerrillas, who sniped at his vessels from the river banks.

When Farragut returned from the "inland sea" in the latter part of 1862, he again advanced the idea of an attack on Mobile. Once again, he was rebuffed. Assistant Secretary of the Navy, Gustavus Vasa Fox, let him down gently: "We don't think you have force enough, and we do not expect you to run risks, crippled as you are . . . my opinion is that wood [wooden ships] has taken risk enough, and that iron will be the next affair." So Farragut and his "wooden walls" marked time in the Gulf awaiting the new iron monitors promised his squadron as soon as Charleston, the unconquerable bastion of secession, had fallen to Union arms.

The wait proved to be lengthy. Charleston defied the Union naval assault, and Farragut's squadron was denied the monitors it so desperately needed to carry the blockade into the bowels of Mobile Bay. The Mississippi beckoned again, and Farragut assisted General Nathaniel P. Banks in reducing the fortress of Port Hudson, which fell on July 9, 1863, just five days after Vicksburg capitulated to General Grant's army. Confederate power was thus decisively broken in the Mississippi Valley.

On his return from the Mississippi, Farragut took a five-month convalescent leave, rejoining his squadron in January 1864. Knowing that the Confederates were strengthening Mobile's defenses and preparing an ironclad blockade-buster, the *Tennessee*, he again appealed to Washington for the matériel with which to close the port. "I am satisfied that if I had one ironclad at this time," he told Welles, "I could destroy their whole force in the bay and reduce the forts at my leisure by cooperation of our land forces, say, 5,000 men."

Washington, however, was not yet disposed to grant Farragut's wish. No matter that Admiral Franklin Buchanan, the Confederate commander at Mobile, had vowed to raise the blockade as soon as the *Tennessee* was ready for action; the monitors Farragut wanted were still battering Charleston's defenses, and the infantry he needed to capture Mobile's forts were away on a fool's errand, gone up the Red River into Louisiana to meet ignominious defeat. Besides, the prevailing attitude in the Administration seemed to be one of "let sleeping dogs lie." So long as the Rebels in Mobile did not bother the blockaders, why bother them? Another seven months would elapse before the pieces finally fell in place and Farragut could launch his long-delayed offensive against the Confederate citadel. By then, the resourceful Rebels had had ample time to prepare for the onslaught.

At the beginning of the war, Mobile was virtually defenseless. There were two old brick forts at the mouth of the bay, both of them run-down and neglected. Fort Morgan, a pentagonal work on the western tip of Mobile Point, and Fort Gaines, opposite on Dauphine Island, commanded a 2,000-yard-wide channel at the entrance to the bay (the only practicable deep-water route). When Buchanan arrived in August 1862, these works were undergunned and manned by a corporal's guard of State troops, barely enough men to work the outmoded guns. Buchanan's first job was to strengthen these forts. He added guns to their batteries, including some powerful rifled pieces, and increased the garrisons. In addition, he erected Fort Powell northwest of Dauphine Island to guard the narrow, shallow-water channel known as Grant's Pass which led to Mississippi Sound. (This passage could not be utilized by the deep-draft vessels of the Union fleet.)

Supplementing the guns of the forts was a forbidding complex of pilings and torpedoes (mines) laid across the main channel, restricting it to a 500-yard-wide safe passage under the ramparts of Fort Morgan. The obstructions were designed by Brigadier-General Gabriel J. Rains, the inventive Confederate mines expert. The eastern end of this barrier (that closest to Fort Morgan) was marked by a red buoy. Beginning at the buoy and running west across the ship channel was a triple line of "infernal machines" (some 180 in all). The pilings covered the shallow westward portion of the channel in the direction of Fort Gaines. Rains's system was so devised that hostile vessels attempting to enter the bay had to choose between crossing the deadly minefield or passing under the guns of the fort and its water battery.

The most important part of the defense, however, was the makeshift fleet of gunboats and ironclads that Buchanan had assembled to deal with Farragut's cruisers. On paper this fleet was quite impressive, consisting as it did of several armored rams, including CSS *Nashville*, nicknamed "the monster" because of its great size. But only a few of these vessels were seaworthy, and the bulk of the force never ventured into the bay. Still, in those days of hybrid navies, one fairly efficient armored vessel could defy any number of wooden battleships with impunity. Buchanan himself had proved this at Hampton Roads when he took on an entire Federal fleet with CSS *Merrimack* and destroyed the *Congress* and the *Cumberland*. In the *Tennessee*, constructed under his close personal supervision, the Confederates had such a warship.

The *Tennessee*, laid down at the Rebel iron foundry at Selma, Alabama, some 150 miles upriver from Mobile, was the most powerful casemated ironclad in the Confederate Navy. Resembling the *Merricmack* in configuration, the sloping sides of her barn-like superstructure were plated with three courses of 2-inch wrought iron armor, giving her a 6-inch composite shield thought capable of resisting the heaviest fire that could be brought to bear against her. Her battery consisted of six heavy guns: four 6.4-inch Brooke rifles in broadside—two on each side—and two 7-inch Brooke rifles on pivot mounts—one at each end of the casemate. In addition, she was fitted with a ram, but her slow speed (6 knots maximum) and lack of agility negated the effectiveness of this weapon.

The *Tennessee* was, indeed, a remarkable vessel, calculated to reduce any of Farragut's ships to charred flotsam in a head-to-head battle. From the standpoint of the marine engineer, however, she was one of the worst vessels ever built—a distinction she shared with others of her ilk. She was slow, balky, and underpowered. Her engines, cannibalized from a Yazoo River steamboat and fitted with extemporized

Confederates at Mobile. Buchanan and Rains had used every resource ingenuity could bring to bear to obstruct the main ship-channel, but little faith was placed in the stopping power of the forts. The real hope of the defense lay in the *Tennessee*. Based on the experience of the *Merrimack* and several similar Rebel ironclads, it was confidently expected that she would batter to pieces or rout any Union warships penetrating the bay.

Washington's policy of delay allowed the Confederates the time they needed to complete their preparations at Mobile. It took more than a year to build the *Tennessee*, and in March she was towed from Selma to Mobile and outfitted for action, receiving her armor and battery. Thus completed, she ventured into the bay in mid-May—a seemingly unconquerable behemoth, mistress of all she surveyed. Farragut, from his station on blockade, could only look on impotently; without monitors to engage the *Tennessee* in shoal water, he did not dare attempt a passage of

Farragut's fleet runs into Mobile Bay under the guns of Fort Morgan.
The leading Union ship, the monitor *Tecumseh*, has struck a torpedo and is keeling over.
In the left foreground, the forward 7-inch gun of the Confederate ram *Tennessee* blazes at the Union fleet.

wooden gears, could barely develop enough horsepower to drive her against a current. Her gunport shutters swung open and shut on crude pins and were liable to jam when hit by shot. Worst of all, her steering chains lay exposed in grooves along her rear decking—a defect later corrected when 1-inch iron plating was bolted over the channels.

The rest of the Confederate fleet available for action in the bay consisted of three lightly armored gunboats: the *Selma*, *Gaines*, and *Morgan*. None of these tiny vessels was very powerful, but they were all quick and maneuverable. They were expected to add the weight of their fire to that of the *Tennessee* but to keep their distance from enemy battleships, since on each the guns were totally exposed and in action at close quarters the gunners were certain to be driven to shelter.

Such was the defensive system employed by the

the forts. As the months passed, he grew impatient, writing home: "I am tired of watching Buchanan and Page, and wish from the bottom of my heart that Buck would come out and try his hand upon us. This question has to be settled, iron versus wood; and there never was a better chance to settle the question." How he longed for a conclusion. But Buchanan, for all his bluster about raising the blockade, was content to stay within the confines of the bay.

By midsummer, however, the impasse was largely ended, and Farragut was preparing for action. Three monitors had arrived in July—the single-turret *Manhattan* from the Atlantic and two twin-turret river monitors, the *Chickasaw* and the *Winnebago*, from the Mississippi. Another single-turret monitor, the *Tecumseh*, captained by Farragut's old friend Tunis A. M. Craven, was due in early August. With these doughty craft in his line of battle, the Union commander would not hesitate to enter the bay and fight it out. The problem of obtaining troops for the landward operations against the forts was resolved almost at the same time. Despite constant drains on his manpower from the Virginia theater, Major-General E.R.S. Canby, the commander of the Military Division of West Mississippi, managed to make 5,000 men under Major-General Gordon Granger available for the operation. Thus, by early August, Farragut had gathered together all the men and matériel he needed to make an attack that ought to have been made two years earlier.

In his original plan Farragut envisaged a simultaneous attack on the forts by the land and naval forces. Granger's men duly "hit the beach" at Dauphine Island on August 3 and promptly invested Fort Gaines, but the Admiral reluctantly postponed the naval assault pending the arrival of the *Tecumseh*, which was being towed from Pensacola by the *Richmond* and was expected at any moment. Farragut's

wooden ships were assigned to the main column, the number equally divided between heavy "battleships" and lesser vessels. Each battleship was paired with a gunboat, which was to be yoked to its port side with heavy cables. Once past the obstructions, however, the gunboats were to cast off and engage the Rebel squadron. Farragut originally intended to lead this column in his flagship, the *Hartford*, but was persuaded to allow the *Brooklyn* to lead because she had four heavy bow-chasers (cannon) and "an ingenious arrangement for picking up torpedoes."

The four monitors, led by the *Tecumseh*, which had finally arrived on the afternoon of the 4th, were to run past the forts to the east and slightly ahead of the main column. Their role, according to Farragut, would be "first, to neutralize as much as possible the fire of the guns which rake our approach; next to look out for the ironclads when we are abreast of the forts; and, lastly, to occupy the attention of those batteries which would rake us while running up the bay."

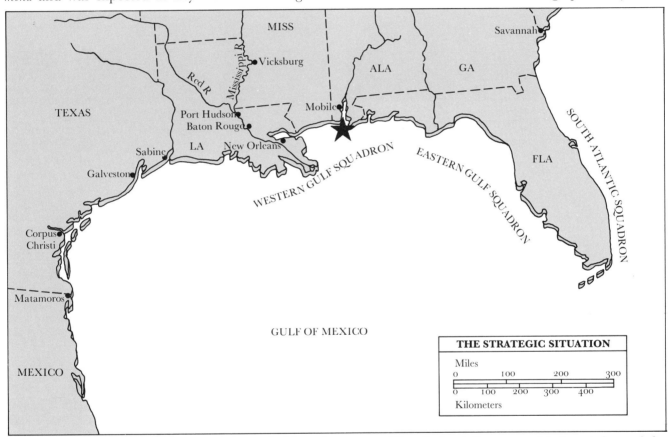

THE STRATEGIC SITUATION

Miles

Kilometers

plan for the naval operation had been fashioned meticulously. Lieutenant-Commander J.C. Watson, the Admiral's aide, related that "Farragut had the carpenter make some little wooden blocks, shaped like boats, with which he experimented on a table or board, on which the points of the compass were traced, to determine the best positions of the vessels with reference to each other in entering the Bay. I used to help him maneuver the little blocks so as to concentrate and maintain as heavy a fire as possible upon Fort Morgan when we should be going in." Having thus "war-gamed" the approach, Farragut issued his orders, prescribing the position of each vessel in the line and various tactical arrangements he wished to be observed.

The time of the attack was set for daybreak on August 5, to take advantage of the early-morning flood-tide, which would help carry the ships past the forts and into the bay. The fleet was to form in two columns: one of wooden ships "in couples, lashed side by side," and one of monitors in single file. Fourteen

The Federal fleet assembled and formed for battle in a dissipating fog at dawn on the 5th. John Coddington Kinney, an army signals officer assigned to the *Hartford*, described the scene: "It was a weird sight as the big ships 'balanced to partners,' the dim outlines slowly emerging like phantoms in the fog . . . All the vessels had been stripped for the fight, the top-hamper being left at Pensacola, and the starboard boats being either left behind or towed on the port side."

Farragut took tea on the *Hartford* while the columns formed in echelon to the right rear so that each vessel was astern of the starboard broadside of the next ahead–a formation that would allow the bow chasers of each ship to play on Fort Morgan while the fleet was running in. Finally, at 5.30 A.M., Farragut rose from his table and, addressing Fleet-Captain Percival Drayton, said, "Well, Drayton, we might as well get underway." Within 15 minutes the great flotilla was churning toward the bay.

At first, the monitors ranged far ahead of the

# THE COMMANDERS

Admiral David G. Farragut, USN

Admiral Franklin Buchanan, CSN

David Glasgow Farragut (1801–70) was the son of George Farragut, a Minorcan *émigré* who served with distinction in the Continental army and navy during the Revolutionary War. In 1808 Farragut's mother died of yellow fever in New Orleans, and young Davy was adopted by Commodore David Porter as a favor to the elder Farragut, then burdened with the care and upbringing of five sons. Farragut's family background and the Porter connection determined his choice of career. At the age of nine he was a midshipman in the U.S. Navy, and during the War of 1812 he was prizemaster of the ship *Alexander Barclay*. Thereafter, until the outbreak of the Civil War, he held ship commands on various stations, fought in the Mexican War, and established the Mare Island Navy Yard in San Francisco Bay.

In December 1861, with 49 years of uninterrupted service behind him, Farragut was appointed Flag Officer of the newly formed Western Gulf Blockading Squadron, a command befitting his as yet untapped high tactical ability. During the next three years, this fleet developed into a primary strike force in the Gulf and the lower Mississippi, carrying the war to the enemy and capturing New Orleans, Galveston, Corpus Christi, Sabine Pass, Port Hudson, and Mobile. These successes earned Farragut the nation's gratitude, and he was lionized as a popular hero. On July 25, 1866, he was promoted Admiral, the rank having been created specially for him by Act of Congress.

Farragut was a remarkably vital man whose boldness and boyish enthusiasm impressed his contemporaries. He had a fondness for red wine, but never drank to excess, and remained alert, trim, and vigorous until the end. But despite this uncomplicated vitality, Farragut was not in the least bit naive; he had all the sagacity of an old sea-dog, and the impetuosity that might have been his undoing on several occasions was only allowed to manifest itself in calculated measures.

Franklin Buchanan (1800–74) is popularly remembered as the man who established the predictable superiority of the armored warship when, as commander of the ironclad *Merrimack*, he won the first round of the Battle of Hampton Roads (March 8, 1862). The scion of a prominent Baltimore family, Buchanan entered the navy at 14 as a midshipman. After service in the Mexican War, he was appointed the first Superintendent of the Naval Academy at Annapolis (1845–47). Subsequently, he served as flag-captain of Commodore Perry's squadron on the famous expedition to Japan. Returning from the Orient, he spent six years on "waiting orders" before being named commander of the Washington Navy Yard in 1859, two years before the outbreak of war.

Buchanan was a strong Unionist, but was repelled by the coercive policy of the Lincoln administration. Anticipating the secession of his native state of Maryland, he resigned his commission on April 22, 1861. Upon entering Confederate service, Buchanan was placed in command of the tiny fleet charged with the defense of Norfolk, Virginia, and the James River. As commander of the *Merrimack*, he was wounded in the action at Hampton Roads. On August 21, 1862, he was appointed Admiral. A short time later, he was transferred to Mobile to organize and command the naval defenses of that city, and he set about his new task with alacrity and skill.

Buchanan was a stern, no-nonsense Presbyterian who abhorred drunkenness. A fellow officer described him as "the *beau idéal* of a naval officer of the old school, with tall form, harsh features, and clear, piercing eyes." As a naval commander, he was courageous but impulsive. When he led the *Tennessee* out to do battle with the entire Union fleet at Mobile Bay, he gave up whatever advantage he might have obtained by waiting and making a night attack. Farragut, whose own audacity was leavened by a healthy dose of common sense, looked on and commented, "I did not think old Buck was such a fool."

main column, and at 6.45 the *Tecumseh* fired the first shots of the battle, loosing a "scaling shot" from each of her two 15-inch guns at the looming gray eminence of Fort Morgan. The fort did not immediately reply, and for several minutes the calm off Mobile Point was broken only by the steady drumming of machinery in motion as the fleet drew slowly ahead. Soon, however, the ships closed the gap between themselves and the fort, and at 7.07 the fort opened fire. Beginning at 7.10 the battleships, led by the *Brooklyn*, replied with their bow-chasers, and within minutes the firing became general.

By 7.30 the *Brooklyn* had overtaken the rear of the plodding column of monitors, and the other wooden vessels, closing in her wake, were contracting the column for the dash past the fort. The crisis of the battle was approaching, and the "wooden walls" strove desperately to beat down the fire from Fort Morgan: first the *Brooklyn* and then each battleship in succession delivered its broadside, again and again. During the next 20 minutes, this fire was furiously sustained, the weight of each broadside exceeding that of Admiral Nelson's fleet at Trafalgar.

In reply, Fort Morgan redoubled its fire, and the Rebel squadron, with the *Tennessee* in the van, eased out from the lee of Mobile Point and into a position behind the minefield from which it could rake the Union vessels as they attempted to negotiate the narrow passage between the red buoy and the fort. The Union vessels, caught in a galling crossfire, were hulled repeatedly, the enemy shells raking the advanced ships fore and aft. At this juncture, the *Brooklyn* began to hesitate, slowing and signaling that the monitors were fouling her path. Farragut, in reply, bade her "Go ahead." Lieutenant-Commander Watson described what happened next: "Instead of going ahead, the *Brooklyn* was seen to be backing, and in doing so her bow swung across the bow of the *Hartford*, closing the narrow passage to the east of the line of torpedoes. Farragut hailed again, and all that could be distinguished of her reply was something about torpedoes."

The cause of all the confusion was the *Tecumseh*, which had turned from the assigned course and made straight for the *Tennessee* as soon as the Rebel ironclad appeared behind the minefield, and at 7.45, when the monitor had drawn to within 200 yards of the *Tennessee*, she struck a torpedo and abruptly sank. As the vessel began to plunge, bow first, her propellor spinning wildly above the waves, Craven and the pilot, John Collins, met at the foot of a ladder leading to the top of the turret and safety. "Go ahead, captain," beckoned the pilot. "No, sir," the gallant Craven declined. "After you, pilot. I leave my ship last." As Collins scrambled away, the *Tecumseh* slid from under him, carrying Craven and 92 others of her complement of 114 with her.

It was a critical moment. The *Brooklyn* was lying athwart the ship channel, unwilling to proceed, yet all the while taking a terrific pounding from the fort, which mistook her for the flagship. The rest of the wooden ships, like the *Hartford*, would soon become stacked up astern of her unless something was done–and done quickly. The danger of collision and piecemeal destruction by the fort's guns was increasing with each passing minute. On the *Hartford*, Signal Officer Kinney described a sight "sickening beyond the power of words to portray . . . Shot after shot came through the side, mowing down the men, deluging the decks with blood, and scattering mangled fragments of humanity so thickly that it was difficult to stand on

the deck, so slippery was it. The old expressions of the 'scuppers running blood,' 'the slippery deck,' etc, give but the faintest idea of the spectacle on the *Hartford*. The bodies of the dead were placed in a long row on the port side, while the wounded were sent below until the surgeon's quarters would hold no more. A solid shot coming through the bow struck a gunner in the neck, completely severing head from body. One poor fellow (afterward an object of interest at the great Sanitary Commission Fair in New York) lost both legs by a cannon-ball; as he fell he threw up both arms, just in time to have them also carried away by another shot. At one gun, all the crew on one side were swept down by a shot which came crashing through the bulwarks.''

Farragut, who had earlier climbed into the *Hartford*'s port main rigging to get a better view of the action, faced the crisis with equanimity. Praying for guidance, he thought he heard a voice inside him command, "Go on!" Then, hailing Drayton and Captain James E. Jouett of the *Metacomet*, he bellowed, "I will take the lead." Almost immediately, the *Metacomet* reversed her paddlewheels, swinging the *Hartford* about to port and clear of the *Brooklyn*. "By this movement," Watson recalled, "we all knew that Farragut had decided suddenly to cross the torpedo field, which he had forbidden any of the ships to do." The *Brooklyn* warned again of torpedoes, but Farragut was determined. As the *Hartford* and her consort began to make headway, he was heard to shout, "Damn the torpedoes! Full speed ahead, Drayton! Hard a-starboard! Ring four bells! Eight bells! Sixteen bells!"

The *Hartford* and the *Metacomet* churned on, magnificently heedless of the danger, and the other vessels fell into line behind; soon the entire fleet had passed the minefield without the loss of a ship. Farragut's abrupt decision to alter course and go on despite the manifest danger of the torpedoes was a daring expedient. There were anxious moments during the passage of the minefield–moments when it seemed that the Union fleet had eluded one predicament only to plunge, bows-on, into another. Several officers reported hearing the snapping of torpedo-primers under the ships, and Watson remembered, "Some of us expected every moment to feel the shock of an explosion under the *Hartford* and to find ourselves in the water."

The high drama of the moment has captivated historians, and Farragut's expression, "Damn the torpedoes!" has become a naval watchword; but in the words of Captain Thornton A. Jenkins of the *Richmond*, Farragut did "the only safe thing possible to do." The risk was great and the attempt bold, but Farragut, characteristically, had weighed the possibilities before the battle. He concluded then, as he told Watson, that "inevitably many of the torpedoes were leaky and would not explode, and a good many have probably drifted from their moorings." As it happened, events proved his judgment correct.

The ordeal of the minefield past, the *Hartford* and her consort steamed into the lower bay, where, for several minutes, they faced the Rebel squadron alone. Here, the Union vessels were confined by the narrow channel of the Middle Ground and were unable to maneuver. Buchanan took advantage of their temporary embarrassment to mount an attack which, had it been pressed with more fervor, might have overwhelmed them. The *Tennessee* led, making a beeline for the *Hartford* as if to ram her amidships, but the Union flagship was too nimble for her adversary

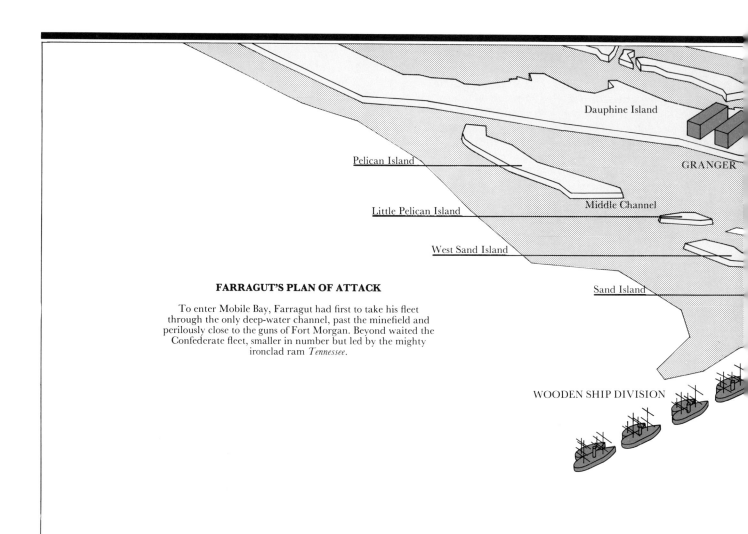

**FARRAGUT'S PLAN OF ATTACK**

To enter Mobile Bay, Farragut had first to take his fleet
through the only deep-water channel, past the minefield and
perilously close to the guns of Fort Morgan. Beyond waited the
Confederate fleet, smaller in number but led by the mighty
ironclad ram *Tennessee.*

---

## THE OPPOSING FORCES

### UNION FLEET
Rear-Admiral David G. Farragut

Monitor Division

*Tecumseh* (Captain Tunis A.M. Craven): single turret, 2
guns.
*Manhattan* (Commander J.W.A. Nicholson): single
turret, 2 guns.
*Winnebago* (Commander T.H. Stevens): double turret, 4
guns.
*Chickasaw* (Lieutenant-Commander G.H. Perkins):
double turret, 4 guns.

Wooden Ship Division
(ships lashed together in pairs)

*Brooklyn* (Captain James Alden): screw sloop, 25 guns, with
*Octorara* (Lieutenant-Commander C.H. Greene):
double-ender, 10 guns.
*Hartford* (flagship, Captain Percival Drayton): screw
sloop, 24 guns, with
*Metacomet* (Lieutenant-Commander J.E. Jouett):double-
ender, 10 guns.
*Richmond* (Captain T.A. Jenkins): screw sloop, 22 guns,
with
*Port Royal* (Lieutenant-Commander B. Gherardi):
double-ender, 8 guns.
*Lackawanna* (Captain J.B. Marchand): screw sloop, 14
guns, with
*Seminole* (Commander E. Donaldson): screw sloop, 8
guns.

*Monongahela* (Commander James H. Strong): screw
sloop, 11 guns, with
*Kennebec* (Lieutenant-Commander W.P. McCann):
gunboat, 6 guns.
*Ossipee* (Commander W.E. LeRoy): screw sloop, 12 guns,
with
*Itasca* (Lieutenant-Commander George Brown):
gunboat, 6 guns.
*Oneida* (Lieutenant C.L. Huntington): screw sloop, 10
guns, with
*Galena* (Lieutenant-Commander C.H. Wells): screw
steamer, 11 guns.

### UNION ARMY
Major-General E.R.S. Canby

Granger's Command
Major-General Gordon Granger

5 infantry brigades (Bailey, Guppey, Clark, Bertram and
Robinson.)
3 battalions of artillery.
1 regiment and 2 companies of cavalry.
Strength: approximately 5,500 men.

Estimated Losses

Army: 7 wounded.
Fleet: 145 killed, 170 wounded, and 4 captured.

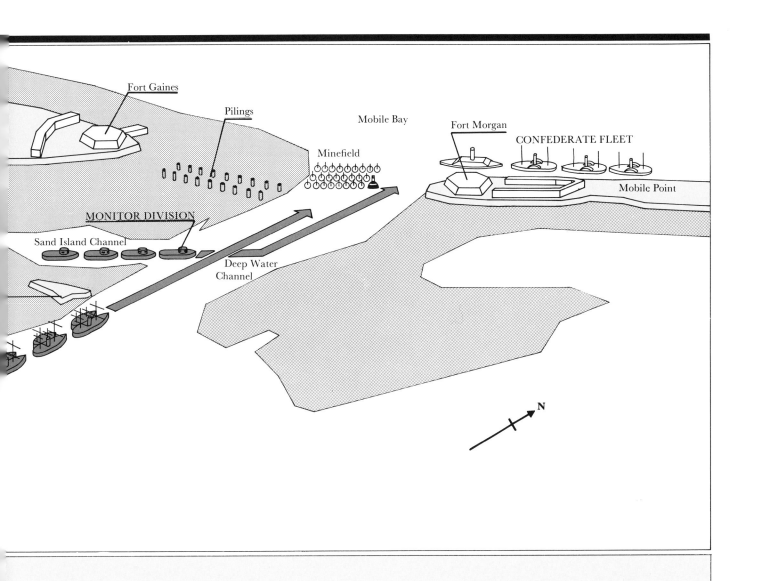

Fort Gaines

Pilings

Mobile Bay

Fort Morgan

CONFEDERATE FLEET

Minefield

Mobile Point

MONITOR DIVISION

Sand Island Channel

Deep Water Channel

N

## CONFEDERATE FLEET
### Admiral Franklin Buchanan

*Tennessee* (flagship, Commander J.D. Johnston): ironclad ram, 6 guns.
*Morgan* (Commander George W. Harrison): side-wheel gunboat, 6 guns.
*Gaines* (Lieutenant J.W. Bennett): side-wheel gunboat, 6 guns.
*Selma* (Commander P.U. Murphy): side-wheel gunboat, 4 guns.

## CONFEDERATE LAND FORCES
### Major-General Dabney H. Maury

Page's Command (Fort Morgan garrison, etc.)
Brigadier-General Richard L. Page

Various commands, totaling about 800 men.

Estimated Losses

Land forces: 1 killed and 3 wounded.
Fleet: 12 killed, 20 wounded, and 280 captured.

and easily evaded the attempt. As the *Tennessee* sheered away to engage the rest of the fleet, the *Hartford* gave her a full broadside at point-blank range, a pounding that would turn most vessels into matchwood. The ram, however, was undisturbed, and amazed Bluejackets looked on in disbelief as the big 9-inch projectiles bounded harmlessly off the casemate.

The *Hartford*'s broadsides did better execution among the Confederate gunboats, driving two of them, the *Gaines* and the *Morgan*, to shelter under the fort's guns. The *Gaines* was shattered in the exchange of salvos and beached by her crew when on the point of sinking, but the *Morgan* later escaped to Mobile under the cover of darkness. The *Selma*, which was managed more skillfully than her sisters, had meanwhile taken up a position above the *Hartford*'s bow, where she darted back and forth, crossing and recrossing ahead of the Union flagship and damaging her with raking shots that coursed through her bowels from stem to stern. Preoccupied as she was, there was little the *Hartford* herself could do to end this torment, but Farragut cast off the *Metacomet*, and Jouett's aptly named vessel chased the *Selma* up the bay and captured her after engaging in a sharp fight at close quarters.

While all this was happening, the *Tennessee* descended on the rest of the Union fleet, intent like some great iron fighting bull on slashing and goring her way through anything in her path. Once again, however, the ram failed in her object, and the fleet slipped past to join the *Hartford* at her anchorage four miles up the bay. Buchanan, having failed twice seriously to damage the Union fleet, returned to Navy Cove, snug under the guns of Fort Morgan. At the Union anchorage, nine wooden ships and three monitors (three gunboats had joined the *Metacomet* in her pursuit of the *Selma*) dropped anchor near the flagship. The crews prepared their breakfast and busied themselves with post-battle housekeeping while Farragut framed a plan to make a night attack on the *Tennessee* with the three remaining monitors. Suddenly—and to everyone's surprise—the still air was rent by the cry, "The ram is coming!" The *Tennessee*, barely visible at four miles but her progress clearly marked by a billowing pillar of black smoke, was returning to the fray.

The sudden reappearance of the Rebel ironclad created a great deal of commotion in the Union fleet: navy signals fluttered aloft and army signalers semaphored messages, the vessels lumbered into motion, jockeying for position, and the Admiral, for a second time, climbed into the *Hartford*'s rigging. "Then," according to Farragut's report, "began one of the fiercest naval battles on record."

"The heavier vessels seemed to contend with each other for the glory of sinking the daring rebel ram, by running themselves up on her decks," wrote Commander James D. Johnston of the *Tennessee*. First the *Monongahela* and then the *Lackawanna*, both big screw-sloops, rammed the iron turtle—but to no purpose; each suffered more damage than it inflicted. Next came the *Hartford*, which struck the ironclad obliquely, bow-on, and sheered alongside her. As the vessels passed, port side to port side, both fired broadsides; the *Hartford*'s shot again glanced off, but the ram's projectiles tore at the innards of the Union flagship, killing eight men.

The *Hartford* had been mauled, her berth and spar decks were a shambles, but Farragut ordered her to put about for another go at the *Tennessee*. While she maneuvered, the *Lackawanna* careered into her star-board side, smashing planking to within two feet of the waterline and sending crewmen flying. As the flagship staggered off, the impetuous *Lackawanna* came on again, still pointing for the ram but plowing dangerously close to the *Hartford* and missing both. Exasperated, Farragut turned to a nearby signal officer and barked, "Can you say 'For God's sake' by signal?" Answered affirmatively, he directed, "Then say to the *Lackawanna*, 'For God's sake, get out of the way and anchor!'" At that, the *Lackawanna* drew off.

The monitors had by now joined the fight, and their intervention proved decisive. The *Chickasaw* took position 50 yards astern of the ironclad, "hanging on to us like a dog," according to the *Tennessee*'s pilot, "and firing the two 11-inch guns in her forward turret like pocket-pistols, so that she soon had the plates flying in the air." This pummeling wrecked the *Tennessee*'s chances. Her steering chains were shot away, and her perforated smokestack collapsed. All her gunports were jammed, and an engineer who tried to repair one was shivered to fragments by the concussive effect of a projectile striking nearby; his remains were shoveled into a bucket and put out of the way. The same shot wounded Buchanan, whose leg was crushed by a splinter jarred loose from the casemate's wooden backing. In a short time, the ironclad was rendered helpless. Unable to maneuver or make steam, unable even to run her guns into battery and reply to the tremendous hammering she was taking, she was observed "lying like a log in the water." When the *Manhattan* brought her 15-inch guns to bear and began a "racking" fire against the previously invulnerable casemate, the *coup de grâce* was administered. At 10 o'clock, some three hours after the battle's first exchanges, the *Tennessee* surrendered.

The capitulation of the *Tennessee* doomed the two forts at the mouth of the bay, and when they fell, as they did after a brief but stubborn resistance, Mobile's usefulness to the Confederacy ended. The victory—Farragut's greatest—had been bought at great cost. Union casualties were 319, including 145 killed. The sinking of the *Tecumseh* was the greatest single ship disaster in the U.S. Navy until World War II. The Rebel fleet lost 12 killed, 20 wounded, and 280 captured, including Buchanan and Johnston. Farragut's triumph left the Confederacy with but one major outlet to the sea—Wilmington, North Carolina. With the blockade now attaining the peak of its efficiency, the effect was crippling. The South was thrown back on her already over-strained and inadequate domestic resources, and the resulting shortages of matériel sapped her powers of resistance as Grant and Sherman powered her remaining armies into ignominious surrender.

As for Mobile, the city persevered until the end. Snug behind her forts and torpedo barrier, she was impervious to naval assault, and General Dabney H. Maury's little army protected her landward flank. When Sherman scourged Georgia in his "March to the Sea," the Alabama delta was isolated and Mobile became a Rebel island. The finish came on April 12, 1865, when Maury abandoned the city to Granger's Federals and retreated west to Mississippi. These final operations cost the Union 1,417 casualties and caused Grant to lament, "I had tried for more than two years to have an expedition sent against Mobile when its possession by us would have been of great advantage. It finally cost lives to take it when its possession was of no importance." Farragut, had he been privy to the General's correspondence, would have understood completely.

Above
A composite photograph showing the interior of Fort Morgan.

The Confederate ram *Tennessee*, idling in calm waters (below), and "lying like a log" in Mobile Bay, surrounded by Union ships and about to surrender.

# NASHVILLE
## December 15–16, 1864

Civilians watch and listen to the battle from the
grounds of the Military College.

The month of November 1864 witnessed a rare and perhaps unparalleled military spectacle: the two great armies of the West, which had been locked in bitter combat for the better part of five months, turned and marched away from each other in opposite directions. The genesis of this remarkable turn of events lay in the impasse which developed on the Georgia front soon after Hood abandoned Atlanta (September 1, 1864) and swung around to the northwest in a move that threatened Sherman's 140-mile-long line of communications with Chattanooga. Leaving one corps to defend Atlanta, which he had denuded of civilians and turned into a military camp, and sending Thomas with two infantry divisions into Tennessee to protect his rear from depradations by Confederate Cavalry, Sherman, in October, turned north to try to snare Hood. But Hood, who, Sherman admitted, could "twist and turn like a fox, and wear out any army in pursuit" could not be brought to book, and Sherman soon gave up the pursuit. On the 22nd, having chased Hood beyond the Alabama line, he took up a position at Gaylesville, Alabama, from which he could "watch" the enemy, then thought to be at Gadsden. Hood, however, was not at Gadsden; he was marching toward the Tennessee River, and his army next appeared at Decatur, 75 miles northwest of Gadsden, on the 26th.

This last move by Hood determined Sherman's strategy, for the Confederate general now seemed bent on an all-or-nothing invasion of Tennessee. For Sherman to follow Hood would be to jeopardize all the gains of the Atlanta campaign and sacrifice the initiative to a ragged army which, by Sherman's own estimate, could not field more than 400,000 men of all arms. This went against the grain, so Sherman determined to match Hood's bold gamble with a stratagem of his own. Reinforcing Thomas in Tennessee with Major-General David S. Stanley's IV Corps and Major-General John M. Schofield's XXIII Corps, plus all the cavalry (much of it dismounted) he could spare, he cut his line of communications with the North, burned Atlanta, and on November 9 began his famous march to Savannah and the sea.

Hood, meantime, had not been idle. Divining Sherman's intent, he modified his original plan of raiding the Union supply line in Tennessee, expanding it to encompass a full-scale invasion of the North, which he hoped would carry him eventually through the Cumberland Gap and into Grant's rear at Petersburg, where, in concert with Lee, he would fall on Grant and defeat him "at least two weeks before Sherman could render him assistance." Far-fetched? Hare-brained? A fantastic scheme? Hood's plan has been called all of these things but in fact it did cause consternation and no small amount of worry in the North. Grant, watching from afar in Virginia and sensing that Louisville and perhaps even Chicago were threatened, later confessed, "I was never so anxious during the war as at that time." But Sherman had promised that Thomas could contain Hood, and so Thomas, with his section of Sherman's army and the vague pledge of troops from General A. J. Smith's command in Missouri, was left to face the Confederate onslaught virtually alone.

By October 31 Hood was at Tuscumbia, Alabama, on the Tennessee River, revictualing his army and awaiting the arrival of Bedford Forrest's cavalry before venturing across the river and into Tennessee. After much delay, occasioned as much by railroad repairs and the rain-swollen river as by the late arrival of Forrest's horsemen, the Confederate army crossed the river on November 21 and began its fateful invasion of Tennessee. Hood's first objective was Thomas's advanced guard, a detachment of 26,500 infantry and 6,500 cavalry under Schofield, which had been thrown forward to Pulaski, Tennessee, in the hope of obstructing the Rebel march toward Nashville. By rapid marches along the Mount Pleasant Turnpike, the Confederate commander hoped to get in Schofield's rear at Columbia and interpose between him and Nashville before the Union general could countermarch to safety.

With Forrest clearing the way, Hood came within an ace of attaining his objective. The two armies converged on Columbia almost simultaneously, but Schofield had the shorter distance to go, and his men got there first, just as Forrest was driving in their cavalry screen. Forrest was turned back, and by the time Hood's infantry had arrived in force on the 27th, Schofield had entrenched the town, covering the bridges across the Duck River. As the two armies faced off along the Duck, Hood conceived an ingenious scheme to pass the river and gain Schofield's flank and rear at Spring Hill, a crossroads town 12 miles north of Columbia. By using Forrest's talented troopers to screen his march, and leaving two divisions of Stephen D. Lee's corps with nearly all the army's artillery to pin Schofield at Columbia, the Confederate commander planned to swing the bulk of his army unobserved across the river above the town and descend on the Union rear before Schofield could react. Cut off from Nashville and pinned between two strong forces, Schofield would have no choice but to surrender. The scheme was, as Hood clinically appraised it, "one of those interesting and beautiful moves on the chessboard of war."

At first, all went well, Forrest's troopers forded the Duck unopposed at Huey's Mills, eight miles above Columbia, on the morning of the 28th. The Union cavalry, under its new commander, Brigadier-General James H. Wilson, who had been sent west by Grant specifically to upgrade the hangdog horsemen of the Military Division of the Mississippi, proved, in Schofield's words, "entirely unable to cope with him [Forrest]," and were driven off to the northeast. At this juncture, and just before his communications with the field army were cut, Wilson managed to get some telegraphic messages back to Schofield warning him of the danger of a Confederate strategic envelopment and pleading with him to "get back to Franklin without delay." For the time being, though, Schofield remained in Columbia. He was expecting reinforcements from Nashville, and his men were worn out from five days of forced marches; despite the manifest urgency of the situation, he would not move until Thomas ordered him to retreat.

Hood's infantry, fully two-thirds of his force, began crossing the Duck in the early morning of the 29th. To the noisy accompaniment of Lee's demonstration at the town, first Benjamin Cheatham's corps, then A. P. Stewart's together with Edward Johnson's division of Lee's corps, passed the river and set out on their hike to Spring Hill. Traveling by dirt roads, the Rebel van drew within sight of the crossroads by 3 P.M. Forrest, of course, was already there, skirmishing with Federal infantry drawn up in a semicircle north of the town.

The Union infantry at Spring Hill belonged to the solitary division of Brigadier-General George D.

Wagner (under the command of General Stanley), which had been hurried northward when Schofield had finally received Thomas's order to retreat at 3.30 A.M. that morning. For the better part of the afternoon and early evening, these troops–numbering in all about 4,000 men–were all that stood between Hood and ultimate victory in the Nashville campaign. What happened next has never been satisfactorily explained and remains a mystery to this day. Hood's infantry, led by Pat Cleburne's élite division, came into line below Spring Hill and advanced toward the turnpike, which was Schofield's lifeline to Nashville. Stanley's men beat off a few half-hearted attacks, and as the afternoon shadows lengthened on the field, the Rebel assault faltered and began to flounder about in confusion. Whole divisions wandered off course or were stopped by conflicting orders: Stewart's corps meandering up the wrong road, countermarched, but came up on the right one too late to be of service. By nightfall, the whole maneuver had degenerated into a

was made to interrupt the Union retreat. By morning Schofield was gone, his leading elements already fortifying the bridges across the Harpeth River at Franklin, just 15 miles south of Nashville.

For Hood, dawn on the 30th brought with it the painful realization that the blunders of the previous day had cost him a great opportunity: "the best which this campaign has offered, and one of the best afforded us during the war." Instead of throttling Schofield, he had been left grasping at air. Enraged, he blamed Cheatham, who in turn blamed him. Before his anger burned itself out, it had settled on the much-maligned troops of the Army of Tennessee, hard-luck soldiers who had proved their mettle in half a dozen bloody encounters, but whom Hood believed incapable of standing up any longer to the rigors of battle. Before the day was out, they would prove him wrong. Once again, Hood set out in pursuit of the elusive Schofield. Following the Columbia Turnpike north past burned-out wagons (the evidence of

Panoramic view of the city of Nashville,
the Union lines, and the battlefield.
The camera, mounted on the roof of a building
on the University of Nashville campus, was in turn pointed due south, then
south-southwest, and then southwest.
In the middleground left are Forts Negley, Casino, and Morton.
Beyond are the hills occupied by the Confederate army.
Some experts believe that these remarkable photographs
were taken while the battle was in progress.

chaotic mess, and the Confederate infantry bivouacked wherever they happened to be–in many cases, within a few hundred yards of the vital asphalt roadway along which the rest of Schofield's army was scurrying to safety.

Union officers were astounded by Hood's ineptitude. Colonel Henry Stone of Thomas's staff noted that, "When night came, the danger increased rather than diminished. A single Confederate brigade, like Adams's or Cockrell's or Maney's–veterans since Shiloh–planted squarely across the pike, either south or north of Spring Hill, would have effectually prevented Schofield's retreat, and daylight would have found his whole force cut off from every avenue of escape by more than twice its numbers, to assault whom would have been madness, and to avoid whom would have been impossible." As the moonless night drew on, Schofield's strung-out force moved past the campfires of Hood's front. But apart from Forrest, who attacked at Thompson's Station, a few miles north of Spring Hill, and a few squads of enterprising infantrymen who roamed the pike firing indiscriminately into the Yankee column, no serious attempt

Forrest's fight) and piles of discarded knapsacks, the Rebel infantry debouched at about 3 P.M. into the plain below Franklin and formed for battle about two miles from Schofield's hastily constructed works ringing the southern approaches to the town.

Schofield had not intended to offer battle at Franklin, but his progress toward Nashville had been held up while his engineers completed repairs on two bridges across the Harpeth River. His troops, mostly veterans, had entrenched a position on the low hills surrounding the town to the south, completing in a few hours a fairly strong bridgehead some two miles in length. The view toward the Confederate line of approach through the Winstead Hills was unobstructed, offering as clear a field of fire as Civil War troops ever saw. The stage was set for the Battle of Franklin, one of the most sanguine of the war, and the Army of Tennessee's last great throw. Few soldiers in either army had anticipated a battle at Franklin, but when it was thrust upon them, they fought it with a savage valor that made a special chapter in the history of man's heroism.

The Confederate line at the foot of Winstead

Hills stretched nearly two miles from flank to flank. From Stewart on the right to Cheatham in the center and left, the whole array massed about 20,000 men–more than had marched the mile to glory with Pickett at Gettysburg. What was about to take place was the greatest charge in the history of the American people. At exactly 3.30 P.M., the Confederates stepped off, deliberately at first, but gaining momentum as they closed the space between themselves and their adversaries. Two brigades of Wagner's division, posted in error outside and in advance of the Union line, were engulfed first, unable to oppose the onrushing wave with anything more than a few rattling, ineffectual volleys. As the Graybacks of Cleburne's and John C. Brown's divisions swarmed over and around Wagner's position, they became enmeshed with the Union troops; some of the latter were taken prisoner, but others were still fleeing through the Confederate line toward their rear. Seeing their opportunity to make a decisive breakthrough, the Rebels began to

the line counted as many as 13 separate attacks during the afternoon and evening, and Hood reported fighting so ferocious "that soldiers were even dragged from one side of the breastworks to the other by men reaching over hurriedly and seizing their enemy by the hair or the collar." Finally, at about 9 P.M., the fighting sputtered out all along the front. Both armies were exhausted, completely fought out. Schofield's troops drew off silently in the inky blackness of the night, making good their escape to Nashville. They had sustained 2,326 casualties–10 percent of their effective strength–and were making their second night march in as many days, but at least the trauma of their long retreat was nearly ended. For the Army of Tennessee, on the other hand, Franklin had crippling consequences; the broken bodies of nearly 6,300 soldiers littered the vast amphitheater of the plain in front of the Union position; losses amounted to a fifth of the army's strength. Gone, too, were 53 field officers and 12 generals, either killed, wounded, or missing. The

shout, "Let's go into the works with them!"

So the Confederate line hurtled onward, filling the air with the wild howling of the Rebel yell. For the troops in the Union center, the crisis of the battle was fast approaching. Their comrades on either side stopped the Confederate rush, but they themselves dared not fire for fear of hitting Wagner's men. In a trice, Cleburne's men were in the main Union works by the Turnpike, capturing guns and colors and scattering the defenders right and left. The fighting swirled up to and around a big gin-house within the Union line, and more and more Rebel brigades crowded toward the gaping breach, adding their weight to Cleburne's spearhead. For a short time, it seemed as if Schofield's army must be overwhelmed, but just then things began to go awry for Hood's triumphant, yelling warriors. Brigadier-General Emerson Opdycke's Union brigade–"Opdycke's Tigers"–which had been lying in reserve a short distance to the rear, shouldered through the crowd of fugitives on the Turnpike and, forming on the run, pitched into Cleburne's command. The stunned Confederates were rocked backward by this compact fresh body of men and, after desperate hand-to-hand fighting, they were driven out of the Union works.

The Battle of Franklin did not end at that point, nor did nightfall end it. The Confederates were reluctant to go back the way they had come and clung sullenly to the outer face of the Union works, disputing its possession until well after dark. Other parts of

dead generals included the valiant Pat Cleburne, John Adams, and O. F. Strahl of Tennessee, J. B. Granbury of Texas, and States Rights Gist of (where else?) South Carolina; their bodies were later laid out on the colonnaded porch of McGavock House, where dark stains made by their blood may still be made out to this day.

A quick head-count revealed that Hood had just over 23,000 effectives left, but despite the absurdly small size of his force, he was determined to go on and besiege Nashville, adopting, he said, "the only feasible means of defeating the enemy with my reduced numbers, viz, to await his attack, and, if favored by success, to follow him into his works." Though he realized he might be venturing forward only to meet overwhelming defeat by an enemy force at least twice as large as his own, he sincerely believed that his men "should face a decisive issue rather than retreat," and that they should make "a last and manful effort to lift off the sinking fortunes of the Confederacy." It was the strategy of despair.

Two days later, on December 2, the ghostlike remnant of the once-proud Army of Tennessee invested Nashville, Tennessee's capital and the railroad center of the Union war effort in the West. The Confederate line, forming a shallow, concave curve for most of its length but hooked-back or refused on the left, was four and a half miles long and covered the southern approaches to the city. Cheatham's battered corps was placed on the right, its own right

# THE COMMANDERS

Major-General George H. Thomas, USA

General John Bell Hood, CSA

George Henry Thomas (1816–70) was a robust, 200-pound giant who made his reputation as a master of defensive warfare. Possessed of a firm, imperturbable personality, "Old Pap" was a dogged fighter whose genius sustained Rosecrans's beleaguered Army of the Tennessee at Murfreesboro, salvaging victory from near-defeat; his bulldog tenacity saved the same force from certain annihilation at Chickamauga, earning Thomas his sobriquet, "The Rock of Chickamauga."

A loyal Viriginian, Thomas graduated from West Point in 1840 and was commissioned in the artillery. After service in the Seminole War and with Bragg's battery in Mexico, he returned to West Point as an instructor in artillery and cavalry. In 1860, as major to the "All-Southern" 2nd Cavalry, he sustained his only wound–an arrow through the chin–in an insignificant skirmish with an Indian war party in the western mountains. When the Civil War began, he was on leave recuperating from the wound, but he immediately volunteered his services to the Union and commanded a brigade of Patterson's force in the Bull Run campaign. Later he was sent to eastern Kentucky to organize and recruit soldiers for the Unionist cause.

It was in Kentucky that Thomas won the first Union victory of the war, defeating Zollicoffer at Logan's Cross Roads. The pattern established there, whereby the Union army switched from the defensive to a devastating offensive at the moment the Confederate attack had spent itself, was later repeated on a grander scale at Nashville; Hood's army, like Zollicoffer's, was effectively destroyed as a fighting force. Significantly, of the three battles of annihilation fought in the war–Logan's Cross Roads, Forrest's defeat of Sturgis at Brice's Cross Roads, and Nashville–Thomas orchestrated two of them. Thus, although his own modesty and self-efffacement prevented his achieving high command until the war's last days, "Pap" Thomas is justifiably accounted one of the Union's greatest generals.

Aged 33 in 1864, John Bell Hood (1831–79) was the youngest officer to attain army command during the Civil War. His rise from brigadier to full general (a temporary rank) and command of the Army of Tennessee in little more than two years was so quick and, in some respects, unmerited that it prompted the caustic Texas Senator Louis T. Wigfall to declare, "That young man had a fine career before him until Davis undertook to make of him what the good Lord had not done–to make a great general of him."

A Kentuckian by birth, Hood graduated from West Point in 1853. After duty with a garrison infantry regiment in California and on the Plains with the famous 2nd Cavalry, he resigned his commission in April 1861 and entered the Confederate Army. His first appointment was as commander of "Prince John" Magruder's cavalry in the Peninsula, then in March 1862 he succeeded Wigfall as commander of the "Texas Brigade," justly renowned as the best fighting unit in Lee's Army of Northern Virginia. Thereafter, he rose rapidly. On October 10, 1862, he was promoted to major-general and given a command of a division of Longstreet's corps, which he led at Fredericksburg, Gettysburg, and Chickamauga. Cruelly wounded at Gettysburg, where his left arm was shattered, he recovered quickly, only to lose his right leg at Chickamauga. Subsequently he had to be strapped into the saddle, but he lost little of his physical vigor and commanded a corps under Johnston in the first phase of the Atlanta Campaign. Succeeding Johnston in July 1864, Hood launched a series of vicious counterblows against Sherman's army but failed ultimately to save Atlanta.

Hood was a lightweight tactician with no pretence to intellectual eminence; he was, nonetheless, a bold leader, without peer as a brigade or divisional commander. Lacking experience and administrative ability, however, he soon found himself at sea as an army commander. In January 1865, at his own request, he was relieved of his position.

extending across the Nolensville Turnpike to the Nashville & Chattanooga railroad. Lee's men were in the center, their lines covering the Franklin Turnpike, and Stewart's corps, taking post on the left, straddled the Granny White and Hillsboro turnpikes. The remaining gap of three miles from the Hillsboro Turnpike to the Cumberland River was unfortified but occupied by Forrest's horsemen.

This open ground proved eventually to be the undoing of Hood's defensive system, for when Forrest and the bulk of his command departed to gobble up Union garrisons elsewhere (as they did almost immediately), the line here was left to be held by one under-strength cavalry division of 1,200 men, barely enough to form a respectable picket line, according to one Confederate trooper. A few detached works, mounting artillery and garrisoned by infantry, with the cavalry forming a mobile reserve, might have better served the Confederates here; but Hood was no engineer and the yawning gap remained, an open invitation to a turning movement.

Within the entrenched position of Nashville, secure behind the big guns of the forts, Thomas's host was marshaling, 55,000 strong, awaiting the moment when its commander would turn it loose to drive off the ragamuffin horde that had penned it up in a bleak, sleet-swept camp where firewood was as scarce as a good hot meal. In the East, too, there was impatience –impatience bordering on hysteria. General Grant could not understand why Thomas, with his superior resources, would not attack and annihilate Hood. Colonel Stone recalled: "From the 2nd of December until the battle was fought on the 15th, the general-in-chief did not cease, day or night, to send him [Thomas] from the headquarters at City Point, Va., most urgent and often most uncalled-for orders in regard to his operations, culminating in an order on the 9th relieving him, and directing him to turn over his command to General Schofield, who was assigned to his place–an order which, had it not been revoked, the great captain would have obeyed with loyal single-heartedness."

If the rain of telegrams from City Point bothered Thomas, he gave no outward indication that he was at all affected. His "army" was indeed strong numerically, but it was under-organized and inexperienced, and he needed time to mold it into an effective fighting force. The dependable core was Schofield's command and three divisions of veterans under Smith, lately arrived from Missouri. The rest of the infantry consisted of fresh recruits in unbrigaded regiments, garrison troops, and convalescents. The need for time to organize and equip was especially pressing in the cavalry. Wilson had inherited a cavalry organization with an impressive paper strength of 50,000 troopers, but the best men and horses had gone with Sherman on his march; of the rest those available for immediate duty numbered about 12,500, mostly dismounted. These men had been chased from pillar to post by Forrest, Morgan, and Van Dorn, but they had never been effectively led or properly armed (according to Wilson, the variety of the arms made them a "museum on horseback"). It was Wilson's job to see to it that this sorry force was efficiently organized and uniformly armed, that the men were mounted and prepared to act as an independent, mobile striking force–the decisive force in the impending battle.

Washington was sceptical about Wilson's ability to mount his cavalry in time for an early blow against Hood and wanted Thomas to attack without him, but Thomas held out against the pressure. He knew that without Wilson any defeat of Hood's infantry would be vitiated by the presence of Forrest's superb command, but he had sworn that "if he [Hood] remains until Wilson gets equipped, I can whip him and will move against him at once." Wilson was finally ready on December 9, his men mounted on horses that were impressed for service from every conceivable source, including Governor Andrew Johnston's stables, street-car companies, and a few circuses, which unfortunately happened to be in the region. More importantly, each trooper was armed with a Spencer seven-shot repeating carbine, a weapon capable of delivering an awesome volume of fire by the standards of the time.

Now Thomas was ready to move on Hood, but the weather had changed abruptly, jeopardizing his chances of success. The temperature plunged 30 degrees on the 7th, ending a week of mild Indian Summer days, and on the 9th a storm of sleet covered the landscape with a sheet of slippery ice, making any kind of movement, mounted or on foot, virtually impossible. Under tremendous pressure from Washington to make the attack despite the weather, Thomas polled his officers on the 10th, seeking their guidance. Their reply confirmed Thomas's own opinion that no attack was feasible until a thaw had set in.

The weather moderated on the 12th, bringing in its train the hoped-for thaw and, by the 14th, mud. It was at last possible to predict a sloughy but comparatively good ground surface for the attack. Needing no further spur, Thomas convened a council of war on the night of the 14th and outlined his plan of battle for the next day. This skillful plan, which in practice became "a perfect exemplification of the art of war" (Schofield's assessment), envisioned a coordinated attack against both Confederate flanks. Major-General James B. Steedman's provisional division, composed mostly of "casuals", convalescents, and raw black regiments not fit for sterner work, was entrusted with the task of demonstrating against the right of Hood's line. While these troops "fixed" the Rebels and diverted Hood's attention from the main effort, Smith's corps-sized force and Brigadier-General Thomas J. Wood's IV Corps (Wood had replaced Stanley, who had been wounded at Franklin), preceded by Wilson's horsemen, would advance through the unfortified gap west of the Hillsboro Turnpike and, pivoting on the center, assail the Confederate left. Schofield's two divisions of XXIII Corps were designated to remain in reserve. Jump-off time was set for 6 A.M.

Dawn on the 15th found the Union forces moving to prearranged positions outside the line of their earthworks under cover of a bank of dense fog. Because of this fog and a major foul-up caused when some of Smith's men deployed across the front of the cavalry, the attack did not get under way until about 8 A.M.–a two-hour delay which, in the last analysis, may have prolonged the life of Hood's army. Steedman's men struck first, having advanced close to Cheatham's line under cover of the fog. The traditional view of this action, based largely on Colonel Stone's narrative, is that Steedman's attack deceived Hood, causing him to reinforce Cheatham with troops drawn from his as yet unengaged center and left, materially weakening Stewart and setting in motion a chain of events that led ultimately to the collapse of his left late in the day. This certainly was Thomas's intent, but it was not, in fact, what happened. Steedman's black brigades attacked

# THE OPENING DAY

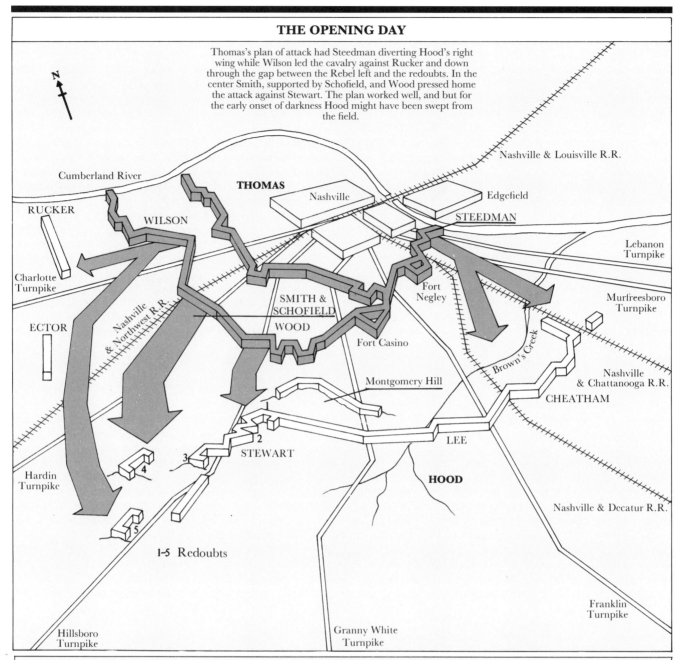

Thomas's plan of attack had Steedman diverting Hood's right wing while Wilson led the cavalry against Rucker and down through the gap between the Rebel left and the redoubts. In the center Smith, supported by Schofield, and Wood pressed home the attack against Stewart. The plan worked well, and but for the early onset of darkness Hood might have been swept from the field.

---

## THE OPPOSING FORCES

### UNION ARMY
Major-General George H. Thomas

#### IV Corps
Brigadier-General Thomas J. Wood

First Division (Brigadier-General Nathan Kimball): brigades of Kirby, Whitaker and Grose.
Second Division (Brigadier-General Washington Elliott): brigades of Opdycke, Lane and Conrad.
Third Division (Brigadier-General Samuel Beatty): brigades of Straight, Post and Knefler.
Strength: 53 regiments of infantry and 7 batteries of artillery.

#### XXIII Corps
Major-General John M. Schofield

Second Division (Major-General Darius Couch): brigades of Cooper, Orlando H. Moore and Mehringer.
Third Division (Brigadier-General Jacob D. Cox): brigades of Doolittle, Casement and Stiles.
Strength: 30 regiments and 4 batteries.

#### Detachment, Army of the Tennessee
Major-General A. J. Smith

First Division (Brigadier-General John McArthur): brigades of McMillen, Hubbard and Sylvester Hill.
Second Division (Brigadier-General Kenner Garrard): brigades of David Moore, Gilbert and Wolfe.
Third Division (Colonel Jonathan B. Moore): brigades of Ward and Blanden.
Strength: 33 regiments and 8 batteries.

#### Provisional Detachment
Major-General James B. Steedman

Provisional Division (Brigadier-General Charles Cruft): brigades of Benjamin Harrison, Mitchell, Grosvenor, Malloy, Morgan and Thompson, plus detachments and unbrigaded troops.
Strength: 5,270 men and 3 batteries.

#### Post of Nashville
Brigadier-General John F. Miller

Various troops, including Mason's brigade, the garrison artillery, and the Quartermaster's Division.

| Cavalry Corps<br>Brigadier-General James Harrison Wilson | brigades of Hammond and Gilbert Johnson.<br>Strength: 29 regiments and 4 batteries. |
|---|---|

Cavalry Corps
Brigadier-General James Harrison Wilson

First Division: Croxton's brigade.
Fifth Division (Brigadier-General Edward Hatch): brigades of Stewart and Coon.
Sixth Division (Brigadier-General Richard W. Johnson): brigades of Thomas J. Harrison and Biddle.
Seventh Division (Brigadier-General Joseph F. Knipe):

brigades of Hammond and Gilbert Johnson.
Strength: 29 regiments and 4 batteries.

Estimated Totals

Thomas's army had an approximate total strength of not fewer than 55,000 men and 170+ guns.
Losses: 387 killed, 2,558 wounded, and 112 captured or missing. Total: 3,057.

## CONFEDERATE ARMY OF TENNESSEE
### General John Bell Hood

Lee's Corps
Lieutenant-General Stephen Dill Lee

Johnson's Division (Major-General Edward Johnson): brigades of Deas, Manigault, Sharp and Brantly.
Stevenson's Division (Major-General Carter L. Stevenson): brigades of Cumming and Pettus.
Clayton's Division (Major-General H. D. Clayton): brigades of Stovall, Gibson and Holtzclaw.
Strength: 50 regiments of infantry and 7 batteries of artillery.

Stewart's Corps
Lieutenant-General A. P. Stewart

Loring's Division (Major-General William W. Loring): brigades of Featherston, Adams and Scott.
French's Division (temporarily attached to Walthall's Division): brigades of Sears and Ector.
Walthall's Division (Major-General E. C. Walthall): brigades of Quarles, Cantey and Reynolds.
Strength: 47 regiments of infantry and dismounted cavalry and 10 batteries.

Cheatham's Corps
Lieutenant-General Benjamin F. Cheatham

Brown's Division:
brigades of Gist, Maney, Strahl and Vaughan.
Cleburne's Division (Brigadier-General J. A. Smith): brigades of Lowrey, Govan and Granbury.
Bate's Division (Major-General William B. Bate): brigades of Tyler, Finley and Jackson.
Strength: 77 regiments of infantry and dismounted cavalry and 9 batteries.

Cavalry Division
Brigadier-General James R. Chalmers

Brigades of Rucker and Biffle.
Strength: 8 regiments.

Estimated Totals

Hood's Army of Tennessee had 174 regiments of infantry and dismounted cavalry, 8 of cavalry, and 26 batteries of artillery, giving him an approximate total strength of 38,000 men and 156 guns.
Losses: approximately 1,500 killed and wounded and 4,462 captured or missing. In addition, 59 guns were lost. Total: approximately 6,000 men and 59 guns.

enthusiastically, driving in the Rebel skirmishers and effecting a lodgment near the railroad, but they were too few to threaten Cheatham's main line seriously.

As Steedman's sham battle progressed, Wilson, on the Union right, initiated Thomas's grand turning movement. The muddy roads in this quarter of the field caused further delays, but the Union advance, if slow, was inexorable; there was little the outnumbered Confederate defenders (900 cavalry of Colonel E. W. Rucker's brigade and 700 infantry of Brigadier-General Matthew D. Ector's brigade) could do to oppose it. Wilson had over 12,000 cavalry in line, with 4,000 troopers, a full division, dismounted as skirmishers. Following, and deploying deliberately, were the massed battalions of Smith's 10,500-man corps. Ector's brigade made a brief show of resistance and then scurried to safety, running between Redoubts 4 and 5 on Stewart's extreme left. As they passed, their comrades in Redoubt 4 called on them for help, but the cry came back, "It can't be done; there's a whole army in your front!" Rucker's men fared little better, being driven pell-mell down the Charlotte Turnpike; it was long past nightfall before they were able to rejoin the main army.

Having cleared the Confederates from the ground west of the Hillsboro Turnpike, Wilson swung his command left, overlapping Stewart's flank and threatening Redoubt 5. Smith's infantry, supported by Schofield's corps, which had been released from its reserve role, now began to pivot on its left, linking with Wood's right opposite Montgomery Hill, a lightly held salient projecting from the main Confederate line just north of Redoubt 1. By 12.30 P.M. the whole Union array had deployed and begun to move forward in unison. General Wood, whose men had remained stationary all morning, described the ensuing scene emotionally: "The pageant was magnificently grand and imposing. Far as the eye could reach, the lines and masses of blue, over which the nation's emblem flaunted proudly, moved forward in such perfect order that the heart of the patriot might easily draw from it the happy presage of the coming glorious victory."

Colonel P. Sidney Post's brigade of Wood's corps took Montgomery Hill at 1 P.M., driving the skirmishers of Major-General W. W. Loring's Confederate division back to the main line behind. At about the same time, Colonel Datus E. Coon's brigade, dismounted, of Wilson's command, joined Brigadier-General John McArthur's division of Smith's corps in assaulting Redoubt 5. Coon's men led, driving along the Hillsboro Turnpike in loose order, their Spencers issuing a shower of lead that scoured the length of the enfiladed Rebel outworks and drove the defenders to seek cover wherever it could be found. The infantry, assaulting head-on, had a harder time of it, having to brave devastating short-range blasts of canister before mounting the works in triumph. With Redoubt 5 in hand, the Federal troops turned next to deal with Redoubt 4. Again, the isolated handful of defenders put up a stiff fight, but soon they were overpowered, hit simultaneously from flank and front. His outworks gone, Stewart now found his line "stretched to its utmost tension." Despite the arrival of reinforcements–Johnson's division of Lee's corps–there seemed little prospect of holding the flimsy trenches along the Hillsboro Turnpike in the face of the mounting strength of the Union attack.

Finally, in the late afternoon, the entire Union line advanced, an irresistible tide of men opposed by the virtually demoralized remnant of Stewart's corps, which for hours had been pummeled mercilessly by the Union artillery. The issue was never in doubt. Smith and Wood took the remaining redoubts and, continuing on, rousted Johnson and Stewart from the trench lines along the Turnpike. Disgracefully, Johnson's division fled before it had fired a shot in its own defense, and Schofield's corps, led by Major-General Darius N. Couch's division, poured through the gap, securing a high ground overlooking the Granny White Turnpike, one of Hood's two remaining retreat routes to the south.

It is quite probable that Hood's army might have collapsed completely that afternoon but for the early onset of darkness. Schofield's corps was entirely fresh, and Wilson had already begun another swing southward and into the vacuum in the Confederate rear. The only organized, resisting Confederates west of the Granny White Turnpike were Major-General William B. Bate's division of Cheatham's corps, shuttled over from the right to shore up Stewart's disintegrating front, and Ector's much-traveled brigade, which had rallied at Shy's Hill when implored by Hood to hold "regardless of what transpires around you." Bate contested Couch's advance in a brief twilight battle, then he too was forced back, joining Ector on Shy's Hill. Bate's fight ended hostilities for the day, and the Union army bivouacked uncomfortably in the damp fields where its advance had halted. Thomas, who had every reason to believe that he had won a great victory, made no battle plan for the 16th. He was satisfied with his men, who had captured two trains, 16 guns, and 1,000 prisoners at minimal cost; his only thoughts were of the pursuit.

But Hood refused to admit defeat. Despite the pounding his much-diminished army had taken, he was resolved to stay on, taking up a contracted line in the Brentwood Hills. His new line, extending from Shy's Hill in the west to Overton's Hill in the east, was three and a half miles long and covered the retreat routes along the Granny White and Franklin Turnpikes. Cheatham, with his two divisions of Bate and J. A. Smith, formed the new left flank, supported by Rucker's cavalry, which wandered in during the night. Stewart's shrunken corps held the center, and Lee's men were posted on the right. The entire line was hastily dug in, and for added protection both flanks were refused southward, following the crestlines of the hills on which they were anchored.

Beginning at daybreak on the 16th, the Union infantry again deployed and started to probe the new Confederate line. There was no immediate resumption of the fighting (the infantry, at least, had no positive orders to proceed), and much of the morning and early afternoon was spent in reconnaissance while the powerful rifled artillery of the Union army was emplaced on hills surrounding the Rebel position on three sides. The cavalry, however, did receive orders, being commanded to "drive the enemy from the hills and push them as vigorously as possible in flank and rear." Accordingly, Wilson swung south and east, infiltrating the rear of Hood's line through the open woods at the foot of the Brentwood Hills.

Wilson's envelopment pushed Rucker's troopers north, and the Union artillery opened a tremendous converging fire on the Confederate line, concentrating on the hills at either end. This cannonade was devastating in its effects. Bate's division, crouched in its shell-swept trenches on Shy's Hill, was ravaged by the fire, which Brigadier-General J. T. Holtzclaw, whose command was posted on Overton's Hill, proclaimed the "most furious I have witnessed, while the range was so precise that scarce a shell failed to explode in the line." Under cover of this mighty bombardment, the Union troops crept close to the Rebel line, and at 3 P.M. an attack was mounted on Overton's Hill. Post's brigade charged from the north, while Steedman's black troops swept in from the east. The attack was gallantly executed, Steedman's men coming on in neatly dressed ranks and Post's veterans by rushes; but the defenders, Major-General H. D. Clayton's division, rose up and poured in withering volleys which decimated the black brigades and cut down Post's men by the dozen. Some of Post's troops broke into the Confederate line, but Post himself was killed by a round of grapeshot and his men were quickly repulsed. The attack broke up in a welter of carnage, and Clayton noted that "It was with great difficulty that the enthusiasm of the troops could be repressed so as to keep them from going over the works in pursuit of the enemy."

At this juncture, with things going so well on his right, Hood weakened his left, shifting troops from Cheatham to Lee, who, after the repulse of Post, did not need reinforcing. This move imperiled the defense in the vicinity of Shy's Hill, the troops ordered away being sent to support Rucker in his losing effort against Wilson. A short time later, at about 3.30, the Rebels contesting Wilson's advance gave way, and the Yankee troopers gained a position astride the Granny White Turnpike south of Shy's Hill. From there they directed a fire against the exposed defenders of the Hill, who were already suffering severely from the artillery crossfire directed against them from front and flank. The cumulative effect of this fire was so devastating that one Rebel private of Bate's division declared, "The Yankee bullets and shells were coming from all directions, passing one another in the air."

It was the beginning of the end for Hood's shaky left flank. McArthur's division stormed the hill from the west at almost the same time as a dismounted cavalry attack by Coon's brigade went in from the south. Bate's men fought back valorously in defense, especially a contingent of Tennesseans under Colonel William M. Shy (whose deeds are commemorated in the hill's name), but, according to an onlooker, "The breach being made, the lines lifted from either side as far as I could see almost instantly and fled in confusion." Hood's Army of Tennessee was decisively broken, transformed in a few minutes into a demoralized mob. Pockets of resistance remained, but, by Smith's account, "Prisoners were taken by the regiment and artillery by batteries." Wilson took up the pursuit immediately, pressing the debris of the Rebel army down the Franklin Turnpike and beyond.

Hood's rearguard, composed of unbroken infantry under Major-General E. C. Walthall, and Forrest's cavalry (which rejoined the army on the 18th), for several days held off the furiously sustained Union attacks. Through their efforts, the bulk of the Rebel army was able to cross the Tennessee River unmolested on the 27th. Thus ended the Franklin and Nashville campaign, a bold offensive which enjoyed fleeting success in its early stages but rapidly degenerated into an unprecedented débâcle for the Army of Tennessee. In Colonel Stone's words, "the whole structure of the rebellion in the South-West, with all its possibilities, was utterly overthrown."

Above
The armored casemate of Fort Negley.

Below
The charge of the Minnesota regiments at Shy's Hill on the second day of the battle.
After a valiant defense, the Confederate line was broken,
and the rout of the Army of Tennessee begun.
Painting by Howard Pyle.

# PETERSBURG

June 15, 1864–April 3, 1865

A Union terror weapon, the "Dictator," in the vicinity of Petersburg. This giant mortar could hurl its 220-pound shells more than 2½ miles; its rail mounting gave it a flexibility new in the art of siege warfare.

In June 1864, the Confederacy was still a strong, viable entity. Despite defeats at Gettysburg, Vicksburg, and Chattanooga in the previous campaigning season, the heartland remained loyal and inviolate. In the West, General Joseph Johnston had breathed fire into the hard-luck Army of Tennessee, and with his skill and their entrenching tools was prepared to keep the "gorillas" of Sherman's three armies from ravaging Georgia. In the coastal areas, many of the more prominent ports were still open to the blockade-runners. Those ports which had fallen had at least not provided invasion bridgeheads into the Deep South, and the invaders were easily contained by local forces.

In the main theater of war, General Robert E. Lee and the Army of Northern Virginia, despite being outnumbered two-to-one, were steadfastly guarding the road to Richmond against Grant's hordes. Lee was doing more than just guarding his capital, he was locked into the Northern jugular vein, draining men, money, and matériel as fast as it could be poured in from the Northern cities, banks, and factories. Especially important was the drain on Northern manpower, used up in the endless attacks, counterattacks, and skirmishes launched against him by Grant. Gone were the cheerful volunteers and steadfast regulars of 1862 and 1863: they were replaced by the draftees, the bounty-hunters, the immigrants (who walked from the boats to the barracks almost without stopping), and by the freed slaves.

"The Army of the Potomac, shaken in its structure, its valor quenched in blood, and thousands of its ablest officers killed and wounded, was the Army of the Potomac no more," wrote its historian, William Swinton. An insight into this wreckage can be found by looking at the army's most famous corps–Major-General Winfield Hancock's II Corps. The glorious corps that had stormed the Bloody Lane at Antietam over the corpses of their first waves; whose division had lost over 4,000 men on Marye's Heights at Fredericksburg but still kept coming; whose regiments had defiantly stood on Cemetery Ridge as Pickett's 15,000 bore down on them; whose men had broken Spotsylvania's Bloody Angle–this corps was not even a shadow of its former self. "Hancock the Magnificent," plagued by a wound from Gettysburg that would not heal, was sapped of all his energy and fought on nerves alone. Major-General John Gibbon, commanding what had once been the finest division of the corps, had seen more men fall in his units in the last two months than he had begun the campaign with. In the Wilderness, II Corps had gone through 20,000 men, including 100 regimental commanders and a score of generals. One company in the 24th Michigan Regiment had only two men left after those 60 days of fighting–one private and his sergeant, just enough to carry the flags on parade. The men were in such a ground-down condition that "the more they serve the less they look like soldiers and the more they look like day-laborers, who had bought second-hand military clothes," commented one of the staff officers. Gibbon himself wrote, "Troops which at the commencement of the campaign were equal to almost any undertaking, became toward the end of it unfit for almost any."

With his forces badly bloodied in the wilderness and at Spotsylvania, and with the nightmare of Cold Harbor still fresh in their memories, Grant now sought to outmaneuver Lee rather than bludgeon him. Convinced that the slaughter of that campaign had at least broken the offensive punch of the Army of Northern Virginia, Grant prepared a risky flank march to the south, across the James River, with the intent of hitting Richmond from below. His target was the railhead of Petersburg, 23 miles south of the Confederate capital. Should it fall, Lee's army would either starve to death or be forced to fight it out in the open to save Richmond. Either course, he was convinced, would spell the end of the Confederacy.

Five railroads, two planked roads, and innumerable thoroughfares met at Petersburg, transforming the small city of 18,000 into the essential supply base for the Virginia theater. A 10 mile-long stretch of trenches, studded with 55 redoubts and protected by thick lines of abatis and chevaux-de-frise, comprised the "Dimmock Line" which guarded the city. But, although parts of it were strongly fortified and the whole place looked well-defended on a map, according to the Confederate General Colston, "with the exception of a few lunettes and redoubts at the most commanding positions, they were barely marked out, and a horseman could ride over them without the least difficulty almost everywhere."

The command of the garrison went to General Beauregard, a man who had fought well against long odds at Sumter, Corinth, and Charleston. An able commander of high social status and influence, he had only 2,200 men to defend the position, most of whom were home guards and reservists. The first test of the General's ability to hold the city had come in early June. Major-General Ben Butler, commanding the Union Army of the James, had sent Brigadier-General August Kautz with a cavalry division and some guns to seize the city. In a fight later known as the "Battle of the Patients and the Penitents," a collection of militia, drummer-boys, and invalids had successfully stood against the Union troopers, defending more by bluff than by physical means. The cavalry thrust had revealed the weakness of the line, however, and this fueled Grant's determination to attack the supposedly weak underbelly of Richmond. On the evening of June 12, 1864, the Union army at Cold Harbor began a march of 50 miles, in the course of which it would cross a half-mile-wide river over 90 feet deep, arriving with its lead elements in front of Petersburg in less than 72 hours.

The move came as a complete surprise to the Union soldiers in the Cold Harbor trenches–and in an army where rumor and security leaks were rife, that was indeed a novelty. The move took Lee by complete surprise also, so much so that he refused to send men south to Petersburg until he had news of Grant's personal arrival there. To lead the advance, Grant chose Major-General William F. Smith and his XVIII Corps of Butler's Army of the James. "Old Baldy" Smith was considered to be one of the better men available for the job. His corps, however, was a bit gun-shy. They had lost heavily at Cold Harbor, a loss only partially compensated by the addition of a raw division of blacks under Brigadier-General Edward Hinks. Still, Smith should be able to overwhelm the small Rebel force before any major reinforcements could come to Beauregard's relief.

At 7 A.M. on June 15, the lead elements of Smith's command arrived on the field. Smith, spying the Confederate works, decided not to attack until he had made a personal reconnaissance of the line and his full corps could be assembled. Beauregard, aware that about 18,000 Yankees were lurking in the woods east of the city, urgently signaled Lee for help. With an average of only one man per four and a half yards of front, the hero of Charleston was understandably upset about doing battle with a full army corps. At

4 P.M., when Smith was finally prepared to give the order to attack, someone noticed that there was no Union artillery on the line. Puzzled, Smith called for his chief of artillery. It seemed that, since no one had told him that an attack was imminent, he had sent the horses off to be watered. After a three-hour delay while the guns were put in position, XVIII Corps moved to the attack.

The Union artillerymen fired as fast as they could to keep the Rebels pinned down. The infantry, advancing in three swarms of skirmish lines, charged the line between the Norfolk and City Point railroads. Beauregard's line quickly crumbled. Hinks's black division alone took five forts, a dozen guns, and 150 prisoners as they overran the Dimmock Line. The Confederates hurriedly collected themselves about a mile to the rear and dug in, hoping at least to slow the Yankees down. True to the spirit of the Union armies in the East, Smith ordered a halt rather than continue his advance to the city. The victory had been too easy, too cheap; it must be a trap, he reasoned, and immediately commanded his corps to dig in and prepare for the Rebel counterattack which he was sure would come with the moonlight.

But there was no Rebel counterattack in the offing. The only force coming to the defenders' aid was Major-General Robert F. Hoke's 5,000-man division, which Beauregard had taken from the line opposite Bermuda Hundred, where it had kept Butler's other troops occupied. The Union force on the other hand had grown to about 38,000 by nightfall as Hancock's corps began to arrive. The famous fighting general was by then in no mood to throw his men into a battle. "I had spent the best hours of the day," he later commented, "marching by an incorrect map in search of a position which, as described, was not in existence." His corps had marched and countermarched all day trying to find the roads and reference points marked on the headquarters map. A five-hour halt for supplies which never showed up further delayed their arrival in the battle zone. Hancock's orders were so confused that not until 5.30 P.M., when a messenger arrived from Smith, did he know that a battle was in progress. Thoroughly exhausted, confused, and seething with professional rage, Hancock refused to launch a night attack into unfamiliar terrain. His infantrymen felt otherwise. After learning of the success of the raw black units, whose soldiers were drunk on victory, Hancock's men pleaded to go in: "Put us into it, Hancock and we'll end this rebellion by tonight!" Even the most common soldier knew that Lee had been outmaneuvered. When the word came down that they were to biouvac rather than fight, according to a contemporary account, "the rage of the enlisted men was devilish. The most blood-curdling blasphemy I ever listened to I heard that night, uttered by men who knew they were to be sacrificed on the morrow." Their fury was justified, for as Beauregard wrote, "Petersburg at that hour was clearly at the mercy of the Federal commander, who had all but captured it, and only failed of final success because he could not realize the fact of the unparalleled disparity between the two contending forces."

On the 16th, Major-General Ambrose Burnside's IX Corps and Major-General Gouvernor K. Warren's V Corps filed into position below Smith and Hancock. At 6 P.M., the Union II and IX Corps threw themselves against Beauregard, who had now built himself up to 10,000 by further stripping his Bermuda Hundred forces. As the soldiers had expected the night before, the attacks were thrown back with brutal efficiency.

When at last he received news that Grant was on the field, Lee decided to march south. His decision came barely in time to save the situation, because Butler, finding his army only lightly opposed, had broken out of his "cage" at Bermuda Hundred and was advancing into the gap between Lee and Petersburg. A spirited attack by Dick Anderson's division, however, rocked the Army of the James back on its heels, and another attack by Pickett the following morning plugged the Bermuda Hundred for good.

On June 17 Beauregard's 14,000 defenders were faced by 80,000 Yankees. The key to the Confederate line rested on two hills guarding the main road into Petersburg. The commander of the Army of the Potomac, Major-General George Meade, ordered Hancock and Burnside to seize them, while Warren tried to extend to the west. At dawn the two corps went forward, bayonets sharpened and canteens tucked into haversacks so they would not rattle. Both hills quickly fell to the surprise attack, but as if the army had a curse on it, the advance stopped. Burnside's support division under Brigadier-General James Ledlie did not advance. A staff officer found Ledlie asleep and, upon waking him, was stunned to find out that he had never received an order to attack. By the time Burnside sent in another division to support his leading unit, the Confederate artillery had had enough time to react, and the support division was broken by its fire. Ledlie finally moved his division out late that night, taking the high ground in front of him by a bayonet attack in the dark, but his force was then in too confused a state to go any farther. Hancock had had similar luck in his attack. His wound inflamed and reopened by the long ride, he turned the command over to General David Birney. Unaware of the overall plan, Birney took the assigned hill but, without any communications from Meade or Burnside, merely consolidated. Beauregard, his center shattered, withdrew to a final line on the outskirts of the town and pleaded with Lee to hurry.

Meade was in a blind rage. For the second time, the city was at the mercy of his army and nobody had taken the initiative to seize it. "I find it useless to appoint an hour to effect cooperation . . . what additional orders to attack you require I cannot imagine," he told officers. "Finding it impossible to effect cooperation by appointing an hour for attack, I have sent an order to each corps commander to attack at all hazards and without reference to each other!"

Beauregard now expected the Yankees to launch a night assault by the light of a moon only two nights short of being full. He wired Lee, "The last hour of the Confederacy has arrived," and retreated still closer to the town. On the morning of the 18th, Meade's entire army charged with fixed bayonets and blaring bugles into the abandoned Rebel line. The surprise at finding the line empty so confused the officers (including Meade) that it was not until noon that a plan was formulated to sort out the units and continue the advance. By then, however, it was too late for an attack to succeed. The hardened veterans of the Army of Northern Virginia had begun to pour into Beauregard's line a little after sunrise, and by 11 A.M. Lee himself had arrived. The odds being reduced to the familiar two-to-one, it became Cold Harbor all over again.

"No, we are not going to charge," an old veteran in the Excelsior Brigade told a young New York recruit, "we are going to run toward the Confederate earthworks and then we are going to run back. We have had enough of assaulting earthworks." The Union attack quickly became pinned down. The older, veteran soldiers knew enough to hug the earth rather than expose themselves to the firepower from the forts. "Lie down, you damn fools, you can't take the forts," the experienced men told the recruits, but many did not listen. The 1st Maine Artillery Regiment, sent into battle as an infantry outfit, leaped up and rushed the Confederate works. Grape and canister swept through the ranks, and in a few minutes 600 out of 900 fell. Burnside and Warren were repulsed also, causing Meade to remark that the men just did not have the spirit they used to have.

Grant called off the slaughter. A few days later, he tried a flank march with two corps on the Jerusalem Plank Road, only to find that A. P. Hill's Rebel corps was already there. In a superbly fought counterattack, the Union troops were beaten back, losing several hundred prisoners. The Petersburg assault had cost Grant 11,386 men in four days, bring-

around a rock into a forward Union rifle-pit, warning, "Tell the fellow with the spy glass to clear out or we shall have to shoot him." An over-anxious Southern recruit opened fire one day and came perilously close to wounding a Yankee soldier on that part of the battle area. To teach him a lesson, his comrades made him march on picket, in full view of the enemy, carrying only a broomstick, an action which gave both sides a rare chance to laugh. But although relations were congenial enough in everyday trench warfare, whenever an attack was launched, quarter was seldom given.

One such attack came in late July. A portion of Burnside's line was held by the 48th Pennsylvania Veteran Volunteer Infantry Regiment, a unit made up largely of anthracite-coal miners from the Schuylkill County coalfields of that state. Their colonel, Henry Pleasants, himself a mine engineer, overheard one of his men remark, as they came under fire from a Rebel fort, "We could blow that damned

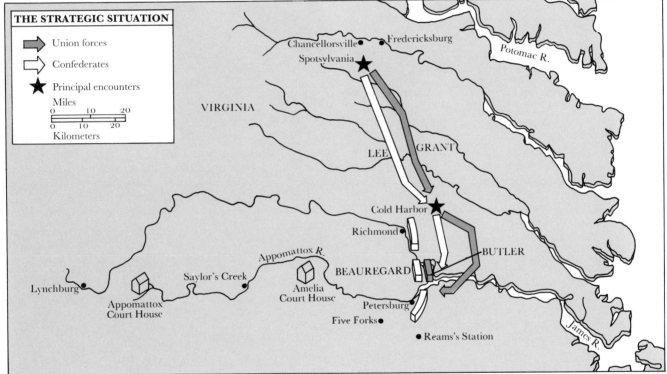

THE STRATEGIC SITUATION

➤ Union forces

▷ Confederates

★ Principal encounters

ing his total for two months to over 75,000 men. With the losses bleeding the army and shocking the citizenry, Grant settled down to a siege with regular approaches. Once again he asked Lincoln for more men, but cautioned him that "the siege of Richmond bids fair to be tedious."

Grant dug in on a five-mile-long line parallel to Lee's works. Trenches, ditches, abatis, covered ways, and forts were strengthened by both sides. At their closest, in the IX Corps zone, the lines were only 150 yards apart, and the sentries continued firing at each other without let-up, a situation exacerbated by the presence of Brigadier-General Edward Ferrero's black division. Whenever the Rebels knew they were faced by black troops, their penchant for bloodletting was unrestrained.

Along the rest of the line, however, the greater distances between the armies made contact less intense. As was their habit throughout the war, the opposing pickets would declare temporary truces, often to the point of warning each other before they were shot. Along the V Corps zone, where the lines were farthest apart and fighting less constant, a Union general climbed the parapet one day to spy the enemy line; a Rebel responded by throwing a note tied

fort out of existence if we could run a mine shaft under it." Pleasants took the idea to Burnside the next day, suggesting that, rather than attack over the field against Pegram's Salient, they attack under it. Using his coal miners, Pleasants would dig a tunnel beneath the battery, fill it with powder, and blow a hole in the middle of Lee's defenses. Burnside was thrilled by the plan and presented it to Meade and Grant, both of whom were sceptical but willing to try anything to break the deadlock.

Even so, the army engineers refused to help Pleasants, saying that to dig a gallery that long was impossible, there being no way to ventilate it. Using a simple bellows-and-draft chimney, however, Pleasants quickly overcame that difficulty. His men worked in round-the-clock shifts, cutting their own lumber and spreading the dirt behind the lines so that the Rebels would suspect nothing. There was no way to hide the noise when they went under the enemy lines, however, and Confederate miners tried, unsuccessfully to countermine. After a while they gave up, convinced that a tunnel that long would never succeed. The coal miners completed the tunnel, and a 75-foot magazine, loading the latter with four tons of powder. The 500-foot-long shaft, with the magazine in place

# THE COMMANDERS

Major-General John Gibbon, USV

Lieutenant-General Ambrose Powell Hill, CSA

**M**ajor-General John Gibbon (1827–96) was the finest divisional commander in the Army of the Potomac. A Regular Army captain of artillery in pre-war days, Gibbon prepared the United States Artillery Manual of 1859, which was widely used during the Civil War. Although three of his brothers had joined the Confederate armies, Gibbon, a Pennsylvanian, remained loyal to his officer's oath, and in 1862 led the famous "Iron Brigade." He was a hard and quite fearless fighter and soon rose to command the men of the Second Division of Major-General Winfield Scott Hancock's II Corps.

Prominent in the campaigns at Second Bull Run, Antietam, Fredericksburg, and Chancellorsville, Gibbon was singled out by Meade after a council of war on the evening of the second day at Gettysburg. Meade told him, with great prescience, "If Lee attacks tomorrow, it will be on your front." Meade was right, and the steadfast conduct of Gibbon's men was a major highlight of the Union victory.

Gibbon and II Corps fought on in a succession of grinding campaigns after Gettysburg, suffering heavy losses. The Wilderness Campaign, in which his division lost 7,000 in two months (many regiments going through two or more complete rosters) had a telling effect upon his ability to order men into battle. At Reams's Station outside Petersburg in late August 1864, Gibbon was humiliated and betrayed when three of his regiments refused to fight, and the glorious II Corps was abysmally defeated. Although he resigned temporarily from his command, Gibbon was back in time to watch the final collapse of the Rebel defenses at Richmond and the surrender of Lee's Army of Northern Virginia, which he had fought for four bitter years.

After the war Gibbon went West, commanding the Regulars in several campaigns against the Indian nations. It was his column which, in 1876, arrived on the field of Little Big Horn to rescue the remnants of Custer's butchered Seventh Cavalry.

**T**he only officer of the Southern Armies to be given an affectionate diminutive sobriquet by his troops, Ambrose "Little Powell" Hill (1825–65) led his famous Light Division to victory in countless battles and skirmishes. A conservative anti-slavery Episcopalian, Hill's Virginia family background was neither plantation nor slave-owning; having graduated from West Point in 1847, Hill nevertheless was loyal to his native state and in 1861 entered the Confederate service.

When Jackson died after Chancellorsville, Lee turned to Hill to take his place. By then Hill had directed the spearhead in the Seven Days Campaign and had held the line with rocks for ammunition when his supplies ran out at Second Bull Run. After Hill's coup against Burnside's men at Antietam, when he arrived late in the day with his Light Division after a 17-mile march from Harpers Ferry, Lee wrote to Jefferson Davis that, after Longstreet and Jackson, "I consider General A. P. Hill the best commander with me. He fights his troops well and takes good care of them."

But although the impulsive qualities that led him to strike, as Colonel Henry Douglas put it, "with the right hand of Mars," made him a success as a commander in charge of a division, Hill seemed overburdened by the responsibility of a full corps, which in Lee's army was equivalent to an army in miniature. While he built an *esprit* among his divisions that made them terrible to face in battle, he had a habit of becoming ill when he felt that Lee was putting an undue amount of faith in him. For all that, his men loved him. Hill made himself continually available to them, visiting them in the trenches and in the hospitals. "In all his career he never advanced a claim or maintained a rivalry. The soul of honor and generosity, he was never engaged in representing the merits of others," wrote one admirer. On April 2, 1865, while trying to reach his command after the Union army had broken through the Petersburg defenses, Hill was felled by a Union skirmisher.

beneath the fort, was ready for explosion in the pre-dawn hours of July 30.

Burnside planned to exploit the gap caused by the blast by massing "the two brigades of the colored division in rear of my first line, in columns of division–'double columns closed in mass'–the head of each brigade resting on the front line and, as soon as explosion has taken place, move them forwards." Once they had broken through, they would continue on to the ridge overlooking the city. The rest of the corps would follow and fan out, widening the gap. Ferrero, the man who had led the final charge across the stone bridge at Antietam under Burnside, prepared his men meticulously for the assault. The black troops rehearsed behind the corps positions, their morale raised considerably at the thought of leading the attack that might end the war. Their campfire minstrels even composed a special verse, which they sang unendingly: "We looks like men a-marchin', we looks like men a-war."

The High Command, however, remaining somewhat sceptical of the whole plan, upset the apple cart at the last minute. As Grant said, "If we put the colored troops in front and it should prove a failure, it would be then said, and very properly, that we were shoving these people ahead to get killed because we did not care anything about them. But that could not be said if we put white troops out in front."

On the night of the 29th, Burnside met with his four divisional commanders. As expected, Ferrero was furious but accepted the order. Burnside, not being a man to take decisions on his shoulders if he did not have to, had his generals choose straws to see who would lead the assault. As if fate were frowning on the army, Ledlie took the short straw. As Brigadier-General Stephen Weed said of him, "He was a drunkard and an arrant coward. In every fight we had been in under Ledlie he had been under the influence of liquor." A military amateur without much combat experience, Ledlie's division was no prize either. One brigade was composed of dismounted cavalry, the other of artillerists who, as Burnside once observed, "are worthless. They didn't enlist to fight and it is unreasonable to expect it of them. In the attack last night I couldn't find thirty of them." If the mine explosion did not do its job, the attacking waves would be butchered. Grant, thinking politically, took some comfort in knowing that it would be whites, not blacks, he was sending to a possible slaughter.

At 3.30 A.M. on July 30, the fuse was lit and the troops were in position. The High Command waited nervously for the explosion. 3.45. 4.00. 4.30, and still no explosion. Pleasants hesitatingly sent his mine boss, Sergeant Harry Reese, to check the fuse. Grant, concerned about wasting all the preparations, ordered the attack to begin, with or without the mine. But before the order could be transmitted, in the words of one of Ledlie's ADCs, "the mine was sprung. It was a magnificent spectacle, and as the mass of earth went up into the air, carrying with it men, guns, carriages and timbers, and spread out like an immense cloud as it reached its altitude, so close were the Union lines that the mass appeared as if it would descend immediately upon the troops waiting to make the charge." Sergeant Reese had fixed the fuse.

The explosion opened up a yawning crater, 170 feet long, 60 feet across, and 30 feet deep, burying or annihilating 278 defenders and throwing the fear of the Lord into the men on either side. It also blew a gap in the defenses nearly 500 yards wide. But at first it was not only the Rebels who ran from the explosion; Ledlie's men also took off at a run, fearful of the wreckage landing upon them. To their credit, their officers reformed them within 10 minutes or so and then they raced across the open space.

Upon reaching the crater, the advancing swarm stopped, as if struck by lightning. The men crowded to the lip of it and stared, open-mouthed in amazement at the debris, then, being shoved into the hole by the push of bodies from behind, proceeded to pull out the half-buried defenders who were still alive. A few more disciplined troops took some of the still-intact guns and faced them toward the Rebel side, trying to form a defense line. The second wave, quite unrehearsed and without the promised aid of the engineers to clear the obstacles, wove their way through them and into the trenches. "The approaches to the Union line of entrenchments at this particular point were so well covered by the fire of the enemy that they were cut up into a network of covered ways almost as puzzling to the uninitiated as the catacombs of Rome," remarked one of these men.

Burnside continued to pour men forward. They kept crowding into the crater, however, although Potter and Willcox tried to extend the gap to the flanks as planned. The position in fact became so bottlenecked that "it was utterly impracticable to reform a brigade in that Crater as it would have been to marshal bees into line after upsetting the hive." In support of the infantry, 144 Union guns kept firing all the while: 80 field pieces, 36 siege guns, and 28 coehorn mortars blasted the enemy positions, seeking also to widen the scope of the attack. But now the Rebels had recovered from the initial shock and bravely stood to their guns around the Crater. Three of the four guns in a fort 400 yards north of the Crater were knocked out, but the defenders kept firing back. Ten of the 16 guns brought up into battery on the sunken Jerusalem Plank Road were dismounted by the barrage, but still fought. Small parties of riflemen made their way back to the rifle pits, and by their efforts kept the mass of attackers penned in the Crater.

The heat, crowding, and lack of food and water soon made the Crater a hellish place for the Union troopers. Lacking senior officers to direct them (Ledlie and Ferrero were both drunk in a dugout), the men became confused. One of the few general officers in the hole was Brigadier-General William Bartlett. He had lost a leg earlier in the war and wore a cork replacement. As he was standing in the middle of the Crater, a Rebel cannon-ball struck his leg with a loud thump and knocked it off. Bartlett, falling to the ground, was immediately surrounded by his men. "Put me down any place where I can sit down!" he cried. "But you are wounded, general, aren't you?" they said. "My leg is shattered all to pieces," he said. "Then you can't sit up, you'll have to lie down," his soldiers urged. "Oh, no," exclaimed the general, "it's only my cork leg that's shattered."

Still Burnside sent in more troops. The black division went in at 7 A.M., still planning to go through the Crater and onto the heights behind it. The black infantry rushed forward in the finest tradition of the army. Although losing about 20 minutes scrambling through the Crater, they reformed and charged ahead. Behind the battle lines, the file-closers kept the ranks in some sort of order. A soldier in the Crater saw them at work: "One of these file-closers was a massively built, powerful and well-formed sergeant, stripped to the waist–his coal black skin shining like polished ebony in the strong sunlight. As he was

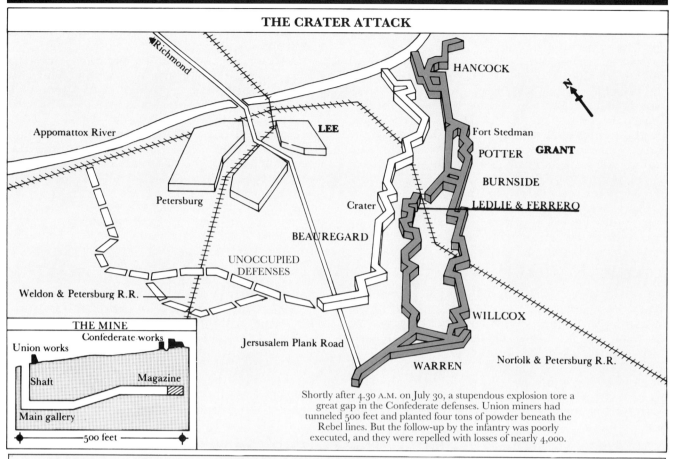

## THE CRATER ATTACK

Richmond

Appomattox River

HANCOCK

LEE

Fort Stedman

POTTER **GRANT**

Petersburg

BURNSIDE

Crater

LEDLIE & FERRERO

BEAUREGARD

UNOCCUPIED
DEFENSES

Weldon & Petersburg R.R.

WILLCOX

Jerusalem Plank Road

WARREN

Norfolk & Petersburg R.R.

### THE MINE

Confederate works

Union works

Shaft

Magazine

Main gallery

—500 feet—

Shortly after 4.30 A.M. on July 30, a stupendous explosion tore a
great gap in the Confederate defenses. Union miners had
tunneled 500 feet and planted four tons of powder beneath the
Rebel lines. But the follow-up by the infantry was poorly
executed, and they were repelled with losses of nearly 4,000.

## THE OPPOSING FORCES (June 1864)

### UNION ARMY
Lieutenant-General Ulysses Simpson Grant

### ARMY OF THE POTOMAC
Major-General George G. Meade

#### II Corps
Major-General Winfield S. Hancock

First Division (Brigadier-General Francis Barlow):
brigades of Miles, Smyth, Frank and Brooke.
Second Division (Brigadier-General John Gibbon):
brigades of Webb, Owen and Carroll.
Third Division (Brigadier-General David Birney):
brigades of Ward and Hays.
Fourth Division (Brigadier-General Gershom Mott):
brigades of McAllister and Brewster.
Strength: 79 regiments of infantry and 11 batteries of
artillery.

#### V Corps
Major-General Gouverneur K. Warren

First Division (Brigadier-General Charles Griffin):
brigades of Ayres, Sweitzer and Bartlett.
Second Division (Brigadier-General John C. Robinson):
brigades of Leonard, Baxter and Denison.
Third Division (Brigadier-General Samuel Crawford):
brigades of McCandless and Fisher.
Fourth Division (Brigadier-General James Wadsworth):
brigades of Cutler, Rice and Stone.
Strength: 62 regiments and 11 batteries.

#### VI Corps
Major-General Horatio Wright

First Division (Brigadier-General Frank Wheaton):
brigades of Brown, Upton, Russell and Shaler.
Second Division (Brigadier-General George Getty):
brigades of Warner, Grant, Neill and Eustis.

Third Division (Brigadier-General James Ricketts):
brigades of Morris and Seymour.
Strength: 47 regiments and 9 batteries.

#### IX Corps
Major-General Ambrose E. Burnside

First Division (Brigadier-General Thomas Stevenson):
brigades of Carruth and Leasure.
Second Division (Brigadier-General Robert Potter):
brigades of Bliss and Griffin.
Third Division (Brigadier-General Orlando B. Willcox):
brigades of Hartranft and Christ.
Fourth Division (Brigadier-General Edward Ferrero):
brigades of Sigfried and Thomas.
Strength: 42 regiments of infantry, 4 of cavalry, and 15
batteries, plus detachments.

#### Cavalry Corps
Major-General Philip H. Sheridan

First Division (Brigadier-General A. T. A. Torbet):
brigades of Custer, Devin and Merritt.
Second Division (Brigadier-General David Gregg):
brigades of Davies and Gregg.
Third Division (Brigadier-General James Wilson):
brigades of Bryan and Chapman.
Strength: 31 regiments and 13 batteries.

#### Artillery Reserve
Brigadier-General Henry Hunt

Strength: 13 batteries.

### ARMY OF THE JAMES
Major-General Benjamin F. Butler

#### X Corps
Major-General Quincy Gillmore

First Division (Brigadier-General Alfred Terry):

brigades of Howell, Hawley and Plaisted.
Second Division (Brigadier-General John Turner):
brigades of Alford and Barton.
Third Division (Brigadier-General Adalbert Ames):
brigades of White and Drake.
Strength: 29 regiments and 9 batteries.

## XVIII Corps
### Major-General William F. Smith

First Division (Brigadier-General William Brooks):
brigades of Marston, Burnham and Sanders.
Second Division (Brigadier-General Godfrey Weitzel):
brigades of Heckman, Stedman and Follet.
Third Division (Brigadier-General Edward Hinks):
brigades of Wild and Duncan.
Strength: 27 regiments and 10 batteries.

## Cavalry Division
### Brigadier-General August V. Kautz

Brigades of Mix and Spear.
Strength: 7 regiments.

## CONFEDERATE ARMY
### General Robert E. Lee

## ARMY OF NORTHERN VIRGINIA
### General Robert E. Lee

### I Corps
### Lieutenant-General James Longstreet

Kershaw's Division (Brigadier-General J.B. Kershaw):
brigades of Henagan, Humphreys, Wofford and Bryan.
Field's Division (Major-General Charles Field): brigades
of Jenkins, G. T. Anderson, Law, Gregg, and Benning.
Strength: 44 regiments of infantry and 14 batteries of
artillery.

### II Corps
### Lieutenant-General Richard S. Ewell

Early's Division (Major-General Jubal Early): brigades
of Hays, Pegram and John Gordon.
Johnson's Division (Major-General Edward Johnson):
brigades of Walker Steuart, Jones and Stafford.
Rode's Division (Major-General Robert Rodes):
brigades of Daniel, Ramseur, Dole, Battle and Johnson.
Strength: 57 regiments and 18 batteries

### II Corps
### Lieutenant-General Ambrose Powell Hill

Anderson's Division (Major-General Richard H.
Anderson): brigades of Perrin, Mahone, Harris, Wright
and Perry.
Heth's Division (Major-General Henry Heth): brigades
of Davis, Cooke, Kirkland, Walker and Archer.
Wilcox's Division (Major-General Cadmus Wilcox):
brigades of Lane, Seales, McGowan and Thomas.
Strength: 61 regiments and 20 batteries.

### Cavalry Corps
### Major-General Wade Hampton

Butler's Division (Major-General M. C. Butler): brigades
of Young, Roser and Aiken.
Lee's Division (Major-General W. H. F. Lee): brigades of
Chambliss and Gordon.
Fitzhugh Lee's Division (Major-General Fitzhugh Lee):
brigades of Lomax and Wickham.
Strength: 25 regiments and 5 batteries.

## Estimated Totals

Grant's Union army had an overall total of 286
regiments of infantry, 42 of cavalry, and 91 batteries.
Numbers varied during the campaign: the Army of the
Potomac had 107,419 men on June 30, 1864, but this
figure was reduced by August 31, with the detachment
of Sheridan and VI Corps, to 58,923; the peak total for
this army was about 124,000 in January 1865. The
Army of the James varied between 36,000 and 40,000.
Losses: in the period June 15 to December 31, 5,099 killed,
24,879 wounded, and 17,576 captured or missing. Total:
47,554.
Losses for the remainder of the campaigns were
comparable; the total killed or wounded for the whole 10-
month period reached about 42,000.
Note. Several commands in the Army of the Potomac
changed leaders during the campaign: most notably,
Burnside was replaced by Willcox, and Hancock was
replaced at first by Birney, then by Humphreys. The
Army of the James was reorganized into two different
corps: XXIV, under Major-General E. O. C. Ord, and
XXV, under Major-General Godfrey Weitzel; it also
acquired a seventh division of infantry.

## RICHMOND AND PETERSBURG DEFENSES
### General Gustave P. T. Beauregard

Ransom's Division (Major-General Robert Ransom):
brigades of Gracie, Kemper, Barton and Lewis.
Hoke's Division (Major-General Robert Hoke):
brigades of Corse, Clingman, Johnson and Hagood.
Colquitt's Division (Brigadier-General Alfred Colquitt):
brigades of Lofton and Ransom.
Whiting's Division (Major-General W. H. C. Whiting):
brigades of Wise, Martin and Dearing.
Miscellaneous troops: brigades of Elliot, Hunton and
Johnson.
Strength: 63 regiments of infantry, 6 of cavalry, and 16
batteries.

## OTHER CONFEDERATE FORCES
At Richmond: Colonel Stevens
At Chaffin's Bluff: Lieutenant-Colonel Maury.
At Drewry's Bluff: Major Smith.
At Chaffin's Farm: Major Stark.
Artillery: Colonel Jones.
Strength: 4 regiments and 20 batteries.

## Estimated Totals

Lee's Confederate army had an overall total of 229
regiments of infantry, 31 of cavalry, and 93 batteries.
Numbers varied during the campaign, and detachments
were sent into the Shenandoah Valley with Early and to
the Carolinas. On June 30 Lee reported 54,751 men fit for
duty; this figure had dropped by August 31 to
34,677, but rose again to a peak of 66,533 in late
December. By March the total was reduced to some
35,000 effectives, of whom only 13,000 went to
Appomattox.
Losses: approximately 28,000 killed and wounded.
(Technically, the loss rate was 100% since the army
eventually surrendered.)
Note. The Confederate command structure changed
midway through the siege. After Early went to the
Valley, John Gordon took command of his division and,
temporarily, of II Corps. Anderson was placed in
command of a IV Corps, composed of the divisions of
Hoke and Johnson. Pickett, who initially fought under
Beauregard at Petersburg, was given a division in I
Corps composed of brigades from Beauregard's old
command.

passing up the slope to emerge on the enemy's side of the crest he came across one of his own black fellows, who was lagging behind his company, evidently with the intention of remaining inside the crater, out of the way of the bullets. He was accosted by the sergeant with 'none ob yo'd–n skulkin' now' with which remark he seized the culprit with one hand and lifted him up in his powerful grasp by the waistband of his trousers, carried him to the crest of the crater, threw him over on the enemy's side, and quickly followed."

The black regiments, 4,300-strong, came into hand-to-hand combat with the Rebels, taking 200 prisoners and a stand of colors, including the recapture of a Yankee flag lost by the first waves. But the time for the assault was over. The Confederate gunners poured in fire from every quarter, and the gray-clad infantry tore furiously at the former slaves. Grant angrily ordered Meade and Burnside to get the men back. Those who tried to cross the open spaces between the Crater and the Union line were cruelly cut down. A trench was dug from the line to the hole, through which many escaped, but only a few at a time. The Union gunners laid down a mass of smoke to screen the Crater, but still a heavy Rebel fire fell upon the men huddled in it.

The Crater attack was a fiasco. It cost Grant 3,798 men, half of them taken prisoner. Despite his desire not to have the blacks slaughtered, their losses were the highest of any of the units involved, amounting to nearly a third of their total strength. The repercussions came fast and furious; the press, the government, the generals, and the soldiers were quick to find scapegoats for what Grant called "the saddest affair I have ever witnesses in the war." The army would soon purge itself of some of the blunderers, but, as usual, only after it had done its butchery.

Grant had one resource above all others which the South could not match: manpower. In the war of attrition he decided he must wage, the cruel arithmetic of numbers would eventually give him victory; but, in addition, it was an election year, the populace was weary of the war, and victory was needed quickly.

Lee's lines were already thinly stretched, covering 35 miles from Fair Oaks, above the White Oak Swamp, along the James to Bermuda Hundred and then along the Appomattox River to the Petersburg forts. Unlike Grant, Lee had to keep the whole line well garrisoned lest his Northern counterpart thrust through a weak link and on to Richmond. With the intention of further stretching that taut, thin line, Grant began moving by his left again. In late August he sent his two best corps, those of Warren and Hancock, to seize the Weldon Railroad that led into Petersburg from the Carolinas. It was not his first attempt to cut that artery. Earlier in the siege, he had let loose a two-pronged cavalry raid against the rail lines. Major-General Phil Sheridan rode from the north in early June, but was well beaten by Wade Hampton (J. E. B. Stuart's successor), who then rode hell-bent to crush the second arm of the attack, mauling two Union cavalry divisions which had been tearing up the Weldon tracks. Deciding that cavalry could not do the job of railroad destruction properly, Grant now dispatched his infantry.

On August 18 Warren's corps, reinforced by a division of cavalry, collided with Henry Heth's division at Globe Tavern, a station on the Weldon line four miles below Petersburg. Meade rushed up troops from the nearby II and IX Corps but, on the 19th, A. P. Hill led in a collection of troops to pound the Union positions. Hill's attack, which included the fire of 30 massed cannon, did not jar the Yankees from the Tavern. But it made the venture less than a Union success: not only did it mark the limit of Warren's advance, he lost 4,500 men, half of whom were taken prisoner when two entire brigades surrendered. Although the rail line was broken, Lee was still able to bring trains within wagon distance of the city. To lengthen or disrupt this wagon route, Hancock tried to cross the Weldon at Reams's Station, some five miles farther down the track from Warren.

Reams's Station confirmed the rot which had been eating at the heart of II Corps. Hill's men drove in on the famous regiments, taking 2,000 prisoners, nine guns, 3,000 rifles, and a dozen battle flags. Three green New York regiments of Gibbon's command refused to fight! Hancock, tears in his eyes, rode the battle line crying to his men, "Come on! We can beat them yet! Don't leave me, for God's sake." Many of the soldiers took off in panic, men who, as General Wilcox observed, "never had come to fight, but to run on the first chance or get into the hospital and ho! for a pension afterwards." "Had our troops behaved as they used to," reported Hancock, "I could have beaten Hill, but some were new, and all were worn out with labor."

That night, his corps reduced by some 750 casualties as well as the 2,000 prisoners and untold stragglers and deserters, Hancock withdrew. The defeat broke his spirit. Hancock and Gibbon soon left the army: Gibbon was to resign, unable to bear the shame (but in a short while returned), and Hancock was sent home, supposedly to organize corps of veterans, but was never used in battle again.

The Confederates, having parried Grant's every thrust, still managed to keep some of the initiative. Six miles downriver from Grant's headquarters, a large herd of cattle had been assembled at Coggins Point to feed the army. Taking three of his brigades with him on a wide, circular ride, Wade Hampton descended upon the depot on September 16. Two brigades attacked the Union camp in the rear, and a third herded the steers away. Hampton's "Beefsteak Raid" embarrassed the Union army in true Stuart fashion. Hampton took 300 men and 2,500 head of cattle into Richmond as his prize; all for the loss of some 60 casualties.

An even more embarrassing episode had taken place in July when Jubal Early, with about 10,000 veterans, had swept through the Shenandoah Valley, "taxing" the locals and sending supplies to Lee. Rather than contentedly sitting in the Valley, Early then drove north. A collection of Union regiments was rudely dispersed at the Monocacy River near Frederick, Maryland, and Early moved toward Washington. As was usual, a panic gripped the government. The defenders of Washington were few in number and quality. The largest cohesive force available was composed of 1,500 quartermaster clerks hastily scraped together by the Quartermaster-General, Montgomery C. Meigs. These men managed to hold Early long enough for VI Corps to reach the capital by water to secure the city. Tired of the opportunities which the Shenandoah Valley offered the South, Grant gave the task of clearing it to Phil Sheridan. With an army of 36,000 men, including VI Corps, the bulk of the cavalry and other troops, Sheridan set off with Grant's instruction to "peel this land." He took a torch to the Shenandoah, destroying over 2,000 barns, 70 mills, and countless bushels of grain, in an estimated 25-million-dollar rampage. Early, forced to send troops to Lee, found himself unable to stop Sheridan.

Grant was impatient at the delays caused by sending troops to clear out the Valley as well as angry at the success of Hampton's "Beefsteak Raid." He ordered Meade to stage a spectacular assault that would gain some ground and attract better publicity. Meade set up two offensives at either end of the line. The first one he launched on September 28, aiming for the Confederate forts at Chaffin's Bluff along the James River, about seven miles below Richmond.

In the pre-dawn darkness, two Union corps rushed Forts Gilmore and Harrison. Major-General E.O.C. Ord's XXIV Corps quickly seized Fort Harrison, but despite three successive assaults by II Corps, Birney was unable to take Fort Gilmore. Lee personally supervised a three-division counterattack on Fort Harrison. It must have broken his heart, just as Reams's Station had shattered Hancock's, to see the three Rebel divisions attack halfheartedly and without proper coordination, falling back from the Union fire in a rabble. Lee ordered them to dig in and seal the breach, thus safeguarding the Richmond approaches along the James.

The second part of Meade's plan came into effect when he was certain that Lee had been drawn north. Two other corps, Warren V and Major-General John Parke's IX (Burnside was no longer with the army) crossed the Weldon Railroad on September 29, heading for the Boydton Plank Road, the major thoroughfare for wagon traffic into Petersburg. From there they were to advance and cut the other railroad, the Southside, and thus maroon Petersburg completely from the South.

Despite pulling a third of his army north to Fort Harrison, Lee had left A. P. Hill with a sufficient force in Petersburg to hold the city. At a two-day battle at Peebles Farm near the Plank Road, Hill and Wade Hampton combined to halt this Union threat. Although the Weldon was still cut, Petersburg remained open to the south. Once again, Grant had failed to break Lee's defenses; even so, he remained firm in his intention to hang on in front of Richmond. Lincoln also was sure that this was the correct strategy; on August 17 he had sent Grant written confirmation of his support: "I have seen your dispatch expressing your unwillingness to break your hold where you are. Neither am I willing. Hold on with a bulldog grip, and chew and choke as much as possible."

Chew and choke was what Grant continued to do. In October he sent the army in again at Petersburg: a move to Poplar Springs Church was turned back in the early days of the month, but still he kept moving. On October 7 Kautz's cavalry raided north of the James, only to be crushed with the loss of all its wagons and guns. Longstreet attempted a follow-up assault, but the Union X Corps threw him back. In mid-October, Butler tried several times to crack the Rebel lines, to no avail, while Grant continued his policy of extending to the left. At Burgess's Mill on the 27th, a massive lunge at the Southside Railroad was turned back by violent Confederate counterattacks.

The only good news for the North in October was Early's defeat at Cedar Creek by Sheridan, but the onset of rain and mud prevented a major follow-through to Richmond. In early November, word came of Sherman's departure from Atlanta and the initiation of his "March to the Sea." With Lincoln's re-election, the pressure to end the war quickly was somewhat relieved; as General Wilcox described events, "From this time forward the operations in front of Petersburg and Richmond, until the spring campaign of 1865, were confined to the defense and extension of our lines, and to offensive movements for crippling the enemy's lines of communication, and to prevent his detaching any considerable force to send south."

The progress of Sherman's armies from the Carolinas, coupled with the news that Sheridan was heading from the Valley to join Grant, forced upon Lee the decision to evacuate Richmond. In the hope of continuing the war to gain some bargaining position for independence, Lee planned to break contact with Grant, link up with Joe Johnston in North Carolina and crush Sherman, and then turn upon the pursuing host under Grant. This almost absurdly ambitious plan was further complicated by the condition of the Army of Northern Virginia. Stretched out over 35 miles of fortifications, with additional cavalry extension, the army had a great deal of ground to cover before it could consolidate. The rations for men and horses were so limited (a pint of cornmeal and two ounces of rotting bacon a day was the average) that Lee was unable to move until the ground hardened, his horses being too weak to pull guns and wagons through the mud.

"I cannot see how we can escape the natural military consequences of the enemy's numerical superiority," Lee told President Davis; he had in mind that the two-to-one odds (Lee had 57,000 in January, Grant 124,000) would be lengthened considerably if Sheridan and Sherman were to arrive. Also, Lee's ammunition was too low to keep up the siege. While Union soldiers were under orders to fire at least 100 rounds a day, Lee's men were rationed to only 18 rounds. At night, the Rebels sifted the earthworks to gather bits of lead and iron fired at them; this became a major source of metal for the ammunition works.

The month of November had been quiet, and in December there had been only one major Union raid, by Warren on the Weldon Railroad. The January rains and floods prevented either side from fighting, but the weather cut the flow of supplies to Richmond, and the city and the army were literally starving. One soldier wrote, "There are a good many of us who believe this shooting match has been carried on long enough. A government that has run out of rations can't expect to do much more fighting." But despite the lack of shoes, clothing, ammunition, food, and reinforcements, the army still had its pride. Lee's men would still fight for him and for their own honor, like a wounded animal who knows the hunt is up, but is determined to resist to the last. In early February Lee became the official Commander-in-Chief of the Confederate armies, such as they were. Although this news reached him in the middle of the disastrous three-day battle at Hatcher's Run, which saw Union troops advance past the Boydton Plank Road, it was the authorization he needed to carry out his breakaway plan.

On March 25, 1865, Lincoln, Grant, and Sherman held a council of war behind the siege lines. A courier reported that a Rebel attack was in progress against the eastern face of the Petersburg lines; it was the last offensive Lee's army would ever launch. Lee had chosen the Union position at Fort Stedman for many reasons. The fort had fallen into disrepair over the winter, since it was too close to the Confederate lines to allow Union workmen to rebuild it; its weakness made it an attractive target. Major-General John B. Gordon had carefully surveyed the area and assured Lee that he could break through the Fort with a few divisions, and perhaps even ruin the Union depots behind it along the military railroad, thus depriving Grant of supplies and also winning valuable time, for it would take the Yankees a few days at least to sort themselves out. Time, not victory, was what Lee wanted. The attack on Fort Stedman should pull Union troops north and east, and away from the roads he would use to evacuate west of Richmond. Given the time to steal a few marches, the Confederates could reach a railhead and move to join Johnston before Grant could catch them. In his last gamble, Lee was as audacious as ever.

At 3 A.M. on March 25, Gordon sent out 50 axmen to clear the abatis to his front, and three parties, each of 100 men, to get in the rear of the Union batteries and forts. Confederates claiming to be deserters surrendered to the Union pickets and then quickly overwhelmed them before they could raise the alarm. Ford Stedman fell in the first rush, and to widen the gap additional columns headed toward Forts Haskell and McGilvery and Batteries XI and XII. The batteries fell, but Fort Haskell, defended by wounded men, gunners, and stragglers from the trenches, gallantly held out. Gordon repeatedly sent in attack columns and sharpshooters to gain the redoubt, whose guns prevented him from widening the gap. Confederate shells burst inside, knocking down the flagstaff. A Union battery on the hill behind opened up on the fort, and small parties of survivors from Stedman and the other forts fought their way through. Parke, whose XI Corps held this part of the line, brought up the six Pennsylvania regiments of John F. Hartranft's division to counterattack.

The defenders, McLaughlen's brigade of IX Corps, were almost overwhelmed; then the Pennsylvanians came to their rescue. Gordon's 12,000 men—a third of Lee's army—were canalized and could not advance with the fire from the forts on either flank enfilading them. Two regiments, the 200th and 209th Pennsylvania, attacked the farthest penetration of the line, the 200th losing 100 men in 20 minutes. Hartranft's remaining regiments, plus some Michigan units, formed a solid semicircular line a mile and a half long around the breach. Gordon, subjected to increasingly heavy converging fire, broke off the attack. About 3,500 Rebels were lost—a full tenth of Lee's army—as opposed to just over 1,000 Yankees, less than one percent of Grant's. The last Rebel offensive had dismally collapsed.

Grant was jubilant. He ordered Sheridan to take his cavalry corps and some infantry and ride behind Lee, cutting off any possible retreat from Richmond. Sheridan set off in appalling weather. The rains poured down and turned the roads into rivers, so much that a common joke in the army was, "When are the gunboats coming up?" But Sheridan refused to be stopped. To parry this lunge at his right flank, Lee sent Pickett and all the cavalry, under W. H. F. Lee, to the junction at Five Forks, on the White Oak Road. At Dinwiddie Court House, Pickett ran into Brigadier-General Tom Devin, "Sheridan's Hard-Hitter," and his cavalry. The dismounted troopers grudgingly gave ground before the Confederate infantry, despite Sheridan's presence and the reinforcements he brought with him. With his mounted bands playing "Nellie Bly" and other popular tunes, Sheridan rode the lines, exhorting his men to hold their ground. A mounted counterattack by George Armstrong Custer's Union division collapsed in the muddy, fire-swept fields, and the cavalry corps fell back. Warren's V Corps, marching up from the right, was the next target of the Confederate infantry. The

Rebels surprised one division, drove it into the second, and were only halted by the arrival of the third division. It took Warren most of the night to restore order.

On April 1, Pickett and Lee pulled their men into a fortified line along the White Oak Road and went to lunch in a quiet spot to bake some fresh-caught shad. That afternoon, with their generals out to lunch, the Confederates were swamped by Sheridan. Urging Warren to force-march his men on to the Rebel flank, Sheridan's dismounted troopers, according to General Horace Porter, used their magazine guns and "created a racket in those pine woods that sounded as if a couple of army corps had opened fire." Warren's corps, although most of it got lost in the woods, rolled down the flank and rear of the Confederate line. Outnumbered three-to-one, outflanked, and taken in the rear, the Rebel force collapsed; 5,000 out of 7,000 were taken prisoner, and Pickett no longer had a division to command.

Grant's excitement was at fever pitch. When Lincoln had suggested he wait for Sherman to come up and take Lee in the rear, he had told him that "it is due to the Eastern armies to let them vanquish their old enemy single-handed"; and Grant prepared to do just that. On April 2, the entire Army of the Potomac threw itself at the Petersburg trenches. Small parties of Confederates tried to slow them down, but to little avail. A. P. Hill died trying to force two Yankees to surrender, as if in fulfillment of his wish not to survive it the town fell. Lee, trying to gain some time, urged 500 men in Battery Whitworth and Fort Gregg to hold back Gibbon's 8,000 surging Bluecoats. he asked the valiant little band to hold for two hours; they held for three before they had to give up. The Confederates fought with desperate courage, but to no avail; the fate of Richmond was no longer in question. All that remained was to get the army out. Factories and military stores were set on fire. The next day, the black troops of the Army of the James marched through the capital of the dying Confederacy.

Lee gallantly tried to link up with Johnston, but his tired army could not outmarch or outfight the victorious troops under Grant and Sheridan, who advanced with new-found strength. Stopping to concentrate his dwindling army at Amelia, Lee searched for an escape road. As his army drove toward the railroad at Appomattox Station, it was attacked and cut in two by Grant's pursuing corps, and on April 6 part of it surrendered at Saylor's Creek. With fewer than 13,000 men and some three score cannon, Lee finally called a halt at Appomattox Court House, his path blocked by Sheridan and two Union infantry corps.

Rather than try for a glorious death, Lee accepted Grant's terms of surrender and capitulated on Palm Sunday, April 9, 1865. The terms were generous: officers kept their swords, the men held onto their horses for the spring planting, and the army was paroled. Within a few days, Joe Johnstone's army also surrendered, and the remaining Confederate forces across the country laid down their arms.

Lincoln urged his countrymen to treat the defeated with charity rather than hate, but his dream for a harmonious reunion of the nation was shattered by the assassin's bullet that took his life less than a week after the surrender. The Radical Republicans—Stanton, Wade, Stevens, and their followers—saw the South as a conquered state, to be chastised, humiliated, and "Reconstructed" as they saw fit. The ruling class of the Old South was destroyed by the new government, which forbade any officer or politician

Above:
The interior of an earthwork fort at Petersburg showing gabions
(wicker cylinders filled with earth)
and abatis (sharpened stakes used as obstructions).

Left
Making gabions for the Petersburg lines.

Below
The Crater.

Below
The charge of Sheridan's cavalry at Five Forks on April 1, 1865.

who had served the Confederacy from taking up a post of any responsibility. The harsh policies of the Reconstruction Congress, coupled with the military occupation by the Northern army, could have inflamed the South into renewed violence, had it not been for the courage and humanity of those men upon whom the burdens of defeat fell heaviest. Robert E. Lee, stripped of all rank and privileges, including his citizenship, urged his people to forget the past and to "make your sons Americans."

Every year, on Memorial Day, the veterans of the fratricidal conflict would gather in the towns and cities to parade, reminisce, and listen to speeches by old officers and comrades. "The generation that carried on the war," said Oliver Wendell Holmes, Jr., in an 1884 Memorial Day observance, "has been set apart by its experience. Through our great good fortune, in our youths our hearts were touched with fire. It was given to us to learn at the outset that life is a profound and passionate thing."

To the surviving soldiers of that war, which had been a frightening, horrible, and bloody event while they lived it, the passage of the years brought a different feeling to their hearts. The sense of comradeship, of drama, and of purpose that they had known in those four brutal years was sorely lacking in the daily labors of farming and merchandising. To many old men who had worn Rebel gray or Union blue, the climactic moments of their lives had come in the days of honor, glory, and chivalry which this, the last of the pre-industrial wars, had given them.

"His army broke up and followed him, weeping and sobbing."
Painting by Howard Pyle
from *General Lee as I knew him*, by A. R. H. Ranson.

# INDEX

*Page numbers in italics refer to illustrations.*

## ACKNOWLEDGMENTS

THE PUBLISHERS WISH TO THANK THE FOLLOWING INDIVIDUALS AND ORGANIZATIONS FOR PERMISSION TO REPRODUCE ILLUSTRATIONS APPEARING IN THE BOOK:

ANN S. K. BROWN MILITARY COLLECTION/BROWN UNIVERSITY; CHICAGO HISTORICAL SOCIETY; *HOWARD PYLE'S BOOK OF THE AMERICAN SPIRIT*; JOHNSON & BUEL, *BATTLES & LEADERS OF THE AMERICAN CIVIL WAR*. VOLS I-IV; LIBRARY OF CONGRESS/BRADY COLLECTION; MANSELL COLLECTION; MARYLAND HISTORICAL SOCIETY; MINNESOTA HISTORICAL SOCIETY; NEW HAMPSHIRE HISTORICAL SOCIETY; OFFICE OF THE CHIEF OF ENGINEERS/NATIONAL ARCHIVES; ORBIS PUBLISHING COMPANY; RADIO TIMES HULTON LIBRARY; US SIGNAL CORPS/BRADY COLLECTION/NATIONAL ARCHIVES; WEIDENFELD & NICOLSON ARCHIVES.

THE MAPS WERE DRAWN BY DAVID POCKNELL AND MICHAEL CAVERS.